Information
Campaigns

SAGE ANNUAL REVIEWS OF COMMUNICATION RESEARCH

Books in This Edited Series:

1: *Current Perspectives in Mass Communication Research*
   F. G. Kline and P. J. Tichenor

2: *New Models for Mass Communication Research*
   P. Clarke

3: *The Uses of Mass Communications*
   J. G. Blumler and E. Katz

4: *Political Communication*
   S. H. Chaffee

5: *Explorations in Interpersonal Communication*
   G. R. Miller

6: *Strategies for Communication Research*
   P. M. Hirsch, P. V. Miller, and F. G. Kline

7: *Children Communicating*
   E. Wartella

8: *Persuasion*
   M. E. Roloff and G. R. Miller

9: *Advances in Content Analysis*
   K. E. Rosengren

10: *Individuals in Mass Media Organizations*
   J. S. Ettema and D. C. Whitney

11: *Nonverbal Interaction*
   J. M. Wiemann and R. P. Harrison

12: *Interpreting Television*
   W. D. Rowland, Jr. and B. Watkins

13: *Organizational Communication*
   R. D. McPhee and P. K. Tompkins

14: *Interpersonal Processes*
   M. E. Roloff and G. R. Miller

15: *Media, Myths, and Narratives*
   J. W. Carey

16: *Advancing Communication Science*
   R. P. Hawkins, J. M. Wiemann, and S. Pingree

17: *Message Effects in Communication Science*
   J. J. Bradac

18: *Information Campaigns*
   C. T. Salmon

Editor
Charles T. Salmon

Information Campaigns:
Balancing
Social Values and
Social Change

Sage Annual Reviews of Communication Research

Volume 18

SAGE PUBLICATIONS
The Publishers of Professional Social Science
Newbury Park   London   New Delhi

For information address:

SAGE Publications, Inc.
2111 West Hillcrest Drive
Newbury Park, California 91320

SAGE Publications Ltd.
28 Banner Street
London EC1Y 8QE
England

SAGE Publications India Pvt. Ltd.
M-32 Market
Greater Kailash I
New Delhi 110 048 India

Printed in the United States of America

Library of Congress Cataloging-in-Publication Data

Main entry under title:

Information campaigns : balancing social values and social change /
    edited by Charles T. Salmon.
        p.   cm. — (Sage annual reviews of communication research ; v.
    18)
        Bibliography: p.
        ISBN 0-8039-3218-9. — ISBN 0-8039-3219-7 (pbk.)
        1. Publicity. 2. Marketing—Social aspects. 3. Communication—
    Social aspects. 4. Social change. I. Salmon, Charles T.
    II. Series.
    HM263.I5195   1989
    659–dc20   89-33256
                                                                        CIP

FIRST PRINTING, 1989

CONTENTS

Preface   7

Acknowledgments   15

PART I: Campaigns and Social Structure

1. Campaigns for Social "Improvement": An Overview of Values, Rationales, and Impacts
   CHARLES T. SALMON   19

2. Community Power and Leadership Analysis in Lifestyle Campaigns
   JOHN R. FINNEGAN, JR., NEIL BRACHT and K. VISWANATH   54

3. Family Planning, Abortion and AIDS: Sexuality and Communication Campaigns
   JANE D. BROWN, CYNTHIA S. WASZAK and KIM WALSH CHILDERS   85

4. The Knowledge-Behavior Gap in Public Information Campaigns: A Development Communication View
   ROBERT HORNIK   113

5. Media Coverage and Social Movements
   CLARICE N. OLIEN, PHILLIP J. TICHENOR and GEORGE A. DONOHUE   139

6. Information and Power: Toward a Critical Theory of Information Campaigns
   LANA F. RAKOW   164

7. Campaigns, Change and Culture: On the Polluting Potential of Persuasion
   RICHARD W. POLLAY   185

PART II: The Campaign Process

8. Publics, Audiences and Market Segments: Segmentation
   Principles for Campaigns
      JAMES E. GRUNIG   199
9. Message Strategies for Information Campaigns: A Social
   Psychological Analysis
      PATRICIA G. DEVINE and EDWARD R. HIRT   229
10. Strategies and Tactics in Political Campaigns
      GARRETT J. O'KEEFE   259
11. Estimating the Magnitude of Threats to Validity of Information
   Campaign Effects
      STEVEN H. CHAFFEE, CONNIE ROSER and
      JUNE FLORA   285

About the Contributors   303

PREFACE

The domain of information campaigns quite accurately has been described as one of the most applied areas of communication research (Rogers & Storey, 1987). Somewhat paradoxically, it is simultaneously one of the most theoretically driven as well, thereby demonstrating that theory and practice need not be mutually exclusive and substantiating Kurt Lewin's maxim that there is nothing so practical as good theory. It is the case, however, that much of the rich theoretical base which undergirds the campaign literature can best be described as theory *for* rather than theory *of* campaigns. That is, researchers have drawn heavily on psychological and sociological theory in order to improve their effectiveness in attaining their objectives. In so doing, they have implicitly adopted a process notion of campaigns, i.e., that campaigns can be viewed in terms of some underlying set of activities, usually consisting of formative research, design, implementation and evaluation (or slight variants thereof).

While this attention to administrative-research concerns has generated a substantial body of theory and research on which campaign organizers can draw, it has tended to distract researchers from the perhaps more compelling questions pertaining to the social context in which campaigns occur. Information campaigns and social marketing efforts represent attempts at planned social change (Kotler & Zaltman, 1971; Rogers, 1973; Zaltman & Duncan, 1977; Kotler, 1978; Paisley, 1981), and it is insufficient to examine inherently social phenomena in a social vacuum. It is equally insufficient to evaluate campaign efforts only in terms of the criteria specified by campaign organizers. Campaigns are extensions of fundamental societal processes of social control and social change inherent within and between all social systems, and as such, are imbued with the values of their creators. Concern for such considerations of change attempts is not peculiar to the discipline of information campaigns but applies equally to all forms of applied social science. As noted social theorist Alvin Gouldner (1969 p. 85) has argued: "It is not enough . . . to examine the intellectual tools of applied social science in terms of their manifest scientific functions as technical instruments. They must also be considered in the light of their latent social functions for the peculiar system of human relations in which they are implicated."

The present volume attempts to provide a social context for examining public information campaigns and social marketing efforts, and can itself be placed in various intellectual contexts. First, the book adopts the explicit theoretical framework of social change (or social changing). As such, the orientation is largely macro or social in nature, with emphasis on such topics as: mobilizing community support for change; social barriers to change efforts; social values implicitly and explicitly promoted by campaigns; and social power of change agents. As McLeod and Blumler (1987) have observed, such macrosocial issues have been underaddressed in the bulk of communication research to date. This volume's emphasis on macro concerns does not mean, however, that micro or individual-level issues are ignored; as Kelman and Warwick (1978) have observed, the study of social change necessarily involves bridging levels of analysis, for at some point, individuals must be changed if society is to be changed.

Secondly, this book represents a merging of the traditions of marketing and strategic communication. According to Kotler and Mindak (1978), the two disciplines have emerged from strikingly different origins, and yet they have grown increasingly similar. Whereas marketing originated from the functions of "selling" and "exchange" and later turned to information dissemination as a result of the rise of a market-driven economy, strategic communication efforts originated with the function of mass information dissemination and have only more recently incorporated elements of the four "levers" of marketing (product, price, promotion and place of distribution). In the realm of ideas and issues, as opposed to products, differences between marketing and public information truly become obscure. Massive public health interventions designed to eradicate AIDS, cigarette smoking or premature heart attack, and sophisticated, multi-media efforts by political groups attempting to elect candidates and influence the social agenda can be labeled information campaigns or social marketing with equal validity. Because information campaign planners have become increasingly concerned with, for example, the psychological "costs" incurred by a smoker attempting to quit or the need for interpersonal support networks to sustain change, they have incorporated social marketing techniques into campaigns which, in eras passed, might have consisted largely of mass mediated messages only. Similarly, social marketers working on such issues as nuclear power, abortion, and gun control increasingly have relied on sophisticated public relations tactics to "win" public support for a particular issue position. Yet, as any successful marketer knows, and as the history of public information campaigns has shown (e.g., Lazarsfeld & Merton, 1948; Doob, 1950; Fine, 1981; Wallack, 1981), mass mediated efforts alone are unlikely to induce any meaningful change. Instead of exclusively focusing on certain modes of information dissemination, researchers should overcome the artificial fragmentation of communication processes and focus on more integrative uses and examinations of communication (Pingree, Wiemann and Hawkins, 1988).

Related to this is the third contextual dimension of this book, its interdisciplinary nature. Wilbur Schramm (1959) once remarked that communication research is a crossroads through which many pass but few tarry. This is certainly the case for the discipline of campaigns, which is based on social theory, employs psychological principles, and can and should be analyzed from quantitative and qualitative perspectives. The authors of various chapters in this book represent a wide variety of traditions, including communication, marketing, social work, public health, sociology and social psychology. Within those traditions, different perspectives are also represented, including international, behavioral, critical, cultural and ethical.

The result of these three orientations is a focus on the fundamental tension between social marketing and these social values influencing and, in turn, influenced by social marketing efforts. The notion of "campaign" itself is inextricably linked with images of conflict and tension, stemming, perhaps, from the term's military connotations and its propagandistic deployment in both World Wars. Campaigners have long spoken of "target" audiences and searched for "magic bullet" theories to guide their "strategies" and "tactics." However, in contemporary usage, the conflictive implications of campaigns emanate from value disputes; because campaigns represent mechanisms to achieve one organization's view of the social good, they necessarily promote certain values to the exclusion of others. It is this balancing of interests and values which unifies the above perspectives and is explicitly or implicitly addressed in several of the chapters.

The volume is organized in two sections, *Campaigns and Social Structure,* and *The Campaign Process.* The first section pays particular attention to the social context in which campaigns are designed, implemented and analyzed. Taken individually, each chapter describes the role of social systems in facilitating or inhibiting social change; taken as a whole, the chapters illustrate the broad range of social concerns which campaigns address, as well as important distinctions between various types of campaigns. In addition, these chapters provide a rich source of ideas for subsequent research on social aspects of campaigns.

In the first chapter, an overview of issues in the study of campaigns in a social context, Charles Salmon expands on the concept of social change briefly described above and explores conflicts of values endemic to three phases of the social marketing process, i.e., problem definition, implementation and evaluation. The central thesis of the chapter is that rationales of "public interest" and "benevolence" often obscure the concomitant underlying social processes of control and change.

The next five chapters describe campaigns seeking various degrees of social change ranging from evolutionary change, in which the system itself is encouraging and even managing the change process, to revolutionary change, in which the system is viewed as explicitly or implicitly obstructing change efforts.

Starting on the evolutionary end of the continuum of change, John Finnegan, Neil Bracht and K. Viswanath describe the steps involved in organizing community-based campaigns, an increasingly popular approach to organized social change in which the system becomes the actual mechanism—not merely the locale—of the change effort. In addition to describing various formative-research approaches used in identifying and recruiting community leaders, the authors describe two specific lifestyle campaigns, the Minnesota Heart Health Program and the Indian National Satellite Project.

The next chapter in this section, by Jane Brown, Cynthia Waszak and Kim Walsh Childers, examines the use of campaigns to control and/or modify sexual behavior. Operating from the premise that sexuality is a social construct, the authors describe ways in which systems use campaigns to control individual behavior in order to promote other social interests. In particular, the authors adopt the perspective that political, social and economic structures of society influence the nature of such campaigns, and then to illustrate their point, offer examples of campaigns conducted in the United States and abroad on family planning, abortion and AIDS.

The next chapter in this section is written by Robert Hornik, who examines the ways in which social structure mediates the effectiveness of developmental campaigns. Citing studies from several international efforts, Hornik presents five structural explanations to account for the often-tenuous relationship between knowledge acquisition and subsequent behavioral change.

Writing about the revolutionary end of the continuum, Clarice Olien, Phillip Tichenor, and George Donohue describe in Chapter 5 the social environment from which social movements and protest campaigns emerge. These campaigns, which attempt to induce major structural change, face a number of formidable structural and institutional barriers. Drawing on the structural model for which they are well-known, the authors describe the role of the mass media in accelerating and decelerating strategic communication efforts by disenfranchised groups.

Lana Rakow, writing from the perspective of critical theory, next elaborates on topics of revolutionary change efforts by questioning the legitimacy of corporations' and governments' inducement of change on the part of individuals. By prescribing a shift in the locus of power from the system to the public, she offers a proposal for redirecting change in such a way that the interests of individuals in society are promoted rather than those of the present power structure.

The final chapter in this section is by Richard W. Pollay, professor of commerce and cultural theorist, who examines the notion of values within the campaign context. Extending his writings on the "unintended" effects of commercial advertising campaigns, he provides direction for research on the cultural aspects of information campaigns and social marketing efforts, and offers an inventory of potential outcomes of campaigns which could serve as dependent variables in empirical studies of campaign effects and effectiveness.

Whereas the first section of the book focuses on various approaches to the study of social structure and campaigns, the second section, *The Campaign Process,* addresses more tactical concerns pertaining to the underlying components of campaigns, namely audience research, planning, organization and implementation, and evaluation.

James Grunig begins this section by providing an inventory of segmentation techniques used to narrowly define audience segments. This chapter integrates material from a number of disparate disciplines and organizes it in terms of a "nested" model of segmentation adapted from the literature of industrial marketing.

Next, two social psychologists, Patricia Devine and Edward Hirt provide a rich offering of social psychological theories which can be applied to a variety of campaign situations. Distinguishing between message-based and behavioral-based modes of persuasion, the authors attempt to reduce campaign planners' reliance on traditional hierarchy notions of persuasion and, instead, suggest other approaches for reaching desired outcomes.

Garrett O'Keefe next provides a state-of-the-art description of the political-campaign process, drawing the topic out of the narrow confines of mass communication and providing information on fundraising, PACs, campaign-organizing principles, and strategic planning.

The final chapter in this section, by Steven Chaffee, Connie Roser and June Flora, provides a rare look at the magnitude of campaign effects relative to other considerations, in this case, threats to validity in quasi-experimental design. Using data from the Stanford Heart Disease Prevention Program, the authors provide a detailed account of conundrums associated with campaign evaluation, and empirically demonstrate the relatively small degree of change that can be expected from massive social interventions.

In summary, by providing a treatment of campaigns that is both intellectually and professionally eclectic, it is hoped that the development of both theory *for* and theory *of* campaigns will be enhanced and not viewed as incompatible by researchers operating from widely divergent perspectives.

REFERENCES

Doob, L. W. (1950). Goebbels' principles of propaganda. *Public Opinion Quarterly,* *14,* 419–442.

Fine, S. H. (1981). *The marketing of ideas and social issues.* New York: Praeger.

Gouldner, A. W. (1969). Theoretical requirements of the applied social sciences. In W. G. Bennis, K. D. Benne, & R. Chin (Eds.), *The planning of change,* (2nd ed., pp. 85–98). New York: Holt, Rinehart & Winston.

Kelman, H. C., & Warwick, D. P. (1978). Bridging micro and macro approaches to social change: A social-psychological perspective. In G. Zaltman (Ed.), *Processes and phenomena of social change.* (pp. 13–59). Huntington, NY: Krieger.

Kotler, P. (1978). The elements of social action. In G. Zaltman (Ed.), *Processes and phenomena of social change* (pp. 169–189). Huntington, NY: Krieger.

Kotler, P., Mindak, W. (1978). Marketing and public relations: Should they be partners or rivals? *Journal of Marketing, 42,* 13–20.

Kotler, P., & Zaltman, G. (1971). Social marketing: An approach to planned social change. *Journal of Marketing, 35,* 3–12.

Lazarsfeld, P. F., & Merton, R. K. (1948). Mass communication, popular taste and organized social action. In W. Schramm (Ed.), *Mass communications.* (pp. 492–512). Urbana: University of Illinois Press.

McLeod, J. M., & Blumler, J. G. (1987). The macrosocial level of communiacation science. In C. R. Berger and S. H. Chaffee (Eds.), *Handbook of communication science.* (pp. 271–322). Newbury Park, CA: Sage.

Paisley, W. J. (1981). Public communication campaigns: The American experience. In R. E. Rice & W. J. Paisley (Eds.), *Public communication campaigns.* (pp. 15–40). Beverly Hills, CA: Sage.

Pingree, S., Wiemann, J. M. & Hawkins, R. P. (1988). Toward conceptual synthesis. In R. P. Hawkins, J. W. Wiemann, & S. Pingree (Eds.), *Advancing communication science: Merging mass and interpersonal processes* (pp. 7–17). Newbury Park, CA: Sage.

Rogers, E. M. (1973). *Communication strategies for family planning.* New York: Free Press.

Rogers, E. M., & Storey, J. D. (1987). Communication campaigns. In C. R. Berger and S. H. Chaffee (Eds.), *Handbook of communication science* (pp. 817–846). Newbury Park, CA: Sage.

Schramm, W. (1959). Comments on "the state of communication research." *Public Opinion Quarterly, 23,* 6–9.

Wallack, L. M. (1981). Mass media campaigns: The odds against finding behavior change. *Health Education Quarterly, 8,* 209–260.

Zaltman, G., & Duncan, R. (1977). Strategies for planned change. New York: John Wiley.

ACKNOWLEDGMENTS

Without the friendship, ideas and efforts of a number of persons, this project never would have reached successful completion. Robert Hawkins, one of three editors of this Sage series, spent countless hours planning, reading manuscripts, editing and patiently supplying encouragement throughout the past year. His coeditors, Suzanne Pingree and John Wiemann, provided excellent analyses of several chapters. The chapter authors were uniformly encouraging and cooperative, even in the face of imminent deadlines. Dianne Rucinski, University of Iowa, provided insightful comments and excellent suggestions in her readings of each of the chapters in this volume. Hye-Ryeon Lee and Kurt Neuwirth, graduate students in the School of Journalism and Mass Communication, provided invaluable research support and ideas. James L. Baughman, a colleague, supplied helpful comments on a draft of the opening chapter. The School of Journalism and Mass Communication offered a supportive environment, generous research support and a congenial atmosphere which greatly facilitated the completion of this project. Finally, Jerry Kline, my doctoral advisor and founding editor of this series, provided the direction and focus which led me on this path in the first place.

PART I

CAMPAIGNS AND SOCIAL STRUCTURE

CAMPAIGNS FOR SOCIAL "IMPROVEMENT": AN OVERVIEW OF VALUES, RATIONALES, AND IMPACTS

Charles T. Salmon

NEARLY FORTY YEARS AGO, G. D. Wiebe (1952) formally launched the field of social marketing with the single question, "Why can't you sell brotherhood and rational thinking like you sell soap?" In other words, can the principles used in the marketing of products be applied to the marketing of ideas, particularly those deemed beneficial to society? In the intervening years, answers to Wiebe's question have consisted of various tests of effectiveness of social marketing programs and information campaigns, where effectiveness has been determined in terms of the interests of those possessing the requisite power and resources to initiate such projects. In retrospect, however, it seems that Wiebe's query might best have been answered with a series of follow-up questions much like the following: "In whose interests is this outcome desirable, and why?" "What circumstances prompted defining conditions in society as a social problem stemming from *lack* of brotherhood?" "To whom will brotherhood be sold—to citizens in society or to legislators in a position to institute meaningful structural reforms?" "How will brotherhood be sold—as an end to racism, as the promotion of peace, as an end to civil disturbances, as tokenism designed to maintain the status quo or as a guarantee of a new labor force for minimum-wage jobs?" And finally, and perhaps most importantly, "What criteria shall we use to determine success, and who shall make that determination?"

Any effort to engineer change in society is a value-laden activity, one in which not all persons agree upon the ends pursued and the means employed to achieve these ends. Instead, each phase of a campaign for social change involves an application and weighing of conflicting interests, some of which will be maximized at the expense of others. At the center of this conflict is the fundamental tension between social control and individual freedoms. Social marketing efforts, by definition, employ mechanisms of social control—e.g., the passage of laws, the inculcation and modification of social norms—to achieve objectives of social change where these objectives are said to be in the best interests of the individuals or systems being changed. As such, social marketing efforts necessarily compromise certain values and interests, often individual freedoms, in order to promote values and interests deemed more socially, economically or morally compelling by the organization sponsoring the change effort. The present essay operates from this premise and examines various conflicts of values arising from three phases of the social marketing process: (1) the definition of a social condition as a social problem meriting intervention; (2) implementation of campaign activities and (3) evaluation of the effectiveness of those activities. The central thesis is that the manifest objectives of social marketing efforts, which are usually framed by their proponents as "prosocial" or "congruent with the public interest," must be examined in terms of their latent social functions and dysfunctions, as well as the values and interests which they supersede. Rather than passively accepting that all social engineering efforts described as in the "public interest" are actually so, one must examine the underlying assumptions of the campaigners as well as the values they are implicitly and explicitly promoting.

THE PROBLEM DEFINITION PHASE

THE NATURE OF THE PROBLEM

An information campaign, like psychotherapy, social work, population control, education, religion, legislation, welfare or even military action, is a form of social intervention prompted by a determination that some situation represents a social problem meriting social action. Depending upon the context, this social situation can take the form of some individual or group, a change agent or agency, making such determinations as: some consumers are unaware (but should not be) of some organization's service which may improve their lives; some social systems are insufficiently "advanced" or "modernized" (and should change); some individuals are engaging in behaviors which bring them pleasure, but which also have a level of risk associated with them that a change agency considers too high (so they should cease these behaviors); or some government is being unresponsive to the needs of certain groups by failing to distribute resources in a manner which a change agency considers equitable (so the government should alter its philosophy of allocation).

In each of the above cases, by defining certain situations as "undesirable" or "in need of change" and then prescribing efforts to change individuals and groups, an organization is attempting to control the process of change, to adapt its political, social or economic environments in a manner which is deemed desirable by the change agency. Change itself is a fundamental and constant condition of society; however, the nature and extent of change are not constant, and instead are variables which organizations seek to control through a variety of strategies, one of which is an information campaign (Paisley, 1981; Rogers, 1973). That some social condition is problematic means only that it has been defined as a problem or threat by someone or some group (Edelman, 1964; Cobb & Elder, 1983). Although this statement may appear self-evident, it needs to be emphasized in the present discussion. It is important because it underscores the relativistic nature of social conditions from which an information campaign emerges as a "solution" to something that some organization has defined as a "problem." The word *defined* is similarly vital in this context because it implies that social problems are not *recognized,* i.e., that social conditions are not inherently problematic or harmful, but, instead, that many chronic conditions exist, but only some are granted "problem" status. This viewpoint essentially reflects the symbolic interactionist perspective on social problems offered by Blumer (1971) and developed by Hilgartner and Bosk (1988), i.e., that definitions or "frames" of social problems compete for acceptance in the public-policy realm and do not reflect objective and non-controversial assessments of conditions.

For example, a number of public information campaigns occur within the domain of public health. This is not to say that every cause of death or illness is the focus of an information campaign; some are and some are not, and the decision whether to sponsor campaigns for a particular social condition involves a number of political as well as medical factors. As Wallack (1981, p. 221) has observed, " . . . these campaigns do not take place in a vacuum but confront strongly vested financial interests and deep-rooted well-established values . . . [C]ampaigns dealing with alcohol, smoking, and most drugs (especially over-the-counter drugs) are inherently political in that they require processes of compromise and conciliation of potentially volatile issues affecting interests not necessarily consistent with public health."

The adversarial nature of campaign contexts and the subjective quality of framing social problems are illustrated in an inventory of possible ways of framing the issue of cigarette smoking, prepared by the Advocacy Institute (1988) for use by antismoking groups in policy debates:

- defenders of health versus profit seekers
- community leaders versus merchants of addictive drugs
- citizens for clean air versus environmental polluters
- children and infants, the family, the poor, women and minorities versus big business
- health scientists versus paid propagandists

While most antismoking campaigns are designed with public health interests paramount, it has been pointed out that some social engineering efforts to eliminate indoor smoking may be more political than substantive in nature. One such attempt, a "Clean Air Act," defined by supporters as a solution to the health implications of air pollution, was passed in New York City, the city with the highest level of carbon monoxide pollution in the nation. If pollution and resulting health hazards were indeed the primary concern of the city, then social engineering efforts would be most appropriately applied to the most egregious problem, and such reforms as the banning of motor vehicle traffic in and around the city and the elimination of noxious fuel sources would be instituted. Yet because these latter outcomes are not as politically and economically viable, they are rejected in favor of less-substantive measures which pose less of a threat to the system. Indeed, the Act itself has been defined as a problem by various groups because it is viewed as discriminating against Blacks and Hispanics (who are disproportionately smokers) and motivated by concerns with profit rather than health. Similarly, it is this profit motive which allegedly led a major airline to restrict smoking on flights because of concern about "the cost of changing filters and cabin air outlets gummed up by tar and nicotine," while publicly framing the restriction as a measure to promote health (*Workers Vanguard*, 1988).

Perhaps the premiere illustration of the politics of problem definition in the domain of campaigns and social marketing is that of the drug "problem." Historically, the use of the term *drug problem* in the context of public health campaigns has uncritically referred to the use of a number of drugs, including alcohol, tobacco, marijuana, cocaine, barbiturates, valium, etc., rather than a single drug (and yet different drugs have greatly different characteristics and associated hazards or dangers). Secondly, most problem definitions have focused on *illegal* drugs rather than legal ones, thereby suggesting that dependence on certain drugs is a problem meriting campaign attention, whereas dependence on other drugs is not. Further, most problem definitions of this type have equated use with *abuse,* thereby implying that those drugs deemed illegal by the medical and governmental establishments cannot be used without abuse.

Campaigns against drugs in the United States date back at least to the nineteenth century and have employed a variety of interpersonal and mass-mediated efforts. From the earliest efforts of the Women's Christian Temperance Union through the first radio broadcast defining drugs as a social "problem" ("The Struggle of Mankind Against Its Deadliest Foe"), fear has been the central theme of antidrug campaigns (e.g., Smart & Fejer, 1974; Feingold & Knapp, 1977; Wallack, 1981). The use of fear appeals is obvious from the titles of anti-marijuana movies in the 1930s, e.g., *Reefer Madness, Assassin of Youth,* and *Marijuana, Weed With Roots in Hell.* Since that time, the National Institute of Mental Health and, more recently, the executive branch of government and the "Just Say No" coalition have inaugurated many nationally coordinated campaigns to address what has been defined as *the* drug problem.

Lost in the extreme patriotic fervor of such efforts, though, are the questions of motivations and values underlying such efforts. In fact, *the* drug problem really refers to *many* possible ways of defining social problems associated with drugs; there is no single problem, just as there is no single drug or single way in which a drug can be used. For example, antimarijuana campaigns conducted by the governmental and medical establishments have implicitly defined the issue in terms of a public health problem in which use of marijuana is seen as contributing to a host of social ills, including impairment of physical health; various psychological maladies; loss of concentration in school; graduation to other, more dangerous drugs; dependence or addiction; and crime motivated by the need to pay for drug usage.

Yet the definition of the marijuana problem could easily be recast. To groups such as the National Organization for the Reform of Marijuana Laws, the "problem" is that of governmental regulation which limits individuals' rights to use the drug for such purposes as recreation in private settings such as the home, treatment of glaucoma, cancer, insomnia, anxiety and epilepsy, and use in religious ceremonies (e.g., by Rastafarians). From this vantage point, the problem definition is one of "infringement on individual liberties."

Of course, these are not the only definitions of "the" problem. Another definition might focus on society's reliance on drugs to solve personal problems, a reliance rivaled only by religion and family support. The common prescription of valium, the widespread availability of over-the-counter drugs in supermarkets as well as in "drug" stores, and the cliche, "Take two aspirin and call me in the morning," as a substitute for a physician's care all speak to the magnitude of the social legitimacy of and dependence upon drugs to solve physical and psychological ailments. Prescription drugs are administered by physicians for problems involving interpersonal relationships, physical pain and intrapersonal feelings of inadequacy. Expenditures on over-the-counter drugs in the United States now exceed two billion dollars annually (*USA Today,* 1989). In other words, the drug problem can be defined in terms of the degree to which the medical community acts as an "institutional pusher" of drugs over which it exercises control of production, distribution and profit, and simultaneously delegitimizes drugs over which it does not exercise this control (Wallack, 1981). Antidrug campaigns, in this context, represent highly selective efforts to discourage use of specific drugs in a culture which, in large measure, is drug-dependent. It is hardly surprising, therefore, that small-scale efforts to reduce dependency on certain delegitimized drugs are destined to fail in the face of formidable institutional support for drugs and parallel social norms, in general, condoning drug use.

DEFINERS OF THE PROBLEM

Given that no single definition of a problem is uniquely accurate, the power to control the framing or defining of an issue is of paramount importance if an organization is to gain acceptance of its proposed solution. Without question, this power resides disproportionately with government, corporations and other institutions possessing legitimacy, social power and resources and access to the mass media. Yet campaigns, in and of themselves are not inherently weapons of the social elite; some campaigns are conducted by socially disadvantaged groups seeking to induce extensive systemic change (e.g., Rada, 1977; Gitlin, 1980; Klandermans & Oegema, 1987). Goals of campaigns can be arrayed on a continuum ranging from developmental or evolutionary to revolutionary change. Political campaigns involving the mainstream Democratic and Republican parties, for example (see Chapter 10 by O'Keefe, this volume), represent institutionalized mechanisms of change within very narrow parameters, continuity from one administration to another with little in the way of radical reform. The adoption of a new cereal or style of clothing similarly constitute forms of evolutionary change which can be viewed as maintenance of the system or transmission of the status quo.

In constrast, other campaigns are sponsored by organizations seeking to alter basic societal assumptions, laws and norms, and seeking to locate the origin of social problems within the system. Social movements reflecting broad social concerns on such topics as civil rights, the right of government to engage in convert military action or the legitimacy of concentration of wealth are examples of efforts to induce revolutionary change.

In general, these latter types of campaigns tend to be less common and less successful than the former. In large measure, this merely mirrors differences in social resources and power between groups seeking evolutionary versus revolutionary change. Challenger groups are often poorly funded and poorly organized; lack of organization, social power and resources, in turn, dictates reliance on less-than-optimal campaign strategies. First, these groups are less able to control the disposition of their messages because they lack the financial resources necessary for the purchase of advertising space. Instead, these groups must rely more heavily on what have traditionally been considered public relations tactics of garnering "free" publicity through the planning of events which are congruent with journalists' definitions of news (see Boorstin, 1961) or the use of news releases and public service announcements. Whereas the use of advertising guarantees that an organization can control the content, placement and timing of a message to enhance the probability that it will reach a desired target audience and have the desired effect, the use of publicity provides no such control for the source, but instead, relegates control solely to a media gatekeeper. This person decides whether information will appear in a mass medium at all and how it will be presented if reported (see Tichenor, Olien & Donohue, 1967; Smith and Rabin, 1978; Goodman, 1981; Baxter, 1981, Turk, 1986). Further, in the case of broadcast information, the gatekeeper controls temporal placement of materials and can relegate information in the form of public service announcements to late-night hours when the viewing audience is small (Hanneman, McEwen, & Coyne, 1973; O'Keefe and Reid-Nash, 1986).

Shoemaker (1984) has found that newspaper editors are more receptive to information from groups perceived as legitimate, viable and centrist (e.g., the League of Women Voters) than from groups percieved as lacking those characteristics (e.g., the Jewish Defense League or the Nazi Party). This conclusion is supported by a number of studies that have documented the media's role in maintaining the status quo (Edelstein & Schulz, 1963; Paletz, Reichert & McIntyre, 1971; and Chapter 5 by Olien, Tichenor and Donohue, this volume). Because of the confluence of financial impediments and journalistic predilections, challenger organizations often must resort to unconventional means in their efforts to draw attention to and define a social problem, including conflict, demonstrations, confrontations and even the slaughtering of animals, all of which gain media attention but simultaneously further delegitimize the group. Albritton and Manheim (1983) and Manheim and Albritton (1986) argue that a campaign's goal of generating publicity without regard to its negative or positive valence is ultimately self-defeating for the group which seeks to gain acceptance of its ideas or practices. This conclusion is similar to that of Todd Gitlin (1980) in his description of how the organization "Students for a Democratic Society" was initially successful in attracting media coverage through the use of staged events but how that success proved to be Pyrrhic as the group was labeled "radical" and "deviant" because of its social agenda and reliance on unconventional means to attract media attention.

LOCATION OF THE PROBLEM

The power to define a situation as a problem carries with it the ability to define the cause or location of the problem, the domain of society to which change efforts will be applied. Just as a social phenomenon is constructed as problematic in terms of the interest of the definer of a situation, the cause or location of a social problem similarly represents a social construction by a particular group. For some groups, lacking social resources, many conditions taken for granted by the majority of citizens may represent problems. Basic institutional arrangements and structure, viewed by many as the pillars of public welfare and the manifestation of the public interest, are viewed by others as impediments to social equality, social justice and social power, and hence, as social problems. Thus, recognition of the location of the problem is predicated upon a change agency's social position. If a group possesses privilege and power, it recognizes as problems those individuals whose actions are incompatible with system norms, whereas those same individuals may view the system itself as a problem. If a sufficiently large number of individuals die of lung cancer, for example, a typical response might be to call for information campaigns to get smokers to stop smoking; alternatively, a response might be to eliminate federal subsidies of tobacco growing. When "enough" individuals die in automobile accidents, a typical response might be to develop campaigns for the passage of laws which will fine passengers for not wearing seatbelts; alternatively, a response might be to require automobile manufacturers to build safer cars and include passive restraint systems (Robertson, 1976). In each case, the threshold for "enough" or "sufficiently large number" of deaths involves a subjective determination by someone that a certain cause of death warrants consideration as a problem (whereas other causes do not). Further, the direction in which the resulting change effort is applied (system versus individuals) follows directly from the problem definition that "wins."

More often than not, the initial response on the part of an agency that has defined a problem is to engineer ways of changing behaviors of individuals or victims affected by a problem rather than addressing the systemic roots of the problem itself, a derivation of the notion of "blaming the victim" (Dervin, 1980; see also Chapter 6 by Rakow, this volume). Particularly in the case of public information campaigns, for which the government is the primary source of funding, it is unusual for funds to be disbursed to change the system rather than changing individuals responding to the system. It is because of this that most campaigns can be viewed as efforts to induce evolutionary rather than revolutionary change. Campaigns usually represent an early attempt by a system to rectify an emerging problem because they are relatively inexpensive and easy to implement and provide the appearance that individuals are able to exercise their free will despite the imposition of a change attempt on them. When campaigns, in and of themselves, are unsuccessful at inducing change, however, they may give way to more stringent forms of change, namely power strategies in which change is legislated or mandated. In any society, such strategies are more potentially threatening to the system, and hence less desirable than strategies in which individuals at least perceive that they are exercising free will.

Further, it can also be argued that some campaigns represent token attempts at change, efforts to deflect criticisms of bias or apathy on the part of government but efforts which are not designed to be maximally effective. For example, it should be obvious by now that short-term, small-scale, media-only campaigns will have little impact on health behaviors that have been ingrained over a lifetime and which are strongly reinforced by individuals' lifestyles, reference groups and family structure. Such campaigns may be effective in altering cognitions and perhaps attitudes within some time period, usually arbitrary and unreasonably short, that has been selected as an appropriate point for evaluation of the campaign (Brown & Einsiedel, 1988). If well-conceived, repeated over time and reinforced through interpersonal intervention, the campaigns may very likely begin to influence behaviors. At the same time, it has been argued that the most powerful determinant of health is socioeconomic status and that by elevating the standard of living and eliminating poverty and illiteracy, the greatest amount of health enhancement could be accomplished (Levin, 1987). Such a solution, however, which is likely to be much more effective than a few public service announcements broadcast at late-night timeslots to resistant viewers, represents, to legitimized change agencies charged with the responsibility of promoting public health, far too drastic a change. Thus, while all public health campaigns can be defined as altruistic efforts to improve society, some—but not all—can also be defined as efforts by the system to control the locus of change in ways deemed desirable by the change agency.

THE IMPLEMENTATION PHASE

As has been discussed above, campaigns occur when an organization has defined a situation as a threat to interests or values to which it is committed. Upon defining a situation in this manner, the organization must next decide whether to intervene and, if so, in what manner. Both decisions explicitly and implicitly involve further applications of social values.

Herbert Kelman (1969) describes these decisions as two horns of an ethical dilemma. At the basis of this dilemma is the widely shared feeling that a core human value which needs to be protected is that of individual freedom of choice. As Kelman (1969, p. 583) describes it, "On the one hand, for those of us who hold the enhancement of man's freedom of choice as a fundamental value, any manipulation of the behavior of others constitutes a violation of their essential humanity."

This sentiment can be traced to the writings of John Stuart Mill (1859) who, in *On Liberty,* wrote that an individual's course of action was best determined by himself or herself, not by some outsider, regardless of the altruism guiding the latter: "He cannot rightfully be compelled to do or forebear because it will be better for him to do so, because it will make him happier, because in the opinion of others, to do so would be wise, even right." "With respect to his own feelings and circumstances," Mill continued, "the most ordinary man or woman has means of knowledge immeasurably surpassing those than can be possessed by anyone else." In other words, Mill felt that interfering with an individual's self determination would, in most cases, result in a loss of personal freedom which would necessarily outweigh any good attained by the intervention. Yet, in some situations, Mill noted, intervention is justified, either if the intervention is made to prevent an individual from engaging in an activity that harms others, if the individual is a child, or if the activity eliciting the intervention is universally deemed disadvantageous to the individual (e.g., selling oneself into slavery).

The second horn of Kelman's dilemma, though, is based upon the realization that society cannot exist in the absence of any form of influence on individual behavior, and certainly efforts to improve society through planned social change are predicated upon the need to influence others. This is the basis, for example, of B. F. Skinner's contention that social engineering is justified—perhaps even mandated—if a society possesses the means of behavior modification and uses those means to create a better society (Skinner, 1971; Rogers & Skinner, 1956). The problem with this position, as Carl Rogers (Rogers & Skinner, 1956), Herbert Kelman (1969), and Aldous Huxley have duly noted, is that one person's vision of utopia is another's vision of dystopia.

Although the majority of the literature of campaigns fails to directly address the dilemma itself, a great deal of work in the broader realms of philosophy and social change theory have focused on elaborate rationalizations for justifying social intervention efforts. Applied to the domain of social marketing, these rationalizations include the freedom-enhancing qualities of certain change strategies, the informative nature of campaign content and promotion of the public and individual interests. In this next section, these justifications are first presented in greater detail and then critically examined.

THE RATIONALE OF RELATIVE FREEDOM ENHANCEMENT

Chin and Benne (1969) have observed that the proliferation of "helping professions" and increased acceptance of the ethical propriety of social intervention itself has resulted in a shift involving the fundamental question asked by social engineers. The question asked in earlier eras, i.e., "should we seek to plan to change?" has been replaced since the 1960s by the question "how [do we] plan particular changes in particular settings and situations?" If we accept as an inevitability the use of planned efforts for social change, the question then becomes one of determining the appropriate strategies to be used in change attempts. This determination often involves considerations of finances, time, ability and willingness of the change target to change, and the nature of the change sought (Zaltman & Duncan, 1977). From the standpoint of ethics, though, the primary consideration is usually that of the extent to which the change strategy inhibits or nurtures freedom of choice (Kelman, 1969).

Several inventories of change strategies have been compiled, including those by Benne and Birnbaum (1969), Chin and Benne (1969), Zaltman and Duncan (1977), and Kotler (1978). For example, Zaltman and Duncan (1977) describe four major categories of strategies, namely power, persuasion, normative-reeducative, and facilitative. In general, these strategies can be differentiated in terms of the degree of personal freedom each one allows. At one end of this continuum is the strategy of power, in which a change agency imposes change on some group, usually through legal mandate or control of financial resources. According to Zaltman and Duncan, this strategy, which is the most freedom-inhibiting, is best suited for situations in which time is limited, opposition is anticipated, the change agency possesses resources valued by the change target, and the change target is either unwilling or unable to change by itself. Perhaps the best examples of this mechanism of social change include Supreme Court decisions on racial integration and abortion.

Next on this continuum is the strategy of persuasion, a strategy considered manipulative but less-overtly repressive than that of power. Persuasion strategies tend to be effective in cases in which resources available to the change agent are limited, the change agency must create needs, motivation and commitment on the part of the change target group, and resistance by the change target is anticipated. Essential to this strategy is bias in the way information is structured and delivered. Many campaigns described as "propaganda" or commercial advertising would be considered to fall into this category.

The third major strategy of social change is described as normative-reeducative, a strategy predicated on the notion that "the relatively unbiased presentation of fact is intended to provide a rational justification for action." This strategy, which is considered far more freedom-enhancing than either of the first two, assumes that information can be considered to be unbiased (a questionable assumption that is addressed later in this essay) and that individuals will act in a similar manner upon exposure to that information. This type of strategy is seen as most effective when individuals believe that a problem exists and lack awareness of some solution to that problem, when a quick change is not required, when long-term financial support is available and when significant systemic change is sought. Many campaigns described as "public information" would be considered as adopting this model of change.

Finally, the fourth major strategy is that of facilitation, in which an organization makes resources available to a system that is interested in changing but which lacks certain material ingredients for change. For this type of change to be effective, a change target must be aware of a problem and must want to change, resistance must be minimal, and the only barrier to change must be lack of resources. Many private foundations and governmental agencies provide grants to organizations seeking to improve communities, promote the arts or otherwise benefit the public welfare. Both the normative-reeducative and the facilitative strategies imply a certain rationality on the part of the change target, where rationality should be defined in terms of actions deemed reasonable by the change agent rather than in absolute terms.

Although information campaigns can be seen as strategies in and of themselves (through persuasion and normative reeducation), they are often essential supplements to other change strategies as well. For example, a facilitative strategy is successful only if the change target is aware of the available resources. Thus, governmental agencies issue "Requests for Proposals" and the like to publicize the availability of funds for worthwhile projects. Similarly, power strategies are effective only to the extent that the change target is aware of the imposed change. Campaigns to publicize a new mandatory seatbelt law should not be viewed as independent change efforts by themselves, but instead, components of a larger, multi-strategic intervention effort. This point has implications for evaluations of social intervention efforts: If an evaluator determines that relatively few individuals respond to information campaigns describing a new mandatory seatbelt law, is it the campaign, or the deployment of a power strategy, which is to be "blamed"? More often than not, the efficacy of the campaign is questioned while the efficacy and appropriateness of the passage of law is unquestioned (e.g., see Gantz, Fitzmaurice, & Yoo, 1987).

The rationale that campaigns are freedom enhancing relative to other potential forms of change is a strong one. However, if one further examines the assumptions of this rationale, it becomes somewhat problematic. First, the degree to which individuals can actually exercise free will is limited by options permitted and promoted by social institutions. Structural-functionalists, for example, argue that individuals merely choose between structurally determined alternatives rather than exercising free will in any absolute sense (see Coser, 1982). Institutionalized processes of social control define and limit potential behaviors in which an individual can engage. From this viewpoint, recipients of information campaign messages can be said to choose from among options allowed by structure but not from the total range of possible behaviors, many of which might even be unknown to those persons. For example, the noted historian David Potter (1954) contends that advertising is effective only to the extent that marketers are first able to inculcate a culture of consumption in a society, a situation in which consumers accept the attractiveness of—and indeed the need for—purchasing consumer goods. In the presence of this engineered social norm, freedom of choice becomes freedom of being able to purchase those products (e.g., automobiles) which marketers have decided to offer, in the form in which marketers have decided to offer them, and which society, through such actions as the construction of highways and reduced support for mass transportation, has made necessities.

Secondly, the rationalization that campaigns may allow greater freedom than might power strategies may understate the extent to which certain mechanisms of social control, social norms or opinion climates, restrict individual choice and action in much the same manner as do power-based forms of social control, such as laws. The intent of many information campaigns, for example, is to alter the prevailing sentiment or climate of opinion regarding some issue. A couple of hundred years ago, for example, tobacco was widely viewed as a panacea, was used in the treatment of several ailments, and was sanctioned by the medical community (Gordon, 1949). As recently as twenty years ago, few people questioned the rights of smokers to smoke in public places, including restaurants. The massive assault on cigarette smoking in the past two decades, however, has created a climate of "health vigilantism" in which smokers are now punished (through guilt, rejection, ridicule) for failing to comply to an emerging social norm (Levin, 1987). Conforming to this social norm, like most, has become virtually a "requisite for good citizenship—a patriotic imperative" (Levin, 1987, p. 57). The power of norms and public opinion to inhibit individual action has long been considered to represent a formidable weapon of social control, often as great as laws (Mill, 1859; Locke, 1961; Noelle-Neumann, 1973, 1974). In the words of John Stuart Mill (1859, p. 220), this form of social control represents "a social tyranny more formidable than many kinds of political oppression, since, though not usually upheld by such extreme penalties, it leaves fewer means of escape, penetrating much more deeply into the details of life, and enslaving the soul itself." In other words, the rationale that campaigns are preferred means of social change because they represent lesser threats to freedom of choice is accurate; however, this relative advantage does not guarantee individual freedom of choice and may, in some cases, be more illusionary than substantive in the context of social norms and power of social institutions.

INFORMATION, NOT PERSUASION

The rationale that public *information* campaigns are more ethical forms of intervention than others, particularly *persuasion* campaigns, is central to a number of justifications of the use of information campaigns to achieve social change. Atkin (1981, p. 265) argues that the former benefit individual receivers or society, whereas the latter benefit the "private self-interest of the sponsoring source." Bauer (1964) and Grunig (1987) both use the term *asymmetric communication* to describe some campaigns which are considered exploitive and manipulative and imply that *symmetric* campaigns, in which organizations disseminate "straight facts," are not only possible but more socially responsible as well. A number of prominent scholars, including Eric Fromm, John Kenneth Galbraith, and Marshall McLuhan, have described the evils of "commercial advertising," contending that it leads to such socially undesirable outcomes as cynicism, anomie, irrationality, neuroticism, self-indulgence, materialism, greed, loss of compassion, and selfishness (Pollay, 1986). In contrast, public information campaigns are described as efforts to "improve the lives of individuals and the fabric of society" (Rice and Paisley, 1981, p. 7).

One of the most vilified words in the political sphere of the English language is *propaganda,* although the term originally referred to the mission of the Catholic Church in disseminating information, propagating the "straight facts" about Catholicism (Qualter, 1962). The word has attracted a number of negative connotations since its inception and now refers to a form of communication in which a communicator "manipulates" others, often without their being aware of the manipulative effort, for the source's own benefit rather than for the benefit of the receiver (Jowett & O'Donnell, 1986). *Misinformation, disinformation,* and even *warnography* are terms similarly used to describe the contents of campaigns which someone considers repugnant or antisocial—or at least with which one disagrees. To Joseph Schumpeter (1965), contemporary usage of the term refers to "any statement emanating from a source that we do not like," and it is this liking or disliking which motivates the value judgment that certain campaigns should be defined as propagandistic whereas other forms of manipulation should be defined as benevolent.

This point is illustrated in an early review of propaganda research by Smith, Lasswell and Casey (1946), in which the authors distinguished between propaganda and education by arguing that the former is concerned with attitudes on *controversial* issues, whereas the latter is concerned with attitudes on *noncontroversial* issues (emphasis added). The problem with this distinction is that it assumes the status quo as noncontroversial, which it is for the "haves" of society. However, it fails to acknowledge that education and many other socially sanctioned forms of transmission of "noncontroversial" values are no less manipulative than are transmitters of "controversial" ones. As noted social psychologist Philip Zimbardo (1972, p. 82) has observed:

> Parents, educators, priests, and psychotherapists, for example, represent some of the most powerful "behavioral engineers" in this society. It is rare that the appropriateness of evaluating what they do in ethical terms is even considered. . . . They function with the benefits of socially sanctioned labels which conceal persuasive intent: parents "socialize," teachers "educate," priests "save souls," and therapists "cure the mentally ill."

And, he might have added, public information campaign planners "improve the lives of individuals," while propagandists "manipulate."

It is this double standard which serves as an unconvincing rationale for praising the dissemination of "facts" and criticizing the use of "persuasion." The definition of social phenomena as problems, the locus of change proposed, and the selection of facts to be presented all involve the imposition of value judgments and attempts to influence individuals. If we purport to give only the "straight facts" in a campaign to promote modernization, for example, we first beg the question of why we are imposing our standard of success on another culture in the first place (Rogers, 1978). Next, are the facts of modernization "progress" and "welfare" or increased pollution and reliance on psychotherapists? In other words, are all aspects of progress necessarily desirable and to all persons equally? The decision regarding which facts are to be cited necessarily stems from an organization's vested interest in the situation. Many recent "straight facts" campaigns in support of mandatory seatbelt laws, for example, have been sponsored by insurance companies and automobile manufacturers. The stated concern justifying these campaigns may be public health and safety, but the vested interest is financial: If mandatory seatbelt laws are passed in a sufficient number of states, automobile manufacturers will not be required to install passive restraint systems, and insurance companies will not have to pay as much in benefits. Should not these facts, which might be of interest to citizens contemplating a referendum, be as prominently mentioned in corporate-sponsored campaigns? Additionally, focusing on the manifest content of "information" campaigns obscures the symbolic persuasive messages which may be present. For example, Paletz et al. (1977) contend that information campaigns sponsored by the Internal Revenue Service and other governmental agencies are inherently persuasive because they portray the government as benificent, capable, and working to promote the interests of the citizens. Such campaigns, according to Paletz et al. (1977), thereby implicitly nurture confidence in and support for institutions while concomitantly suppressing political participation on the part of the citizenry.

In practice, the use of the "information-not-persuasion" rationale realistically should be considered a strategy employed by an organization to gain acceptance of its activities and to deflect criticism of its intent rather than some absolute indication of its moral or ethical imperative.

PROMOTION OF PUBLIC AND INDIVIDUAL INTERESTS

Related to the justification based upon the distinction between factual and persuasive campaigns is the rationale that some campaigns are warranted because they promote the public interest and enhance the lives of individuals in society. To Paisley (1981), for example, one of the key concepts in considering some campaigns as "public" is that of reform, where *reform* is defined as "any action that makes society better or makes the lives of individuals better," and where the term *better* is defined in terms of dominant or emerging social values in a specific society at a specific point in time. Rogers and Storey (1987), using a notion similar to that of Atkin (1981) described above, make the point that the locus of benefit of some campaigns rests with the source, in the case of commercial or private interest campaigns, versus with the receiver, in the case of public information campaigns. The distinction is not intended to imply mutual exclusivity, because most campaigns can be evaluated in such a way that both source and receiver are said to benefit, but instead, to refer to the predominant locus of benefit.

The rationale that some campaigns promote public and individual interests rests upon some consensual notion of what actually constitutes these interests. Yet there is no single conceptual or operational definition of the concept "public interest" and even less consensus regarding how to achieve it (or them). The classic articulation of the concept stems from an eighteenth century notion that some "common good" exists and can be determined, and that this good should serve as the obvious "beacon light" of policy (Schumpeter, 1965; see also Sorauf, 1957). This, in turn, meant that for most reasonable citizens the public will or desired course of action was synonymous with the common good. Inspired by this notion of the public interest, a number of attempts have been made to identify a set of core interests which could truly be considered "public" in the sense of being universally shared within a particular society. But this raises the important point that interests are defined in terms of a specific culture and in terms of economic, social psychological and spiritual values. Some inventories of these interests include such conditions as health and the maximization of individuals' economic satisfaction (Schumpeter, 1965); wealth, well-being, affection, skill, respect, enlightenment, freedom and power (Lasswell, 1962); and enhancement of individual freedom (Kelman, 1969). Regarding this last interest, that of individual freedom, it generally is argued that the public interest is not merely the sum of individual interests (as is the case, for example, with the conventional definition of public opinion, which treats that concept as the aggregation of individual opinions). As Bertrand Russell once remarked, this would be a reasonable algorithm only if the sum total of selfish individual actions could be equated with the maximum happiness of the community, which is seldom the case.

Thus the first problem with the public-interest rationale is that there exists no single definition regarding what constitutes the public interest, and thus little hope that we can validly argue that our campaign efforts are promoting anything but interests valued by some, but not all. In the words of Warwick and Kelman (1978, p. 393): "There is [very little] consensus on what constitutes personal well-being and individual freedom—on the definition of the 'ideal man' to which social change ought to be directed. The choice of goals in this area depends on one's view of what is good for man, of what is happiness, and of how individuals should relate to the state and surrounding society." The value that probably comes closest to having universal endorsement is that proposed by John Stuart Mill, i.e., physical safety, and this humanitarian value is the basis for virtually all public health campaigns.

Yet, even if we assemble the greatest philosophers, psychologists, marketers, sociologists and other high priests of social engineering and compel them to define a single public interest, we are then confronted with the even larger problem regarding how best to achieve that interest. The value "personal well-being" is, in the abstract, a desirable end in most cultures. Yet there is no unique way of promoting this interest, and many approaches which are intended to promote it necessarily restrict other, equally viable interests.

Gerald Dworkin (1979) and John Kleinig (1984) have analyzed a number of social interventions in terms of the concept of paternalism, defined as "the interference with a person's liberty of action justified by reasons . . . of welfare, good, happiness, needs, interests or values of the person being coerced." The term is a derivative of the sixteenth century notion of patriarchalism, in which the interference in the lives of individuals is justified in terms of the good of a group or society rather than an individual. The increasing acceptance of the philosophy of paternalism, according to Kleinig (1984), has been the result of the rise of the liberal society and concomitant adherence to the belief that society has an obligation to enhance the opportunities for and realization of personal fulfillment. The paradox of paternalism, similar to the dilemma posed by Kelman, is that the goal of self-fulfillment is achieved, in part, through the abrogation of personal freedom. Thus the term "benevolent manipulation" is used to describe paternalistic efforts to change someone for his or her own good, or at least, a change agency's vision of that good.

Paternalism refers to a class of activities rather than a single activity. Common to all types of paternalistic efforts is the assumption that a change agency is in a position to determine what is in the best interests of an individual targeted for change. In some cases, the change target may be seen as lacking the requisite skill or knowledge to make a decision that is in the best interests of that person. An information campaign to address this type of problem would be considered "weak" paternalism in Kleinig's model. In other cases, an individual may be the object of a social intervention that does not consider the person's capacity to make an informed decision. In this case, the intervention would be considered "strong" paternalism. Some of these types of intervention are considered preferable to others in an ethical sense because they involve fewer limitations on self-determination. For example, weak paternalism is viewed as more ethical than strong, because a change agency has at least considered whether or not the change target is capable of change without intervention.

Antismoking campaigns have long been predicated upon the justification of paternalism. The typical assumptions of public health specialists, for example, are that: (1) many smokers want to quit but cannot because of the addictive qualities of the activity; (2) many smokers began smoking and developed this addiction when they were young, impressionable and vulnerable and now are "trapped" in this behavior as adults; (3) even if smokers don't say they want to quit, society has an obligation to save these people from themselves; and finally, (4) that social and physical costs incurred by the societal majority (increased costs of insurance premiums, threat of secondary smoke, loss of productivity to the system) justify the abrogation of the minority faction's freedom. Campaigns explicitly designed to help smokers in the first two cases (addiction, peer pressure) thus are considered more ethically justifiable than are those for which the motivation is the third case, e.g., a desire to prevent individuals from doing something which brings them pleasure (although some might further argue, with some justification, that this pleasure is the result of a false sense of consciousness induced by cigarette marketing practices). Campaigns motivated by desire to assuage costs to the majority can be justified by John Stuart Mill's edict that intervention is warranted to prevent an individual from harming another, although this rationale is more compelling when the costs are physical rather than merely financial in nature.

THE EVALUATION PHASE

It is popular, in some circles, to regard activities based upon the precepts of science and the scientific method as less susceptible to social pressures and value judgments than are other social phenomena. Pollsters, for example, counter criticisms that their polls are biased in favor of legitimized interests and issue positions by adroitly cloaking their procedures with the mantle of science and pleading that numbers are ideologically neutral. While numbers themselves may be neutral, the means through which numbers are procured and interpreted certainly are not. In evaluation research, an organization must decide, among other things, how to interpret a successful intervention, what contextual factors are to be examined and controlled for, and what time frame constitutes an appropriate period of study. Each of these decisions is strongly influenced by a complex of value judgments.

CRITERIA FOR SUCCESS

The past forty years have witnessed a plethora of evaluations of small-scale campaigns, some concluding that efforts were unsuccessful while other were claiming success. Despite some pessimistic conclusions to the contrary, campaigns indisputably are *capable* of inducing effects (see also Lau, Kane, Berry, Ware, & Roy 1980 for a review of more than a dozen strategic communication efforts judged to have tangible effects; Puska, McAlister, Pekkola, & Koskela 1981; Gillespie, Yarbrough, & Roderuck 1983; O'Keefe 1985; Salmon, Loken, & Finnegan 1985; Mittlemark, et al. 1986; and Flora, Roser, Chaffee, & Farquhar 1988). However, not every campaign actually will be judged effective, largely because effectiveness cannot meaningfully be defined in absolute terms. Instead, it is solely a subjective determination resulting from expectations and values of the evaluator.

The subjective nature of campaign effectiveness is a direct result of the heterogeneity of the class of activities known as campaigns. Information campaigns are not merely mass media campaigns, although most employ mass media vehicles in conjunction with interpersonal delivery systems. In the past, campaigns have relied on: broadcasting, print media, billboards, and direct mail versus other, more exotic vehicles, such as Colonel Muammar Qaddafi's purchase of an ice hockey team to promote his "Green Book" on the team's jerseys (Schmemmann, 1987); hour-long television programs (Mendelsohn, 1973) versus decade-long, multiple-intervention saturation efforts (Farquhar et al., 1985; Mittlemark et al., 1986); elaborate formative research versus none. Some campaigns have attempted to alter highly involving personal habits while others have attempted to induce ephemeral and trivial behaviors. Some have been heavily funded by governmental agencies, while others have relied on voluntary efforts and miniscule budgets. In other words, the search for a definitive answer to the question, "Are campaigns effective?" is a search for a minotaur, as the functions, durations, potentials, and levels of creativity and resources are exceptionally heterogeneous. Further, because we have often tended to focus on the "trees," that is, those discrete, obvious, visible and often short-term mass media efforts aimed at the general population, we have tended to ignore the "forest, " that is, those pervasive yet disguised long-term efforts aimed at legislative bodies as well as citizens and conducted by literally hundreds of trade associations, governments (foreign and domestic), and interest groups. As a result, we have but scant knowledge of the collective impact of campaigns on the nexus of social values and institutions that comprise the social context of campaigns.

Mirroring this diversity in campaign composition, duration and intensity is similar diversity in criteria for success. Historically, evaluations of campaigns have consisted of examinations of *effectiveness* rather than *effects,* with the former term referring to those outcomes expected or intended by the campaigner and the latter term including unexpected or unintended outcomes (see Chapter 7 by Pollay in this volume). The best example of this distinction is provided in the classic study of the United Nations Information campaign (Star & Hughes, 1950), perhaps the most often-cited study in the campaign literature, one which is used to support what has now become an obligatory conclusion that campaigns—and indeed the mass media—do not have particularly strong effects (e.g., see reviews by Klapper, 1960; Bauer, 1964; Atkin, 1981). Yet if we reexamine the data provided by Star and Hughes, we find that such conclusions may be overstated. First, Star and Hughes tended to frame findings in negative light, such as the following:

> "The slogan, 'Peace Begins with the United Nations—the United Nations Begins with You' . . . was not recalled by 51 per cent of the people." (p. 397)

A different interpretation of the same data is that 49 percent of the citizens *did* recall the slogan after the six-month effort, a result that would be hailed by contemporary social and commercial marketers, yet an effect that was interpreted as evidence of ineffectiveness at the time. In the face of such interpretations, we would do well to remember the advice of the noted philosopher and pragmatist William James, who once observed that "success" is calculated by dividing one's achievements by one's expectations; when campaign planners have had high expectations, resulting achievements have been considered evidence of "ineffectiveness," whereas in the context of low expectations, those same achievements would have been considered evidence of effectiveness.

A second example from this same campaign, which allegedly provided evidence of the the failure of the "strong effects" paradigm of mass communication, concerns the finding that the campaign did induce knowledge-gap effects in the community. That is, the "information rich" apparently benefited more from the campaign than did the "information poor," and this was viewed as evidence of failure. What exists, therefore, is a case in which a selective effect was interpreted as lack of effectiveness, which, over the years, has been incorrectly translated by reviewers as evidence of lack of strong media effects. In fact, the knowledge-gap outcome is an empirically verifiable effect, but it is an indication of failure or ineffectiveness only in the context of the value system of the campaigner. As described by Tichenor, Donohue and Olien (1970), who coined the term "knowledge gap," the phenomenon is not inherently dysfunctional for a system, not necessarily evidence of failure, and can, in some cases, actually facilitate social change. To commercial marketers, knowledge gaps are not indicative of failure but can be indicators of success; that is, efficient market segmentation and media selection are expected to result in knowledge gaps between market segments. Only because public information campaigns are predicated upon the value judgment that information is not proprietary and should be made equally available to all members of society (Bloom & Novelli, 1981; see also Ettema, Brown, & Luepker, 1983), knowledge gaps may be considered indicators of a poorly conceived campaign but certainly not as evidence of weak effects.

The highly subjective interpretation of evaluative data is evident also in declarations of campaign successes by a number of public health and other nonprofit organizations. Because many of these organizations must rely on less-expensive, uncontrolled forms of communication, e.g., news releases, public service announcements, etc., they have tended to evaluate the effectiveness of their efforts in terms of placement, i.e., whether they were successful in placing their materials in news columns. Thus, several campaign organizers have described their efforts as "successes" or "failures" based solely upon placement in the media (e.g., Pietrodangelo, 1983; Maloney & Peterson, 1985; Mannheim & Albritton, 1986). This may be considered a case in which a campaign is interpreted as "effective" without having any demonstrable effect. That is, placement does not guarantee whether the news items were noticed, read, recalled or acted upon or had any effect on audience members whatsoever. The unrealistic expectation that information will have effects by mere placement can be considered an extension of the "third-person effect" described by

Davison (1983) and studied by Rucinski and Salmon (1989). In short, effective campaigns have been defined as those which have no discernible effects (i.e., where effectiveness is determined solely in terms of placement), and paradoxically, some ineffective campaigns have been defined as those which have demonstrable effects (but those effects were either unexpected or less-than-expected).

TIME FRAME

As mentioned above, the vast majority of campaigns documented in the literature are brief, and their evaluations rarely cover a period of time much longer than the campaign itself. Yet the various impacts stemming from a campaign may occur over generations rather than weeks and thereby go undetected. An example of this occurs with developmental campaigns designed for such outcomes as preventing infant mortality, reducing the birth rate, or improving the health behaviors of residents of developing nations. In each case, the short-term consequences of the campaigns may be judged to be effective and functional for the system. Indeed, effectiveness and functionality for the maintenance of the system often are considered synonymous because those in charge of determining criteria for effectiveness are those in charge of funding and initiating the campaign efforts in the first place. Rarely, if ever, are evaluations conducted in terms of the many conflicting interests and values affected by campaign efforts. However, short-term outcomes defined as "successes" by the system may engender problems which exceed those originally addressed by the campaigns. Campaigns to reduce infant mortality and disease can be evaluated in the narrow context of effectiveness, i.e., by tabulating the number of infants who die by a certain age or the number of adults who die from a certain disease targeted for extinction. Yet these campaigns, if "effective," also increase the population base, thereby straining the system's resources and possibly leading to unemployment, poverty and civil disorder. These threats to a system, in turn, are used as justifications for government's further attempts at social engineering to solve the problems created by the first "solution."

In a related manner, many public health campaigns in the United States can be said to have divergent outcomes if evaluated in terms of short-term versus long-term criteria. Public health campaigns do not prevent death; if effective, they merely delay it and perhaps alter the ultimate cause of death. An effective anticancer campaign may be considered one in which a cohort dies of premature heart attack rather than cancer. Because of public policies which tend to favor fragmented rather than holistic approaches to health, these same deaths, in turn, could be interpreted as evidence of "failure" by campaign evaluators working for a campaign to reduce incidence of premature heart attack. If the anticancer campaign is effective in delaying death, it may exacerbate demands on limited social resources, e.g., Social Security, medicare and other forms of insurance, and increase personal financial and emotional costs. Economic interpretations of campaign effectiveness are not preferred by the author, but economic rationales for campaign efforts are commonly used by public health organizations to justify the abrogation of individual freedoms (e.g., the desire not to wear a motorcycle helmet or not to wear a seatbelt) in the interests of reducing social costs.

CONTEXTUAL FACTORS

Campaigns are not conducted in a social vacuum; they represent one mechanism of change in direct competition with others. With commercial campaigns, this is obvious as we are daily exposed to competing messages for Coke versus Pepsi, for General Motors versus Ford, and so on, and thus the success of one organization's messages cannot be considered in isolation. In this context, it is useful to think in terms of Kurt Lewin's notion of how change occurs. To Lewin, a behavior at some point in time is the result of a dynamic balancing of forces working in opposite directions. Some of these forces can be considered "driving" forces, whereas other, opposing forces can be construed as "restraining" forces. The interaction of these two sets of forces creates an equilibrium point at which a behavior is "frozen." To induce change, i.e., to "unfreeze" a behavior, one must either increase the magnitude of the driving force or decrease the magnitude of the restraining force, at which point a new equilibrium will emerge. Campaigns, for example, represent only one social force among many driving and restraining forces. For every campaign message intending to dissuade consumers from illegal drug use or cigarette smoking, there are literally dozens of forces—including campaign messages from organizations espousing competing philosophies—similarly at work. According to Smith (1972), when cigarette commercials were still allowed on television, they outnumbered antismoking public service announcements four-to-one. Further, competing messages are not restricted to those that are obviously discernible as advertising. Concerned that public service announcements were "tuned out" by viewers, entertainment moguls such as Grant Tinker and Norman Lear have embedded persuasive messages in entertainment programming so that their influence will more subtly evade psychological defenses of viewers. The most recent effort involves decisions to "plant favorable dialogue" about the designated driver concept in the scripts of television shows (Rothenberg, 1988).

Other driving and restraining forces emanate from a variety of social influences. The more traditional and probably more powerful social anchors of religion, education, social class, family and peer groups constitute powerful forces operating simultaneously with a campaign on an individual or system. Most trade associations attempting to influence legislation on a relevant issue regularly conduct low-visibility campaigns through placement of materials in news columns and editorials. In recent years, classrooms have become increasingly popular communication vehicles for groups seeking social change. The International Brotherhood of Teamsters (1987) provides curriculum planning units to elementary school teachers in an attempt to educate children about the importance of unions in society. Several innovative campaigns have been developed for use in schools to educate children about public health issues (Hawkins, Gustafson, Chewning, Bosworth, & Day, 1987; Mittlemark et al., 1986). Many of these campaigns are so subtle (e.g., see also Burnham, 1987; Feldman, 1988) that they may not be recognized as campaigns at the time and are rarely included in reviews of campaign effectiveness. The goal of many such organizations is to monopolize an information environment through the deployment of a variety of mutually reinforcing strategies and tactics. As Lazarsfeld and Merton (1948, pp. 508–509) noted, "To the extent that opposing political propaganda in the mass media are balanced, the net effect is negligible. The virtual monopolization of the media for given social objectives, however, will produce discernible effects upon audiences." In certain societies and under certain social conditions (e.g., wartime), conditions approximating monopolization are possible and may be more successful by creating social cohesion (Lazarsfeld & Merton, 1948; Coser, 1956). In the absence of such drastic conditions, campaign planners have little hope of achieving true monopolization and, instead, compete with other campaigners for limited media attention under relative zero-sum conditions (Salmon, 1986).

The implications of these contextual factors are important for campaign evaluators. First, it is important to temper expectations of campaign success with a realistic appraisal of the competitive environment in which the campaign is vying for success. In a highly monopolistic situation, in which campaign planners are able to saturate a system with mutually reinforcing messages, expectations should be higher than in a very competitive situation. In the latter case, an outcome of "no change" may actually signify that the campaign was enormously successful in resisting the powerful nature of competing driving forces operating concomitantly. Yet historically, autopsies of "failed" campaigns have led campaigners to blame "obstinate" audiences or "weak" media effects rather than their own, unrealistic expectations of success. Second, it is important to evaluate campaigns in terms of both manifest and latent functions. Because campaigns operate in complex social and political environments, the manifest purposes of campaigns (e.g., to eradicate unhealthy behaviors) may actually be less important to the campaign sponsors than the latent purposes (e.g., to deflect criticisms that the government is doing nothing to solve a problem). Campaigns which employ half-hearted efforts such as a few public service announcements to cure complex and long-standing social ills probably have been designed for symbolic rather than substantive purposes. In examining such campaigns only at the manifest level and declaring them "failures," evaluators risk making egregious errors concerning the effectiveness of these efforts—as defined in terms of the goals of the sponsors, not the targets, of the campaign efforts. Third, we must expand our focus and examine the effects and effectiveness pertaining to campaigns "embedded" in other social institutions, including schools, worksites, and entertainment programming on television. Because these campaigns are prolific yet subtle, they are particularly worthy of researchers' attentions.

CONCLUSION

To synthesize the above discussion and answer Wiebe's question raised in the introduction of this paper, there is some evidence that well-designed, well-executed and competently evaluated campaigns, for which there are generally low expectations of success, can be and have been construed as effective and defined as "pro-social" by their organizers. Yet this question, important in the narrow confines of administrative research, pales in comparison to questions involving the underlying propriety and latent social functions of these efforts. Because every decision to engage—or refrain from engaging—in social intervention necessarily involves conflicts of values, campaigns represent weapons in conflicts of interests.

In general, most social marketing efforts are conducted by groups possessing social power and resources. Sponsors of these efforts usually define the location of a social problem in the public sphere and then rationalize their persuasive efforts in terms of the public interest. In contrast, other social marketing efforts are attempted by socially disadvantaged groups, which are more likely to define the location of the same social problem in the system itself. Yet because these challenger groups often lack legitimacy and resources and because the magnitude of the change sought is great, these efforts are far less likely to succeed. As a result, some campaigns take on the characteristics of class conflict, in which the values and interests of the dominant class are likely to be successfully imposed—in the name of benevolence—on the less powerful.

The valuation of interests thus becomes of paramount importance in policy decisions regarding social interventions. Few reasonable persons would contend that government and other social institutions have no right whatsoever to exert controls. As staunch a libertarian as John Stuart Mill would argue that certain values, most notably physical safety, must be protected because they are fundamental to the pursuit of secondary values. Yet as Kelman (1969) has observed, all forms of social manipulation are ethically questionable, and a high burden of proof rests with a change agency contemplating some campaign. We must not passively accept that a social marketing effort described as "pro-social" is actually so; we must question the motives, interests and impacts pertaining to each such effort. Campaigns to improve us, to make our nation stronger, to bring about progress or to make us happier should all be subjected to critical scrutiny. Campaigns which instill fear or which turn smokers or the overweight into pariahs—for their own "good"—should be examined for their dysfunctional as well as their functional consequences. Campaigns which attempt to eliminate all risk from life should be questioned, for risk can be pleasurable as well as threatening.

When intervention is necessary, it should follow Dworkin's (1979) principle of the "least restrictive alternative," i.e., the form of intervention which least inhibits individual freedoms. In most cases, a public information campaign, as intrusive and value-laden as it can be, is still a less restrictive alternative than are some other, more coercive forms of social change. To the extent that resource-poor challenger groups have the same access to campaign resources as do their more powerful establishment counterparts, then campaigns represent an even more attractive mechanism of social change (Laczniak, Lusch & Murphy, 1979). Many campaigns are inspired by humanitarian and egalitarian principles and implemented by well-intentioned crusaders. Paradoxically, this is the case for campaigns both supporting and opposing such positions as legalized abortion, prohibition of alcohol, and the need for economic development in Third World nations. On the other hand, many other efforts to promote the public interest are merely cloaked in the mantle of sanctimony in an effort to gain public support. But all campaigns, regardless of the sincerity of motives, implicitly or explicitly abrogate individual freedoms while endorsing one vision, among many, of the social good.

REFERENCES

Advocacy Institute (1988). *Smoking control media advocacy*. Paper presented to Mass Communications and Public Health: Complexities and Conflict, Rancho Mirage, CA.

Albritton, R. B., & Manheim, J. B. (1983). News of Rhodesia: The impact of a public relations campaign. *Journalism Quarterly, 60*, 622–628.

Atkin, C. K. (1981). Mass media campaign effectiveness. In R. E. Rice & W. J. Paisley (Eds.), *Public communication campaigns*. (pp. 265–279) Beverly Hills, CA: Sage.

Bailey, J. (1973). An evaluative look at a family planning radio campaign in Latin America. *Studies in Family Planning, 4*, 275–278.

Bauer, R. (1964). The obstinate audience: The influence process from the point of view of social communication. *American Psychologist, 19*, 319–328.

Baxter, W. L. (1981). The news release: An idea whose time has gone? *Public Relations Review, 7*, 27–31.

Benne, K. D., & Birnbaum, M. (1969). Principles of changing. In W. G. Bennis, K. D. Benne, & R. Chin (Eds.), *The planning of change* (2nd ed., pp. 328–335). New York: Holt, Rinehart & Winston.

Bloom, P. N., & Novelli, W. D. (1981). Problems and challenges in social marketing. *Journal of Marketing, 45*, 79–88.

Blumer, H. (1971). Social problems as collective behavior. *Social Problems, 18*, 298–306.

Boorstin, D. (1961). *The image or what happened to the American Dream.* New York: Atheneum.

Brown, J. D., & Einsiedel, E. F. (1988). Public health campaigns: Mass media strategies. In E. B. Ray & L. Donohew (Eds.), *Communication in health care contexts: A systems perspective.* Hillsdale, NJ: Lawrence Erlbaum.

Burnham, J. C. (1987). *How superstition won and science lost: Popularizing science and health in the United States.* New Brunswick, NJ: Rutgers University Press.

Chin, R., & Benne, K. D. (1969). General strategies for effecting changes in human systems. In W. G. Bennis, K. D. Benne & R. Chin (Eds.), *The planning of change.* New York: Holt, Rinehart & Winston.

Cobb, R. W. & Elder, C. D. (1983). *Participation in American politics: The dynamics of agenda building* (2nd ed.) Baltimore, MD: Johns Hopkins University Press.

Coser, L. A. (1956). *The functions of social conflict.* New York: Free Press.

Coser, L. A. (1982). The notion of control in sociological theory. In J. P. Gibbs (Ed.), *Social control: Views from the social sciences* (pp. 13–22). Beverly Hills, CA: Sage.

Davison, W. P. (1983). The third-person effect in communication. *Public Opinion Quarterly, 47,* 1–15.

Dervin, B. (1980). Communication gaps and inequities: Moving toward a reconceptualization. In B. Dervin & M. J. Voigt (Eds.), *Progress in communication sciences* (vol. 2, pp. 73–112). Norwood, NJ: Ablex.

Douglas, D., Westley, B., & Chaffee, S. H. (1970). An information campaign that changed community attitudes. *Journalism Quarterly, 47,* 479–487.

Dworkin, G. (1979). Paternalism. In P. Laslett & J. Fishkin (Eds.), *Philosophy, politics and society* (Fifth Series, pp. 78–96). New Haven: Yale University Press.

Edelman, M. (1964). *The symbolic uses of politics.* Urbana: University of Illinois Press.

Edelstein, A. S., & Schulz, J. B. (1963). The weekly newspaper's leadership role as seen by community leaders. *Journalism Quarterly, 40,* 565–574.

Ettema, J. S., Brown, J. W., & Luepker, R. V. (1983). Knowledge gap effects in a health information campaign. *Public Opinion Quarterly, 47,* 516–527.

Feingold, P. C., & Knapp, M. L. (1977). Anti drug-abuse commercials. *Journal of Communication, 27,* 20–28.

Feldman, A. (1988). *Selling the electrical idea in the 1920s: A case study in the manipulation of consciousness.* Paper presented to the annual meeting of the Association for Education in Journalism and Mass Communication, Portland, OR.

Fleisher, G. A. (1973). A study of a radio/TV campaign on safety belt use. *Journal of Safety Research, 5,* 3–11.

Flora, J. A., Roser, C., Chaffee, S. H., & Farquhar, J. W. (1988). *Information campaign effects of different media: Results from the Stanford Five City Project.* Paper presented to the annual meeting of the Association for Education in Journalism and Mass Communication, Portland, OR.

Gantz, W., Fitzmaurice, M., & Yoo, E. (1987). *Seat belt campaigns and buckling up: Do the media make a difference?* Paper presented to the annual meeting of the Midwest Association for Public Opinion Research, Chicago, IL.

Gillespie, A. H., Yarbrough, J. P., & Roderuck, C. E. (1983). Nutrition communication program: A direct mail approach. *Journal of the American Dietetic Association, 82,* 254–259.

Gitlin, T. (1980). *The whole world is watching: Mass media in the making and unmaking of the new left.* Berkeley: University of California Press.

Goodman, R. I. (1981). Selecting public service announcements for television. *Public Relations Review, 7,* 25–33.

Gordon, B. L. (1949). *The romance of medicine.* Philadelphia: F. A. Davis Company.

Grunig, J. E. (1987). *Symmetrical presuppositions as a framework for public relations theory.* Paper presented at the Conference on Communication Theory and Public Relations, Normal, IL.

Hanneman, G., McEwen, W., & Coyne, S. (1973). Public service advertising on television. *Journal of Broadcasting, 17,* 387–404.

Hawkins, R. P., Gustafson, D. H., Chewning, B., Bosworth, K., & Day, P. M. (1987). Reaching hard-to-reach populations: Interactive computer programs as public information campaigns for adolescents. *Journal of Communication, 37(2),* 8–28.

Hilgartner, S. & Bosk, C. L. (1988). The rise and fall of social problems: A public arenas model. *American Journal of Sociology, 94,* 53–78.

International Brotherhood of Teamsters (1987). *Why the need for a union? Past, present and future.* Paper presented at the Teaching Labor Studies Seminar, Madison, WI.

Jowett, G. S., & O'Donnell, V. (1986). *Propaganda and persuasion.* Newbury Park, CA: Sage.

Kelman, H. C. (1969). Manipulation of human behavior: An ethical dilemma for the social scientist. In W. G. Bennis, K. D. Benne, & R. Chin (Eds.), *The planning of change* (pp. 582–595). New York: Holt, Rinehart & Winston.

Klandermans, B., & Oegema, D. (1987). Potentials, networks, motivations and barriers: Steps towards participation in social movements. *American Sociological Review, 52,* 519–531.

Klapper, J. (1960). *The effects of mass communication.* New York: Free Press.

Kleinig, J. (1984). *Paternalism.* Totowa, NJ: Rowman and Allanheld.

Kline, F. G., Miller, P., & Morrison, A. (1974). "Adolescents and family planning information: An exploration of audience needs and media effects. In J. Blumler & E. Katz (Eds.), *The uses of mass communications* (pp. 113–136). Beverly Hills, CA: Sage.

Kotler, P. (1978). The elements of social action. In G. Zaltman (Ed.), *Processes and phenomena of social change* (pp. 169–189). Huntington, NY: Robert E. Krieger.

Laczniak, G. R., Lusch, R. F., & Murphy, P. E. (1979). Social marketing: Its ethical dimensions. *Journal of Marketing, 43,* 29–36.

Lasswell, H. D. (1962). The public interest: Proposing principles of content and procedure. In C. J. Frederich (Ed.), *Nomos V: The public interest.* New York: Atherton.

Lau, R., Kane, R., Berry, S., Ware, J., & Roy, D. (1980). Channeling health: A review of the evaluation of televised health campaigns. *Health Education Quarterly, 7,* 56–89.

Lazarsfeld, P. F., & Merton, R. K. (1948). Mass communication, popular taste and organized social action. In W. Schramm (Ed.), *Mass Communications* (pp. 492–512). Urbana: University of Illinois Press.

Levin, L. S. (1987). Every silver lining has a cloud: The limits of health promotion. *Social Policy, 18(1),* 57–60.

Locke, J. (1961). *An essay concerning human understanding* (vol. 1). London: Dent.

Maccoby, N. (1977). Reducing the risk of cardiovascular disease. *Journal of Community Health, 3,* 100–114.

Maloney, S. K., & Peterson, D. J. (1985). Placement of health promotion columns in suburban newspapers—An analysis. *Public Health Reports, 100,* 368–370.

Mannheim, J. B. & Albritton, R. B. (1986). Public relations in the public eye: Two case studies of the failure of public information campaigns. *Political Communication and Persuasion, 3,* 265–291.

Mendelsohn, H. (1973). Some reasons why information campaigns can succeed. *Public Opinion Quarterly, 37,* 50–61.

Mill, J. S. (1859). On liberty. In J. M. Robson (Ed.), Collected works of John Stuart Mill (Vol. XVIII). Toronto: University of Toronto Press.

Mittlemark, M. B. et al. (1986). Community-wide prevention of cardiovascular disease: Education strategies of the Minnesota Heart Health Program. *Preventive Medicine, 15,* 1–17.

Morrison, A., Kline, F. G., & Miller, P. (1976). Aspects of adolescent information acquisition about drugs and alcohol topics. In R. Ostman (Ed.), *Communication research and drug education.* Beverly Hills, CA: Sage.

Noelle-Neumann, E. (1973). Return to the concept of powerful mass media. *Studies of Broadcasting, 9,* 67–112.

Noelle-Neumann, E. (1974). *The spiral of silence: Public opinion—Our social skin.* Chicago: University of Chicago Press.

O'Keefe, G. J. (1985). Taking a bite out of crime: The impact of a public information campaign. *Communication Reserach, 12,* 147–178.

O'Keefe, G. J., & Reid-Nash, K. (1986). *The uses and effects of public service advertising.* Paper presented to the Midwest Association for Public Opinion Research, Chicago, IL.

Paisley, W. J. (1981). Public communication campaigns: The American experience. In R. E. Rice & W. J. Paisley (Eds.), *Public Communication Campaigns* (pp. 15–40). Beverly Hills, CA: Sage.

Paletz, D. L., Pearson, R. E., & Willia, D. L. (1977). Politics in public service advertising on television. New York: Praeger.

Paletz, D. L., Reichert, P., & McIntyre, B. (1971). How the media support local governmental authority. *Public Opinion Quarterly, 35,* 80–95.

Pietrodangelo, D. (1983). Child abuse: Making the public aware. *Public Welfare,* (Fall), 31–35.

Pollay, R. D. (1986). The distorted mirror: Reflections on the unintended consequences of advertising. *Journal of Marketing, 50,* 18–36.

Potter, D. (1954). *People of plenty.* Chicago: University of Chicago Press.

Puska, P., McAlister, A., Pekkola, J., & Koskela, K. (1981). Television in health promotion: Evaluation of a national program in Finland. *International Journal of Health Education, 24,* 238–250.

Qualter, T. H. (1962). *Propaganda and psychological warfare.* New York: Random House.

Rada, S. E. (1977). Manipulating the media: A case of a Chicano strike in Texas. *Journalism Quarterly, 54,* 109–113.

Rice, R. E., & Paisley, W. J. (1981) Preface. In R. E. Rice & W. J. Paisley (Eds.), *Public communication campaigns.* Beverly Hills, CA: Sage.

Robertson, L. S. (1976). The great seat belt campaign flop. *Journal of Communication, 26,* 41–45.

Robertson, L. S., Kelley, A. B., O'Neill, B., Wixom, C. W., Eiswirth, R. S., & Haddon, W. Jr. (1974). A controlled study of the effect of television messages on safety belt use. *American Journal of Public Health, 64,* 1071–1080.

Rogers, C. R., & Skinner, B. F. (1956). Some issues concerning the control of human behavior. *Science, 124,* 1057–1066.

Rogers, E. M. (1973). *Communication strategies for family planning.* New York: Free Press.

Rogers, E. M. (1978). The rise and fall of the dominant paradigm. *Journal of Communication, 28,* 64–69.

Rogers, E. M., & Storey, J. D. (1987). Communication campaigns. In C. R. Berger & S. H. Chaffee (Eds.), *Handbook of communication science.* Newbury Park, CA: Sage.

Rothenberg, R. (1988, September 7). Social engineering—How far should TV go? *Wisconsin State Journal,* p. 1C.

Rucinski, D. M., & Salmon, C. T. (1989). *The other as the "vulnerable voter."* Paper presented to the American Association for Public Opinion Research, St. Petersburg, FL.

Salmon, C. T. (1986). Message discrimination and the information environment. *Communication Research, 13,* 363–372.

Salmon, C. T., Loken, B., & Finnegan, J. (1985). Direct mail in a cardiovascular health campaign: Use and effectiveness. *Evaluation and the Health Professions, 8,* 438–452.

Schmemann, S. (1987). Qaddafi foiled as an ice hockey patron. *The New York Times,* p. 48.

Schumpeter, J. A. (1965). *Capitalism, socialism and democracy.* London: Unwin University Books.

Shoemaker, P. (1984). Deviance of political groups and media treatment. *Journalism Quarterly, 61,* 66–75.

Skinner, B. F. (1971). *Beyond freedom and dignity.* New York: Knopf.

Smart, R. G., & Fejer, D. (1974). The effects of high and low fear messages about drugs. *Journal of Drug Education, 4,* 225–235.

Smith, F. A. (1972). Health information during a week of television. *New England Journal of Medicine, 286,* 516–520.

Smith, B. L., Lasswell, H. D., & Casey, R. D. (1946). *Propaganda, communication, and public opinion.* Princeton, NJ: Princeton University Press.

Smith, D., & Rabin, K. H. (1978). What broadcasters want in public service spots. *Public Relations Review, 4,* 29–36.

Sorauf, F. (1957). The public interest reconsidered. *Journal of Politics, 19,* 616–638.

Star, S. A., & Hughes, H. G. (1950). Report on an educational campaign: The Cincinnati plan for the United Nations. *American Journal of Sociology, 55,* 389–400.

Tichenor, P. J., Olien, C. N., & Donohue, G. A. (1967). Predicting a source's success in placing news in the media. *Journalism Quarterly, 44,* 32–42.

Tichenor, P. J., Donohue, G. A., & Olien, C. N. (1970). Mass media flow and differential growth in knowledge. *Public Opinion Quarterly, 34,* 159–170.

Turk, J. V. (1986). Information sudsidies and media content: A study of public relations influence on the news. *Journalism Monographs, 100.*

USA Today. (1989, January 3). Achoo! Could it be flu? p. 1A.

Wallack, L. M. (1981). Mass media campaigns: The odds against finding behavior change. *Health Education Quarterly, 8,* 209–260.

Warner, K. E. (1977). The effects of the anti-smoking campaign on cigarette consumption. *American Journal of Public Health, 67,* 645–650.

Warwick, D. P., & Kelman, H. C. (1973). Ethical issues in social intervention." In G. Zaltman (Ed.), *Processes and phenomena of social change* (pp. 377–417). Huntington, NY: Robert E. Krieger.

Wiebe, G. D. (1952). Merchandising commodities and citizenship on television. *Public Opinion Quarterly, 15,* 679–691.

Workers Vanguard (1988 May 20) Warning: Anti-smoking crusade dangerous to your rights.

Zaltman, G., & R. Duncan (1977). *Strategies for planned change.* New York: John Wiley.

Zimbardo, P. G. (1972). The tactics and ethics of persuasion. In B. T. King & E. McGinnies (Eds.), *Attitudes, conflict, and social change* (pp. 84–99). New York: Academic Press.

Chapter 2

COMMUNITY POWER AND LEADERSHIP ANALYSIS IN LIFESTYLE CAMPAIGNS

John R. Finnegan, Jr., Neil Bracht and K. Viswanath

INTRODUCTION

THE CURRENT GLOBAL PHENOMENON of community-based campaigns has been stimulated in part by developing inter-disciplinary theories about ways to solve social problems and to improve the quality of life. Like all public information campaigns, community-based efforts seek to "generate specific outcomes or effects . . . in a relatively large number of individuals . . . usually within a specified period of time . . . through an organized set of communication activities" (Rogers & Storey, 1987, p. 821). Such campaigns have especially sought changes in health behavior and agricultural methods and typically have involved several campaigns or campaign cycles. They therefore differ from other kinds of campaigns by seeking complex, long-term outcomes, often in several related behavioral areas defined as "lifestyle," (daily living and work habits); by the use of multiple strategies for intervention, and by an emphasis on "community" as the nexus of social relations which form individuals' behavior.

The rationale underlying these community-based campaigns is that social and cultural influences are crucial factors in learning and adopting behavior patterns and importantly, that these influences are experienced by individuals through social aggregates and networks that make up communities (Eisenstadt & Shachar, 1986). This is particularly true of health outcomes, in which cross-cultural comparisons have revealed striking behavioral differences associated with varying levels of adult chronic disease (Keys, 1980; Blackburn, 1983). In this view, population-wide behavior change requires close attention to the social and cultural influences and socializing mechanisms that form behavior in the first place. Multiple intervention strategies have been developed due to the complexity of changes sought and the time it takes for the adoption of these changes by community populations (McAlister, Puska, Koskela, Pallonen, & Maccoby, 1980; Maccoby & Solomon, 1981; Blackburn, Luepker, & Kline, 1984; Puska, Nissinen, Tuomilehto, et al., 1985; Elder, Hovell, Lasater, Wells, & Carleton, 1985; Farquhar, et al., 1985; Stunkard, Felix, & Cohen, 1985; Mittlemark, et al., 1986). Not surprisingly, planners of these kinds of campaigns have increasingly emphasized formative research as a set of evaluation methods to enhance the potential for achieving social and behavioral change (Palmer, 1981; Windsor, Baranowski, Clark, & Cutter, 1984).

One of the most important dimensions of these community-based campaigns is their emphasis on mobilizing whole communities as an overall strategy to enhance the potential for individuals to change. But how should one approach the analysis of communities in such campaigns? What are key concepts and variables about communities, and how do these combine as practical applications to generate information useful in making strategy decisions? To answer these questions, this chapter reviews several perspectives on community leadership and power and shows how analysis of these perspectives may be useful in managing campaigns seeking social and behavioral change. The chapter draws often on two examples of campaigns conducted in different social settings to illustrate approaches to analyzing community leadership and power. The first is the Minnesota Heart Health Program (MHHP), a federally-funded research and demonstration project that promotes the adoption of healthier lifestyles in three Midwest communities. The second is the Indian National Satellite Project (INSAT), a long-term satellite-television project promoting rural development, including improved health habits and agricultural techniques.

COMMUNITY APPROACHES TO SOCIAL CHANGE

Community-based approaches arise from applied interdisciplinary approaches to planning and managing efforts to achieve lifestyle behavior outcomes in community settings (Suchman, 1967; Archer, Kelly, & Bisch, 1984; Brown, 1984; Rifkin, 1985; Bracht, 1988). Developing disciplines, such as social marketing, for example, borrowed concepts, strategies, and techniques from their commercial counterparts for the promotion of ideas and behavior rather than products (Kotler & Zaltman, 1971). From an innovation-diffusion perspective, investigators have noted that key elements of the promotion process may be manipulated to stimulate social and behavioral change (Rogers & Shoemaker, 1971). These have included technology (strategies and techniques); social organization (relationships, structures, organizations); ideology (knowledge, beliefs, attitudes); the availability of resources; and the development of social and behavioral change agents. Political and policy-making researchers have described the process of stimulating social and behavioral change variously as "agenda-building," increasing citizen participation, and mobilizing for social action (Alinsky, 1946; Beal & Hobbs, 1964; Cobb & Elder, 1972; Milbrath & Goel, 1977). Community-development and community-organization researchers have described the process as "empowering" communities, or building "capacity" for social action based on an ideology of localism, coalition-building, and mass participation (Goodenough, 1963; Biddle & Biddle, 1965; Mayer, 1972; Berger & Neuhaus, 1977; Blau & Alba, 1982; Riessman, 1983; Rappaport, Swift, & Hess, 1984).

Three themes unify these views about the process of seeking long-term social and behavioral change. First is the emphasis on powerful social forces influencing individuals' behavior—the idea that behavior is formed and influenced by the dominant culture and individuals' social relations in the context of their communities (Barth, 1961; Aiken, 1970; Coleman, 1977). Communities form individuals' behavior both symbolically and tangibly. As agents of the dominant culture, communities transmit values and norms that symbolically circumscribe some behavioral choices and encourage others. As systems of exchange and influence relationships, communities establish opportunities for people to behave in some ways but not in others.

A second common theme is that communities themselves may be mobilized to act as change agents to achieve social and behavioral outcomes. Conceptually, mobilizing communities to act as change agents means that they both give legitimacy to values and norms for desirable behavior and make the social and physical environment more conducive for individuals to act. Practically, mobilizing communities means engaging networks of public and private organizations and special interest groups to channel their resources (personnel, time, money, goods, services) in coordinated activity in a broad range of interpersonal, group and mass communication strategies (Crosby, Kelly, & Schaefer, 1986; Brown & Detterman, 1987). Legitimacy is particularly important to community-based campaigns because it is the process through which social leaders "give sanction, justification, (and) the license to act," influencing the rest of the community to adopt desired changes (Rogers & Shoemaker, 1971, p. 280). But an equally important tangible outcome is that groups with power to allocate resources may change their capacity to provide opportunities for individuals to engage in behavior-change activity. Such capacity may include organizations acting as channels to reach individuals with specific behavior change strategies; the adoption of strategies themselves by organizations and the providing of a framework for individuals to influence others as volunteers working for behavior-change goals. The latter two particularly involve expanding organizational capacity in the transfer of technology, knowledge and skills.

A third theme stresses that campaign planning needs to be systematic and data-based, not only to identify traditional audience, source, message and channel variables, but also to identify specific powerful individuals and groups who may mobilize their support and resources to act as change agents.

To summarize briefly, a rich and varied literature about community analysis is available for campaign planners seeking additional strategies to manage the process of social and behavioral change. It is eclectic and interdisciplinary, and the techniques lend themselves to a wide variety of applications in different campaign settings and even different social settings. These techniques may be used to analyze community power and influence to: (1) identify leaders and organizations most effective in giving legitimacy to campaign messages and activities, (2) identify community organizations and leaders most effective in sustaining long-term coordinative activity to reach campaign goals, (3) generate media and other education campaign strategies tailored to community social and cultural traditions, (4) deal with potential community conflict surrounding campaign goals and activities, and (5) create long-term impact on the allocation of community resources for the achievement of campaign goals.

COMMUNITY ANALYSIS

Community-based campaign planners do not rely exclusively on any single idea of *community*. Definitions are diverse and depend, to a great extent, on campaign goals and objectives. For example, communities may be defined spatially in the sense that residents identify with and participate in relationships in a geographically bounded locale (Eisenstadt & Shachar, 1986). They may be defined geopolitically as formal governmental jurisdictions. They may be defined institutionally as a set of interacting formal organizations. They also may be defined as systems of power and influence with formal and informal functions for the management of conflict and competition, the allocation of resources and the formation of public policy (Aiken, 1970; Nix, 1969; Eisenstadt & Shachar, 1986).

Whatever the disciplinary perspective, there emerge some common concepts about communities that campaign planners regard as important in the formation of strategies: space, social institutions, social interaction, and social control (Warren, 1963; Eisenstadt & Shachar, 1986). These encompass some key characteristics on which communities may be compared and contrasted and which may be used in the campaign planning process: complexity (size, specialization of functions); linkage and relationships (the interaction of formal organizations); power and influence (control over resources, coordination, centralization or dispersion); dependence-autonomy and formality (of various social relationships); community identity; and social integration (cohesion).

Analysis of these areas is, of course, limited by available resources. Decisions must be made about which variables are more or less important, and how formally or informally analyses should be conducted. Analyses also should be integrated with other formative-research strategies (e.g., focus groups, marketing surveys, available information sources) which may provide additional useful information for developing and adjusting community-based strategies.

For example, Table 2.1 describes a community analysis process generalized from the Minnesota Heart Health Program (MHHP). It incorporates four distinct phases pertaining to ten areas of analysis. Objectives, methods, and approximate completion times are shown for each analysis area. These results are compiled in a comprehensive community casebook, which is used by campaign-planning teams for each education community. In general, these methods are used to enumerate community organizations, to analyze community leadership and power structures as well as sociopolitical conditions, and to provide feedback to planners about campaign effects, both on individuals and on community organizations and relationships.

Analyses in phase I and II usually occur about one year prior to the beginning of intervention. Data collected in these phases are used to make critical initial decisions about the community-based strategy. These include, for example, assessment of public attitudes and behavior as a measure of community "readiness" for the campaign, and identification and assessment of the community power structure's capacity to direct resources to enhance citizen participation and the achievement of campaign goals.

Phase I includes the collection of baseline measures, and study of community leadership and power. Baseline survey data not only provide information about individuals' risk-factor-related behavior and prevention knowledge and attitudes, but also about community attachments, including organizational memberships and the time each person has been a resident in the community. In addition, information is gathered from available data sources about demographics and economic and political activity. Special attention is devoted to how these might impinge upon campaign goals. Community leadership and power structures are evaluated in this phase through structured interviews with key informants.

Phase II marks the end of preliminary assessment and the beginning of formal strategy development and implementation. All major community organizations and groups are enumerated by functional sectors, based on various community and organizational directories and interviews with key informants. Community capacity for campaign involvement is assessed in terms of potential resources and previous community experience with social action projects. Campaign planners make decisions about community leaders, activists, and organizations that ought to be represented on the program's community advisory boards and various risk-factor and delivery-system task forces. Once formed, these coordinative groups take a direct role in campaign planning.

In phase III, community analysis provides feedback to adjust campaign strategies through regular cross-sectional phone surveys of the public and through surveys of special community groups, such as health-care professionals. Cross-sectional surveys every six months assess the public's awareness of the program, ability to recall or to

Table 2.1 Summary of Community Analysis Activities: Objectives and Methods

Analysis Area	Objectives	Method	Time Requirement
Phase I			
1. Baseline Population Surveys	Determine comparability levels between educated and comparison town. Includes health behaviors and medical history.	Independent survey, SES data plus risk factor status. (400–500 population sample)	2 months for each town
2. Community Leadership Study	Assess community power base and develop list of names of possible membership on community advisory boards/task forces.	Interviews with officials and reputed influentials.	3 months
3. General community characteristics, structure and history. Special issues/concerns.	Analyze demographic, economic and institutional structures of the community as they impinge on MHHP health promotion efforts. Well-informed staff ensures smoother entry into the community.	Interviews (above) provide some of this information, along with state and local studies, census information and review of related historical and other social indicator sources.	2 months
Phase II			
4. Local organization inventory includes identification of entrepreneur groups involved in risk status improvement.	Develop information on all major local organizations and groups by functional sectors: 1. Voluntary/Service Groups 2. Religious 3. Labor/Business	Review of various directories and contacts with local informants. Some information collected during leadership interviews. Information made available in community casebook.	3 months

4. Education
5. Recreation/Entertainment
6. Government
7. Professional (non-health)
8. Media/Communications
9. Health/Medical

5. Community capacity/resources for implementing campaign	Review current organizational resources and document past efforts in community action projects. Anticipate special problems, community issues and/or recent conflicts.	Information derived from above interviews and information from other local persons and archival (newspapers) materials. Summary statement developed.	3 months

Phase III

6. Survey of special community organizations and health groups including health professionals inventory: nurses, pharmacists, etc.	Assess awareness and activity levels of groups—particularly in health programs. Monitor changes over time. Obvious examples are the Health Department, local medical clinics, hospitals, wellness programs, etc.	Survey of officers from selected organizations. Use of professional directories. Information summarized in community casebook.	1–2 months
7. Special surveys conducted in such areas as food buying and restaurant patterns, use of health services, membership in organizations.	Gain more detailed information on local households and organizations in order to assess educational and media approaches.	Rapid surveys of households—and use of findings from ancillary research projects (e.g., smoking patterns in worksites).	Varies

(continued)

61

Table 2.1 Continued

Analysis Area	Objectives	Method	*Time Requirement*
Phase IV			
8. Ongoing community events analysis. This includes update of organizational and community information by local staff.	Monitor from period of first contact all MHHP-generated activities that occur in community. Areas include: Direct Education Community Organizations Media Health Screening Professional Education	Weekly tracking and collection of data from local campaign field staff with monthly feedback.	2 hours staff time per week
9. Survey of social change in comparison communities.	To study all institutional sectors (education, health, business, etc.) in comparison cities to document social/health changes, unusual events that provide broader context for interpreting findings from educated communities.	Principally unobtrusive measures from existing social/economic data	1 year
10. Description and history of campaign in each education community.	Qualitative study of staff and community perspective on project.	Independent writers conduct an oral history of project.	6 mos.—1 year.

recognize its name, and participation in various program activities through organizations in various community sectors.

Phase IV analysis continues to assess program impact on community structures and their capacity to carry on prevention activities after intensive intervention ceases. The purpose of this phase is to identify key community processes, organizations, and leaders that might "incorporate" prevention activities and continue to plan, develop, and implement them with only occasional consultation from university-based investigators. Three kinds of data are used in these analyses. A computerized register is used to record all intervention activities and contacts as a sequential-event history. This is used to generate information about the nature and patterns of campaign activity in different community sectors. Data are collected weekly by local community staff to assist in evaluating how campaign strategies actually were implemented. This is further supplemented through a formal oral history of the project's development conducted by independent observers who interview key actors involved in community boards and task forces. Finally, data are collected from available documentary sources and interviews with key organizations in reference communities to assess institutional-sector involvement in prevention activities. This provides a base for comparing and contrasting the "natural" evolution of prevention efforts in noncampaign communities with that of intervention communities. Of key interest here is whether such extensive campaign efforts suppress or foster prevention activity; that is, whether community capacity actually increases in intervention communities, and in what ways.

COMMUNITY POWER AND LEADERSHIP

A lifestyle campaign such as MHHP thus makes use of a number of quantitative and qualitative formative analysis techniques including cross-sectional surveys, focus groups, oral history, analysis of existing data sources and community power and leadership analysis. The last of these is perhaps the most important element of phase I and II, since it focuses on community power as essential to the success of community-based campaigns.

Domhoff and Dye (1987) have recently noted that all studies of power structures have two basic components: (1) generating a list of key actors who are connected to each other and to important organizations and issues, and (2) generating a content analysis of various kinds of documents (e.g., letters, memoranda, minutes, proposals, policies) that illustrate interaction among these actors. Both parts of the analysis may be conducted more or less formally, depending on applications of the information, but both direct investigators to study who has power, how it is converted and used to accomplish different kinds of outcomes, and how key actors interact (Liebert & Imershein, 1977; Nix, 1969).

There are essentially four types of community power structure and leadership analysis methods available to community-based campaign planners: positional, reputational, decision making, and community-reconnaissance. They are based on somewhat different assumptions about community structure and function and developed originally for formal sociological studies of communities and other social aggregates. This is an important point because while community-based campaign planners tend to be eclectic in their use of various techniques, selection of a specific method often carries a fairly well-constructed theoretical view of important variables.

The four methods emerged from the classic debate about the nature of power that pitted "elitists" such as Mills (1956) and Hunter (1953) versus "pluralists" such as Dahl (1958, 1961). For about the last decade or so, researchers have noted that while much of this ongoing debate was based on different views about the structure of power, assumptions reflected not so much contradictory stances as differences in emphasis (Liebert & Imershein, 1977; Domhoff & Dye, 1987). Moreover, the methods often arrive at reasonably similar descriptions of how power is structured.

While the original elitist-pluralist debate is perhaps no longer as hotly contested as it once was (Burton & Higley, 1987), there are some distinctly different variations in the definition of, and search for community power. Liebert and Imershein (1977) have noted, for example, that the structuralist tradition continues to emphasize "systematic power" arising from the capacity of dominant economic actors to effect public policy. In this view, communities do not often function as self-contained systems, since their interorganizational networks reach beyond community boundaries (Lincoln, 1977; Turk, 1977; Stone, 1980). Variations of the decision-making method are a staple of this pluralist approach.

Another view also emphasizes systemic power, but within a framework that defines power as the control of resources arising from exchange relationships and *influence* as the conversion of power through "intra-elite networks" to accomplish some larger social change (Coleman, 1977; Laumann, Marsden, & Galaskiewicz, 1977; Cook, Emerson, Gillmore, & Yamagishi, 1983; Gartrell, 1987). Variations of the positional and reputational methods developed by Mills (1956) and Hunter (1953) and the hybrid community-reconnaissance method (Nix, 1977) are used in these kinds of studies and often generate highly sophisticated dyadic and network models and graphic representations.

THE POSITIONAL METHOD

The positional method derives from the "power elites" perspective of Mills (1956) and seeks to establish interconnections among a broad range of formal organizations, usually at a state, regional, or national level (Silk & Silk, 1980; Kurtz, 1987). Publicly available information often is used to establish "interlocks" among government, business-industry and nonprofit sector leaders and organizations that control the flow of money, information and the allocation of other community resources (Domhoff & Dye, 1987). A typical study begins with the enumeration of organizations and their leaders in major community sectors and establishes how they are connected to each other (interlocking directorates; exchange relations, such as contract ties; family ties, etc.). Informally, such studies may involve little more than building trees showing interconnections, or they may use formal models to address such issues as the centralization or dispersion of power in networks and the flow of money, information, or other resources they control (Coleman, 1977; Laumann & Pappi, 1976; Cook et al., 1983; Domhoff & Dye, 1987; Gartrell, 1987).

This method has the advantage of identifying important organizations and leaders in key community sectors, based on authority over resource allocation. However, it has been criticized for too heavily emphasizing power as the authority which attaches to formal positions while neglecting community influence—an important dimension of power, not necessarily accrued only on the basis of formal authority.

Nix (1977), for example, observed that while formal authority is a source of power over allocation of resources and therefore makes those who hold high positions "legitimizers"[1] in the community, formal authority extends only as far as organizational boundaries. Community influence, on the other hand, may be enhanced by formal authority, but it is exercised largely through coordinative intergroup settings and is, in part, a function of leaders' personal abilities to effect their desires. Such groups (e.g., chambers of commerce, community charity funds, community improvement associations, professional associations, and so on) are the means of rectifying, managing and coordinating competitive and potentially conflicting group interests and goals to realize mutually beneficial outcomes.

Freeman and his colleagues (1963), discussing the scope and influence of leaders, described two types in addition to legitimizers that may be involved in coordinative groups. They observed that not all legitimizers will be involved in such settings, nor will all have the communication skills to realize their goals. However, the approval of legitimizers will be needed in some way to facilitate community action.

A second set of community leaders are called "effectors." These are individuals who do not have the formal authority to control key resources but may hold positions secondary to those who do. Effectors may also have technical or professional skills and be more active in community decision making than legitimizers. It has been noted that in small communities, legitimizers and effectors tend to be the same people, but that as communities grow in size and specialized functions, the two groups diverge (Nix, Dressel & Bates, 1977). It has been noted further that in large cities, effectors frequently "carry the burden of initiating and effecting community change except for the approval and prestige lent by legitimizers."

A third set of community leaders have been labeled "activists"— individuals who join organizations and play a minor role in policy decisions because of a lack of technical knowledge, but who largely carry out tasks.

REPUTATIONAL METHOD

Originally developed by Hunter (1953) in his classic study of the power structure of "Regional City," the reputational method involves structured interviews with key individuals who are asked to identify those whom they believe to be the most powerful or influential in the community. A tree of influence and interconnection thus is built through patterns of nominated individuals.

The method works from the assumption that leadership, power, and influence are complex phenomena, in which power over resources arises from exchange relationships and is converted to community influence through leaders' personal communication skills of persuasion and negotiation (Coleman, 1977; Burt, 1977; Nix, 1977; Beaulieu & Ryan, 1984). In practice, the method proceeds by first identifying some key positional leaders and asking questions about who is influential (Hunter, 1953). Although the results of this method often parallel those of the positional method (Walton, 1968), the reputational method does not assume that formal authority alone determines broader community influence. Both legitimizers and effectors are therefore likely to be located in this kind of analysis.

Data gathered from this method may be analyzed informally or through quantitative analysis of blockmodels (White, Boorman, & Brieger, 1976; Deseran & Black, 1981), multidimensional scaling (Laumann & Pappi, 1976), graphic representations (Alba & Moore, 1978) or other variations examining the centrality or dispersion of power and influence in different community sectors (Galaskiewicz, 1979; Cook et al., 1983; Bonacich, 1987).

Some conclusions from this research support the idea that in smaller communities there is less differentiation of types of leaders. That is, legitimizers and effectors tend to be the same individuals (Nix, 1977). However, in larger, more complex communities, leaders are more differentiated. Moreover, there are relatively few leaders with across-the-board influence (Hunter, 1953; Nix, 1977; Galaskiewicz, 1979). Finally, some investigators have observed problems in relying on actors' self-reports of associations and interactions and have noted the need for external validation of their accounts (Galaskiewicz, 1979; Hammer, 1980; Deseran & Black, 1981).

THE DECISION-MAKING METHOD

The observation that community influence is seldom exercised across-the-board is one basis for the decision-making method. Because broad community influence accrues only to a few leaders— given the complexity and pluralism of communities—the decision-making approach analyzes the exercise of power in specific issues, decisions, and policies. Through case studies relying on interviews and documents of organizations, groups, and individual actors, the method seeks to recreate decision-making processes (Dahl, 1958;

1961; Ornstein & Elder, 1978). The beginnings of this approach are evident in the work of Lasswell (1936), who discussed analyzing policy outcomes as "who gets what, when, and how." Dahl (1958, 1961), however, is credited with formalizing the approach in his classic study of power and decision making in New Haven.

Some difficulties with this method include the time and expense of participant-observation techniques; the difficulty of selecting important typical events or policy processes; and the difficulty of being able to observe key decisions being made (Nix, 1977). This is especially true in smaller communities, in which key decisions may be made informally. While the method may be successful in uncovering the role of effectors and activists in larger communities, it may be less successful in uncovering the role of legitimizers, who often are not directly involved in the more public aspects of the policy process.

COMMUNITY RECONNAISSANCE METHOD

Recognizing that each of these methods may be useful in studying community power, Nix and Seerley (1971) and Nix (1977) sought to maximize their strengths and minimize the weaknesses of the methods in calling for a "modified positional-reputational approach." The purpose of this approach is to analyze multiple aspects of community power to discover "some of all kinds of leaders," including those of traditionally underrepresented minority groups (McCain & Hofstetter, 1982), and to reveal patterns of association among community elites and interorganizational groups involved in decision making.

Procedurally, the method involves six steps: (1) determining the geopolitical area of study, (2) developing the interview schedule, (3) selecting respondents, (4) conducting interviews, (5) summarizing and analyzing findings, and (6) making additional observations to confirm or uncover associational patterns. Step 1 involves developing the sampling frame by analyzing the community as a collection of jurisdictional and organizational sectors. Such an enumeration assures that careful thought is given to the major public and private sectors and actors and their various subdivisions. Developing the interview schedule in step 2 focuses on the specific questions to be asked respondents in several areas of concern. Primarily, the interviewer asks respondents to nominate a half-dozen or more individuals deemed influential both in the community and in the more limited realm of respondents and other community sectors. Additional questions are asked to assess repondents' views of the community's economic diversity and its autonomy or dependence in relation to other communities and major local institutions, the extent and kind of coordinative groups, and the numbers and types of community factions (Nix, 1977).

Selecting respondents in step 3 may be accomplished through two methods: a positional panel approach, in which leader-respondents are selected on the basis of their formal authority in critical community sectors; or a "snowball" technique of interviewing a few known community influentials and asking them to nominate others, who are interviewed in turn. The number of interviews to conduct in step 4 depends, in part, on the size of the community, and whether it is split into multiple factions. As a rule of thumb, Nix and Seerley (1971), and Nix (1977) recommend at least fifteen interviews in cities of 10,000 to 100,000 population and about half that number for communities of 5,000 or fewer.

Summarizing and analyzing findings in step 5 is aimed primarily at characterizing the community power structure. This includes identifying types of leaders, as described earlier; determining the extent of leaders' power and influence; mapping interconnections and relationships among individuals, organizations, and groups and identifying patterns in community decision making. In step 6, the patterns may be further characterized by their degree of factionalization, centralization or dispersion across groups.

An issue of ongoing concern in community analysis generally is the gap between methods for comparative analysis of power structures (especially the positional approach) and the more typical use of case studies. To bridge this gap, Burt (1981) has suggested a technique for gathering "ersatz network data" from only a few key informants across many communities. He compared such data to previous community research and found them to be reliable in predicting community power structures.

While the methods described here are flexible, their use by campaign planners depends on the goals of community-based strategies. That is, a relatively simple goal of engaging community influentials in symbolic legitimation of a campaign may not involve as extensive analyses as a goal of engaging them in a process of channeling substantial resources for long-term impact on the community's coordinative capacity to carry on campaign activity. A project as extensive as

MHHP, for example, sought to do both. Thus the program carried out a variation of Nix's community reconnaissance method, not only to identify influentials but also to involve them directly in the campaign planning (Bracht, 1988).

THE MINNESOTA HEART HEALTH PROGRAM (MHHP)

The Minnesota Heart Health Program uses education, mass media, community organization and environmental strategies in such arenas as worksites, churches, schools, restaurants, grocery stores, physicians' offices, and other community organizations (Carlaw, Mittelmark, Bracht, & Luepker, 1984; Jacobs et al., 1986; Mittelmark et al., 1986). Typical of U.S. efforts in this area, MHHP is a multiple time-series design that includes three pairs of matched communities that are surveyed and observed in Minnesota, North Dakota, and South Dakota. Demographic, risk-factor and behavior data are collected annually on the adult populations of these communities (Jacobs et al., 1986). MHHP is similar to projects in California (Stanford Heart Disease Prevention Project), Rhode Island (Pawtucket Heart Health Program) and Pennsylvania (Community Health Improvement Program).

MHHP's community-based approach emanates from additional goals of citizen participation in the design and implementation of the campaign and in eventual community ownership through a joint investigator-community partnership (Carlaw et al., 1984; Bracht, 1988). The purpose is to help the community use its structure and resources to give legitimacy to campaign messages, recommendations, and activities, but also to provide for long-term activity (such as public policy changes and the adoption of specific education programs) as tangible opportunities for people to act in desired ways. The program specifically sought to establish citizen advisory groups and task forces oriented to risk-factor campaign areas (e.g., smoking, eating, physical activity, blood pressure) and important campaign delivery channels (e.g., mass media, physicians and health professionals, worksites, restaurants and grocery stores), and thus to provide opportunities for citizen participation beyond normal campaign contacts. This focus on community was based, in part, on evidence that positive health outcomes are related to social support mechanisms (Schafer, 1981; Rook, 1984; Maida, 1985; Ward, 1985).

Interviews were conducted initially with major positional leaders who were asked to identify others reputationally influential in the community. These influential individuals were interviewed in turn. Interviews included questions about individuals and organizations with general and specialized influence in the community, specifically with respect to health issues and projects. Interviewees were requested to give examples of prior community programs in health or other areas, stating who was involved and giving reasons for the programs' success or failure. In the first of MHHP's three education communities (population = 35,000), this process resulted in some 50 interviews. In the two larger communities (population = 112,000 and 88,000 respectively), about double that number were conducted in a 12 month period.

This initial analysis guided MHHP decisions about the make-up and size of advisory boards and risk-factor and delivery-system task forces. For example, in the first community analyzed, a business leader mentioned ten or more times as influential might be asked to serve on the advisory board. However, an individual mentioned only once but revealing a strong interest in smoking cessation, might be asked to serve on the smoking-cessation task force.

In the second community, a regional city, MHHP's community analysis was conducted along similar lines, but it also was validated by an independent study conducted by local investigators (Dulka, 1982). In this community, there was somewhat greater differentiation between community "legitimizers," "effectors," and "activists," as described earlier. This resulted in a community advisory board heavily drawn from "legitimizers," and a much larger health promotion task force including predominantly "effectors" and "activists."

In the third community, a metropolitan suburb, the leadership study reflected greater positional status. That is, heads of organizations were mentioned most often as influential. Key organizational actors (chamber of commerce, schools, human services, public health, city council, etc.) became the nucleus of this community advisory board.

Power structures in the second and third MHHP communities were far more fluid and differentiated than in the first community. For example, more than half of the original advisory board members in the first community continued to serve after 7 years. There was greater turnover in the second and third communities. The greater turnover reflected the larger pool of available leadership and also the larger pool of important community organizations.

In addition to determining the composition of boards and task forces, however, community analyses also are useful in other kinds of campaign decisions. In MHHP, for example, community analysis also permitted the identification of organizations likely to be influential channels of campaign information, and those organizations likely to incorporate campaign programs and messages in the long-term. This encouraged MHHP to develop program strategies most conducive to gaining this kind of support. Examples include an annual physical activity challenge involving dozens of worksites and thousands of employees in friendly competition to become more active (Blake et al., 1987) and a community-wide smoking-cessation contest, for which prizes were donated by community organizations, and which, in the largest of the education communities, became sponsored and organized by a major insurance company.

Decisions about mass-media strategies also were made, in part, on the basis of community analysis. For example, beyond the usual techniques of generating news stories and public service announcements, MHHP engaged in collaborative efforts with selected media outlets to produce special material tailored to each community. Overall, media strategies emphasized the activities of community residents and influentials, rather than those of investigators and field staff.

An early media effort involved a tabloid-sized newspaper insert produced and distributed collaboratively with the daily newspaper. It featured a series of profiles of community influentials who served on the community advisory board and task forces. These individuals were interviewed about the values they saw in the program, its benefit to the community, and their personal reasons for becoming involved. The same strategy was followed in several other print and electronic efforts featuring locally recognized individuals attempting to quit smoking, becoming more physically active, receiving blood pressure checks and demonstrating low-fat, low-sodium recipes.

Community analysis also was helpful in identifying key influentials to deal with potential public controversy surrounding the program. Although cardiovascular disease campaigns do not typically generate a great deal of community conflict, some controversy is inevitable.

This is true especially in rural areas in which some food producers may perceive program goals to be detrimental to their interests. For example, although MHHP's eating-pattern message was framed in positive terms (i.e., recommending consumption of fruits, vegetables, legumes, low-fat dairy products, lean meats, fish, and poulty), some food producers occasionally interpreted the message as a recommendation to avoid their products. Community influentials, including some directly involved in agribusiness, were helpful more than once in addressing conflicts either through public explanation or interorganizational coordination to allay fears that MHHP opposed food-producer interests. This also was true in other areas in which some health-care interests perceived MHHP as posing competition for market share, rather than one of its intended purposes of providing a new level of coordination of various interests' prevention activities.

INDIAN NATIONAL SATELLITE PROJECT (INSAT)

A somewhat different class of community-based campaigns has occurred in the Third World, aimed at changing the health and agricultural habits of mainly rural residents (Bordenave, 1977a, b, c, d; Berrigan, 1979; Tuluhungwa, 1981; Hall, 1985). These campaigns have used mainly broadcast and print media in combination with strategies involving community leaders to generate discussion and consensus about changing living and work habits.

The Indian National Satellite Project (INSAT) is typical of projects of this kind. Beginning in the mid-1970s as the Satellite Instructional Television Experiment (SITE), India arranged with the United States to lease a satellite for a year to telecast health and agricultural programs to some 2,400 villages in six states (Agrawal, Doshi, Jesudasan, & Verma, 1977; Eapen, 1979 a, b; Mody, 1979; Agrawal, 1981; Gore, 1983). Television sets were placed in each community, and arrangements were made for their access and use. Evaluation of SITE showed that insufficient attention had been paid in the campaign to the social aspects of the behavior-change process (Agrawal et al., 1977; Agrawal, 1981). Although evaluation found significant changes in knowledge, it also found that more attention in future efforts needed to be devoted to community variables in order to enhance the likelihood of behavior change. These included the location and size of villages, levels of development and the social structure of communities in terms of caste and demographics and how these combined as power and influence that might aid in more effective future campaigns.

Community analysis approaches described here have been developed mainly on the basis of western concepts of social structure. That is, power and community influence are viewed as dependent on position (authority), class, involvement in coordinative settings and personal communication skills. Community analysis techniques have also been applied effectively in non-Western settings. However, the nature of the dominant social and cultural setting leads to a number of differences in their application.

Based on the SITE experience discussed earlier, the task for INSAT project planners was to devise formative methods giving government campaign planners better insights into rural Indian community structure—insights that could enhance their development of educational television that would be more effectively tailored to community needs. Previous formative efforts had focused heavily on interviews with those in official positions, which appeared to result in a somewhat unidimensional view of community dynamics (Agrawal, 1981). These efforts needed to be broadened to better account for leadership and influence through a crucial structural variable in Indian social organization: caste.[2]

Of specific interest to INSAT community analysts was the extent to which lower classes had differential access to community resources and programs and the conditions under which they would have access to a community television facility carrying health and agricultural programming. INSAT was interested in better tailoring messages and programming to more effectively supplement village programs conducted by various agricultural and medical extension services. Furthermore, they were interested in how communities might be better mobilized to use televised information in their daily activities. Some brief background about castes and their role in Indian society will serve to make community analysis procedures in this cultural and social setting clearer.

Castes are hierarchical endogamous units, divided into a number of subcastes or subunits, having their origin in ancient Sanskrit writings. Ascribed at birth, caste membership determines marriage and kinship ties and occupational and exchange relationships. In combination with language, caste is one of the major divisors of Indian society (Gangrade, 1971). There are four main castes: *Brahmins, Kshatriyas, Vysyas* and *Sudras. Brahmins* were ascribed the top position in the hierarchy, mainly as priests, scholars, administrators and teachers. *Kshatriyas* were the ruling or warrior caste, whose job it was to rule, administer, protect and fight. They, too, were learned and, with *Brahmins,* dominated the ruling and ideological arms of the state. The *Vysyas'* main profession was commerce and banking. While they were third in the hierarchy, they nevertheless enjoyed many privileges and free access to many facilities. And, of course, they were economically powerful. Last came the *Sudras,* followed by the *Harijans* who were responsible for menial jobs and once possessed only limited civil and religious rights. This is only an approximation of caste structure. Castes are not always so unified or clearly delineated, and they are divided further into subcastes and also along occupational lines.

A major difference between the Western concept of class and the Indian caste has to do with social mobility. While an individual may move up or down in a class system, in a caste system, it is entire communities which may change their position, rather than individuals (Beteille, 1965). While various reforms have considerably eroded the social stigma attached to membership in the lowest castes, the system overall continues to channel political, economic, and social power. Caste groups have foundations and trusts initiating various social welfare programs (e.g., scholarships, loans) and, in some cases, they even have marriage bureaus. Caste and class in terms of social and economic power are highly-correlated (Sharma, 1986; Narain, Pande, & Sharma, 1976). There also is a close relationship between political parties, elections, and caste (Bhambri, 1986). Political bargaining and mobilization continues to occur along caste lines in, for example, preferential quotas in parliament and state legislatures, and in various legislative activities involving loans, and educational, economic, and agricultural subsidies for lower castes.

INSAT community analysis was conducted in several phases. In the first phase, analysts selected the survey sites—five villages of different size (population 500 to 8,000), complexity and configuration in the state of Andhra Pradesh.[3] Two villages functioned as holy sites and thus attracted a regular flow of pilgrims from the surrounding area. Priests occupied particularly important positions in these villages. The other three villages included upper caste groups, but not Brahmins in key power positions.

In the second phase, analysts identified key community leaders beginning first with village leaders in the *panchayat samithi* (the village council, an elective body), followed by caste leaders, other officials such as the village doctor, other medical staff, extension agents, the village school teacher, and groups of men and women in different caste groups.

In the third phase, analysts assessed community geography to identify key caste segments. In general, dominant castes live in well-built homes, closer to the center of villages. Other castes are scattered around the center, yet within village boundaries. The lowest castes typically live outside of the village proper, while the Harijans (mainly farm laborers for land owners) live farthest away, linked typically by a single, unpaved road. Thus, on the basis of this geographic-spatial analysis, community analysts were able to assess which castes (those living near the center) typically dominated the community.

In the fourth phase, interviews were conducted using an open-ended schedule, asking about major community health problems, opinion leaders, access to community facilities and programs, and what could be done to improve both. The first groups contacted were official village leaders, including the elected president of the village council (generally from the upper caste), and other officials, both elected and appointed. This was intentional, since as legitimizers, this group's collaboration is required for the success of most programs.

Leaders were first apprised of the nature of the INSAT project and the purpose of the interviews. They supplied information on their villages' institutional infrastructures, including hospitals, council buildings, temples, schools (primary and secondary), the nearest regional center, and access to medical and educational facilities. Each was asked to assess major problems (health-related problems in this case) major village needs and to assess the adequacy of government resources and the success or failure of various government efforts to alleviate rural problems.

Another group of community elites interviewed included the village physician, medical assistant, extension agents, the village school teacher, and so forth. Although these individuals were generally more educated and were not native, they had chosen the village as home usually to practice a profession. These interviews elicited information on the numbers of patrons of the interviewees' institutions, their perceptions of problems and potential solutions and how television might be useful in supplementing their needs and roles.

Analysts also interviewed traditional village midwives, some of whom received training and equipment from the government.

A second series of interviews was conducted with members of dominant caste groups like the *Brahmins, Reddies,*[4] or *Vysyas,* who were relatively better educated, economically better-off and lived near the center of the villages, according to their dominant position. Interviews also were conducted with lower-caste groups living in the village itself and with the lowest groups living outside the village proper.

The fifth phase involved the collection of other kinds of documentation, including statistics, photographs, and official records.

In the sixth phase, interviews and documentation were summarized as an assessment of each village, including: (1) an identification of main groups, castes, and leaders; (2) an enumeration of community facilities and their spatial orientation; (3) a summary of major problems, perceptions, and solutions by the different leaders and caste-group representatives; and (4) a summary of access and information needs by the different groups in relation to the use of television programming.

As analysts expected, the information needs of the groups differed, based upon their caste, class and occupational status. For example, serious medical treatment needs of the dominant-caste/class members were met by doctors in the village or in the nearest regional town, to which many had access. Minor ailments were treated at home, using indigenous techniques, or through the local clinic. From a public health point of view, members of this group lived in relatively more hygienic conditions, ate better and were better informed about various preventive measures. Other groups—especially the *Harijans*—showed great need not only for sanitary facilities but for information on basic preventive public health measures. They possessed very little information on pre- and post-natal care, child care, vaccinations, causes or sources of disease and treatments for simple injuries. Importantly, they did not mention access to medical facilities in the nearest town. Their dependence on local facilities was total. Poverty, coupled with limited access to better facilities because of geographical, economic, and cultural limitations, also produced in them a sense of alienation and mistrust of officials. Yet, this did not prevent them from articulating grievances or indicating a consciousness of their political power as a bloc.

These analyses are expected to be useful to program planners, not only in tailoring information to the needs of various groups but also in using television to complement existing outreach strategies, particularly to lower-caste groups. Moreover, engaging caste opinion leaders is likely to assist in securing access to facilities and in better mobilizing caste groups to view, discuss, and use information and programs.

CONCLUSION

Community analysis makes an important contribution in the developmental stages of campaign planning as a way of providing feedback to monitor the role of organizations and as part of a broadly-conceived planning process incorporating appropriate outcome analysis strategies (Windsor, Baranowski, Clark, & Cutter, 1984). At the very least, community-analysis methods, as a type of formative research, can assist planners in avoiding some major strategy mistakes based on ignorance of community social and cultural traditions and how communities work as aggregates of different kinds of power and influence. Beyond this, community analysis informs "empowerment" strategies to mobilize community power and influence, enhancing the potential for achieving overall goals and adjusting strategies. The use of community analysis methods is justified primarily on the assertion that individuals are more likely to change when they have adequate social support, a point often made in the campaign literature.

But the use of community analysis presupposes that there also are outcome-analysis strategies in place to observe campaign-related changes in community-level variables. That is, while campaign-outcome evaluations usually examine change among individuals, there has been much less examination of campaign-related changes on community structural variables. There are a number of models available to inform this kind of outcome analysis, drawn from ethnographic, environmental-ecological and policy-analysis research traditions, as well as a hybrid model that seeks to link systemic changes to effects on individuals (Davidson, Redner, & Saul, 1983).

From a campaign perspective, community analysis would seem to be justified to the extent that investigators can make the case in outcome measures that community-based strategies actually affected elements such as: (1) the allocation of community resources to achieve campaign goals; (2) numbers of community interorganizational connections; (3) levels of community interorganizational activity; and (4) the longevity of the aforementioned, following the cessation of intense, highly visible campaigning.

Some preliminary analyses in MHHP have looked at the issue of network density as one way of operationalizing a community-level campaign effect (Weisbrod, 1988). Some initial favorable results appear to lend support to the hypothesis that engaging community leadership in campaigns may increase connections among a greater number of organizations involved in preventive activity, compared to communities without a campaign. Also, more than 70% of heart health programs initiated in MHHP intervention communities were maintained following the withdrawal of federal campaign funds.

Analysis of community power and leadership thus is beginning to be justified also through true community-level outcomes. Much work remains both in the specification of outcomes and in their validation through longitudinal studies comparing communities with and without community-based campaign interventions.

NOTES

1. That is, those whose approval is usually required to assure the success of a community undertaking.

2. While caste as one type of social formation is the primary focus of this description, it should be noted that other factors such as class, gender, age, education, occupation and community size were also included in the analyses.

3. Analyses were also conducted in other states, as well as in other districts of Andhra Pradesh. The focus here is on one set of community surveys as part of the much larger analysis effort, drawing on the third author's personal experiences. This summary does not represent official views of the Indian government.

4. That is, a dominate caste group whose influence stemmed from control of land (Elliot, 1977; Bernstorff, 1977).

REFERENCES

Agrawal, B. C. (1981). Anthropological applications in communication research and evaluation of SITE in India. *Media Asia 8,* p. 3.

Agrawal, B. C., Doshi, J. K., Jesudasan, V., & Verma, K. K. (1977). *Satellite instructional television experiment: Social evaluation-impact on adults* (Vols. 1, 2). Bangalore, India: Indian Space Research Organization.

Aiken, M. (1970). The distribution of community power: Structural bases and social consequences. In M. Aiken & P. E. Mott (Eds.), *The structure of community power* (pp. 487–525). New York: Random House.

Alba, R. D., & Moore, G. (1978). Elite social circles. *Sociological Methods and Research, 7,* 167–188.

Alinsky, S. D. (1946). *Reveille for radicals.* Chicago: University of Chicago Press.

Archer, S. E., Kelly, C. D., & Bisch, S. A. (1984). *Implementing change in communities: A collaborative process.* St. Louis: C. V. Mosby.

Barth, E. A. (1961). Community influence systems: Structure and change. *Social Forces, 60,* 58–63.

Beal, G. M., & Hobbs, D. (1964). *The process of social action in community and area development.* Ames: Cooperative Extension Service, Iowa State University.

Beaulieu, L. J., & Ryan, V. D. (1984). Research note: Hierarchical influence structures in rural communities: A case study. *Rural Sociology, 49,* (1), 106–116.

Berger, P. L., & Neuhaus, R. J. (1977). *To empower people: The role of mediating structures in public policy.* Washington, DC: American Enterprise Institute for Public Policy Research.

Bernstorff, D. (1977). Political leadership in Andhra Pradesh. In B. N. Pandey (Ed.), *Leadership in South Asia.* New Delhi: Vikas Publishing.

Berrigan, F. J. (1979). *Community communications: The role of community media in development.* Paris: UNESCO.

Beteille, A. (1965). *Caste, class and power.* Berkeley: University of California Press.

Bhambri, C. P. (1986). Caste and politics in India. In K. L. Sharma (Ed.), *Social stratification in India* (pp. 79–87). New Delhi: Manohar.

Biddle, W. W., & Biddle, L. (1965). *The community development process: The rediscovery of local initiative.* New York: Holt, Rinehart & Winston.

Blackburn, H. B. (1983). Research and demonstration projects in community cardiovascular disease prevention. *Journal of Public Health Policy, 4,* 398–421.

Blackburn, H. B., Luepker, R. V., Kline, F. G. et al. (1984). The Minnesota Heart Health Program: A research and demonstration project in cardiovascular disease prevention. In J. Matarazzo, C. Weiss, J. A. Herd, N . Miller, & S. Weiss (Eds.), *Settings for health promotion in behavioral health: A handbook for health enhancement and disease prevention.* New York: John Wiley.

Blake, S. M., Jeffery, R. W., Finnegan, J. R., Crow, R., Pirie, P., Ringhofer, K., & Fruetel, J. (1987). Process evaluation of a community-based physical activity campaign: The Minnesota Heart Health Program Experience. *Health Education Research: Theory and Practice 2 (2),* 115–121.

Blau, J. R., & Alba, R. D. (1982). Empowering networks of participation. *Administrative Science Quarterly, 27,* 363–379.

Bonacich, P. (1987). Power and centrality: A family of measures. *American Journal of Sociology, 92 (5),* 1170–1182.

Bordenave, J. E. D. (1977a). *A critical analysis of the case studies. Communication and Rural Development.* Paris: UNESCO.

Bordenave, J. E. D. (1977b). *Communication theory and rural development: A brief review. Communication and Rural Development.* Paris: UNESCO.

Bordenave, J. E. D. (1977c). *National radio study campaigns for civic education—United Republic of Tanzania. Communication and Rural Development.* Paris: UNESCO.

Bordenave, J. E. D. (1977d). *Pilot project in the use of communication media for adult education—Senegal. Communication and Rural Development.* Paris: UNESCO.

Bracht, N. F. (1988). Use of community analysis methods in community-wide intervention programs. *Scandinavian Journal of Primary Health Care, Supplement 1,* 23–30.

Brown, E. R. (1984). Community organization influence on local public health care policy: A general research model and comparative case study. *Health Education Quarterly, 10 (3/4),* 205–233.

Brown, L. D., & Detterman, L. B. (1987). Small interventions for large problems: Reshaping urban leadership networks. *Journal of Applied Behavioral Science, 23 (2),* 151–168.

Burt, R. S. (1977). Power in a social topology. In R. J. Liebert & A. W. Imershein (Eds.), *Power, paradigms, and community research.* (pp. 251–334). Beverly Hills, CA: Sage.

Burt, R. S. (1981). Comparative power structures in American communities. *Social Science Research, 10,* 115–176.

Burton, M. G., & Higley, J. (1987). Invitation to elite theory: The basic contentions reconsidered. In G. W. Domhoff, and T. R. Dye (Eds.), *Power elites and organizations* (pp. 219–238). Beverly Hills, CA: Sage.

Carlaw, R., Mittelmark, M., Bracht, N. F., & Luepker, R. V. (1984). Organization for a community cardiovascular health program: Experiences from the Minnesota Heart Health Program. *Health Education Quarterly, 11 (3),* 243–252.

Coleman, J. S. (1977). Notes on the study of power. In R. J. Liebert and A. W. Imershein (Eds.), *Power, paradigms, and community research.* (pp. 183–198). Beverly Hills, CA: Sage.

Cobb, R. W., & Elder, C. D. (1972). *Participation in American politics: The dynamics of agenda-building.* Baltimore, MD: Johns Hopkins University Press.

Cook, K. S., Emerson, R. M., Gillmore, M. R., & Yamagishi, T. (1983). The distribution of power in exchange networks: Theory and experimental results. *American Journal of Sociology 89 (2),* 275–305.

Crosby, N., Kelly, J. M., & Schaefer, P. (1986). Citizens panels: A new approach to citizen participation. *Public Administration Review, 46,* 170–178.

Dahl, R. A. (1958). A critique of the ruling elite model. *American Political Science Review, 52 (June),* 463–469.

Dahl, R. A. (1961). *Who governs?* New Haven, CT: Yale University Press.

Davidson, W. S., Redner, R., & Saul, J. A. (1983). Research modes in social and community change. In E. Seidman (Ed.), *Handbook of social intervention.* (pp. 99–118). Beverly Hills, CA: Sage.

Deseran, F. A., & Black, L. (1981). Research note: Problems with using self reports in network analysis: Some empirical findings in rural counties. *Rural Sociology, 46, (2),* 310–318.

Domhoff, G. W., & Dye, T. R. (Eds.) (1987). *Power elites and organizations.* Newbury Park, CA: Sage.

Dulka, M. (1982). The power structure of Moorhead, Minnesota. *Journal of Social and Behavioral Sciences* (pp. 1–38). Moorhead, MN: Moorhead State University.

Eapen, K. E. (1979a). SITE: A learning experience. *Media Asia, 6,* 1.

Eapen, K. E. (1979b). Cultural component of SITE. *Journal of Communication, 29,* 4.

Eisenstadt, S. N., & Shachar, A. (1986). *Society, culture, and urbanization.* Newbury Park, CA: Sage.

Elder, J. P., Hovell, M. F., Lasater, T. M., Wells, B. L., & Carleton, R. A. (1985). Applications of behavior modification to community health education: The case of heart disease prevention. *Health Education Quarterly, 12,* 151–68.

Elliot, C. (1977). Caste and faction among the dominant caste: The Reddis and Kammas of Andhra. In R. Kothari (Ed.), *Caste in Indian politics* (pp. 129–171). New Delhi: Orient Longman.

Farquhar, J., Fortmann, S., Maccoby, N., Haskell, W. L., Williams, P., Flora, J., Taylor, C. B., Brown, B. W., Solomon, D. S. & Hulley, S. (1985). The Standford five-city project: Design and methods. *American Journal of Epidemiology, 122,* 323–34.

Freeman, L. C., Fararo, T. J., Bloomberg, W., Jr., & Sunshine, M. H., (1963). Locating leaders in local communities: A comparison of some alternative approaches. *American Sociological Review, 28,* 791–798.

Galaskiewicz, J. (1979). *Exchange networks and community politics.* Beverly Hills, CA: Sage.

Gangrade, K. D. (1971). *Community organizations in India.* Bombay: Poplar Prakashan.

Gartrell, C. D. (1987). Network approach to social evaluation. *American Review of Sociology, 13,* 49–66.

Goodenough, W. A. (1963). *Cooperation in change.* New York: Russel Sage Foundation.

Gore, M. S. (1983). *The SITE Experience.* (Reports and papers on mass communication No. 91). Paris: UNESCO.

Hall, B. L. (1985). International Council for Adult Education. *Mtu ni Afya: Tanzania's health campaign.* Toronto, Ontario.

Hammer, M. (1980). Some comments on the validity of network data. *Connections Bulletin of the International Network for Social Network Analysis, 3,* 13–15.

Hunter, F. (1953). *Community power structure: A study of decision makers.* Chapel Hill: Universtiy of North Carolina Press.

Jacobs, D. R., Luepker, R. V., Mittelmark, M. B., Folsom, A. R., Pirie, P., Mascioli, S., Hannan, P. J., Pechacek, T., Bracht, N., Carlaw, R., Kline, F. G., & Blackburn, H. B. (1986). Community-wide prevention strategies: Evaluation design of the Minnesota Heart Health Program. *Journal of Chronic Disease, 39,* 775–788.

Keys, A., (Ed.) (1980). *Seven countries: A multivariate analysis of death and coronary heart disease.* Cambridge, MA: Harvard University Press.

Kotler, P. & Zaltman, G. (1971). Social marketing: An approach to planned social change. *Journal of Marketing, 35 (3),* 3–12.

Kurtz, D. M. (1987). Who runs Louisiana? Institutions and leaders at the state level. In G. W. Domhoff & T. R. Dye (Eds.), *Power elites and organizations* (pp. 126–151). Newbury Park, CA: Sage.

Lasswell, H. D. (1936). *Politics: Who Gets What, When, and How.* New York: McGraw-Hill.

Laumann, E. O., Marsden, P. V., & Galaskiewicz, J. (1977). Community-elite influence structures: Extension of a network approach. *American Journal of Sociology, 83 (3),* 594–631.

Laumann, E. O., & Pappi, F. U. (1976). *Networks of collective action: A perspective on community influence systems.* New York: Academic Press.

Liebert, R. J., & Imershein, A. W. (1977). *Power, paradigms, and community research.* Beverly Hills, CA: Sage.

Lincoln, J. R. (1977). Organizational dominance and community structure. In R. J.

Leibert & A. W. Imershein (Eds.), *Power, paradigms, and community research* (pp. 19–50). Beverly Hills, CA: Sage.

Maccoby, N., & Solomon, D. S. (1981). Heart disease prevention: Community studies. In R. E. Rise & W. Paisley (Eds.), *Public communications campaigns* (pp. 105–126). Beverly Hills, CA: Sage.

Maida, C. A. (1985). Social support and learning preventive health care. *Social Science and Medicine, 21 (3),* 335–339.

Mayer, R. R. (1972). *Social planning and social change.* Englewood Cliffs, NJ: Prentice-Hall.

McAlister, A., Puska, P., Koskela, K., Pallonen, U., & Maccoby, N. (1980). Psychology in action: Mass communication and Community organization for public health education. *American Psychologist, 35* (4), 375–379.

McCain, T. A., & Hofstetter, C. R. (1982). Leaders of opinion for ascertainment in the black community: The method is the message. *Social Science Journal, 19,* 25–44.

Milbrath, L. W., & Goel, M. L. (1977). *Political participation: How and why do people get involved in politics?* (2nd ed.). Chicago: Rand-McNally.

Mills, C. W. (1956). *The power elite.* New York: Oxford University Press.

Mittlemark, N., Luepker, R. V., Jacobs, D., Bracht, N., Carlaw, R., Crow, R., Finnegan, J. R., Grimm, R. H., Jeffery, R. W., Kline, F. G., Mullis, R. M., Murray, D. M., Pechacek, T., Perry, C. P., Pirie, P. L., & Blackburn, H. B. (1986). Community-wide prevention of cardiovascular disease: Education strategies of the Minnesota Heart Health Program. *Preventive Medicine, 15,* 1–17.

Mody, B. (1979). Programming for SITE. *Journal of Communication, 29,* 4.

Narain, I. L., Pande, K., & Sharma, M. L. (1976). *The rural elite in an Indian state.* New Delhi: Manohar.

Nix, H. L. (1969). Concepts of community and community leadership. *Sociology and Social Research, 53,* 500–510.

Nix, H. L. (1977). *The Community and its involvement in the study planning action process.* (U.S. Dept. of Health, Education and Welfare Publication No. (CDC) 78–8355.) Washington, D.C.: U.S. Government Printing Office.

Nix, H. L. Dressel, P. L., & Bates, F. L. (1977). Changing leaders and leadership structure: A longitudinal study. *Rural Sociology, 42 (Spring).*

Nix, H. L., & Seerley, N. R. (1971). Community reconnaissance method: A synthesis of functions. *Journal of the Community Development Society, 2 (Fall),* 62–69.

Ornstein, N. J., & Elder, S. (1978). *Interest groups, lobbying and policymaking.* Washington, D.C.: Congressional Quarterly Press.

Palmer, E. (1981). Shaping persuasive messages with formative research. In R. E. Rice & W. J. Paisley (Eds.), *Public communication campaigns* (pp. 227–238). Beverly Hills, CA: Sage.

Puska, P., Nissinen, A., Tuomilehto, J., et al. (1985). The community-based strategy to prevent coronary heart disease: Conclusions from the ten-year study, *Publication,* 147–193.

Rappaport, J., Swift, C. & Hess, R. (Eds.) (1984). *Studies in empowerment: Steps toward understanding and action.* New York: Haworth Press.

Riessman, F. (1983). The new politics of empowerment. *Social Policy, 14,* 2–3.

Rifkin, S. B. (1985). *Health planning and community participation: Case studies in South-East Asia.* London: Croom Helm.

Rogers, E. M., & Shoemaker, F. F. (1971). *Communication of innovations: A cross-cultural approach.* (2nd ed.). New York: Free Press.

Rogers, E. M., & Storey, J. D. (1987). Communication campaigns. In C. R. Berger & S. H. Chaffe (Eds.), *Handbook of communication science* (pp. 817–846). Newbury Park, CA: Sage.

Rook, K. S. (1984). Promoting social bonding: Strategies for helping the lonely and socially isolated. *American Psychologist, 39,* 1389–1407.

Schafer, C. (1981). The health-related function of social support. *Journal of Behavioral Medicine, 4 (4),* 381.

Silk, L., & Silk, M. (1980). *The American establishment.* New York: Basic Books.

Stone, C. (1980). Systemic power in community decision-making: A restatement of stratification theory. *American Political Science Review, 74,* 978–990.

Stunkard, A. J., Felix, M., & Cohen, R. (1985). Mobilizing a community to promote health: The Pennsylvania County Health Improvement Program (CHIP). In J. C. Rosen & L. J. Solomon (Eds.), *Prevention in health psychology,* (pp. 143–190). Hanover, VI: University Press of New England.

Suchman, E. A. (1967). Preventive health behavior: A model for research on community health campaigns. *Journal of Health and Social Behavior, 8,* 197–209.

Tuluhungwa, R. N. (1981). A communication strategy for development. In M. Meyer (Ed.), *Health education by television and radio* (pp. 30–37). Munich: K. G. Saur.

Turk, H. (1977). An interorganizational view of pluralism, elitism, conflict, and policy outputs in large communities. In R. J. Liebert & A. W. Imershein (Eds.), *Power, paradigms, and community research* (pp. 51–78). Beverly Hills, CA: Sage.

Walton, J. (1968). Differential patterns of community power structure: An explanation based on interdependence. In T. N. Clarke (Ed.), *Community structure and decision making: Comparative analyses* (pp. 441–459). San Francisco: Chandler.

Ward, R. A. (1985). Informal networks and well-being in later life: A research agenda. *Gerontologist, 25,* 55–61.

Warren, R. L. (1956). Toward a reformulation of community theory. *Human Organization, 15,* 8–11.

Warren, R. L. (1963). *The community in America.* Chicago: Rand-McNally.

Weisbrod, R. (1988). *Community incorporation research project.* (Unpublished report, Minnesota Heart Health Program) Minneapolis: University of Minnesota Division of Epidemiology.

White, H. D., Boorman, S. A., & Brieger, R. L. (1976). Social structure from multiple networks: Blockmodels of roles and positions. *American Journal of Sociology, 81,* 730–780.

Windsor, R. A., Baranowski, T., Clark, N., & Cutter, G. (1984). *Evaluation of health promotion and education programs.* Palo Alto, CA: Mayfield.

Chapter 3

FAMILY PLANNING, ABORTION AND AIDS: SEXUALITY AND COMMUNICATION CAMPAIGNS

Jane D. Brown, Cynthia S. Waszak and Kim Walsh Childers

SEXUALITY AND COMMUNICATION CAMPAIGNS

SEXUALITY IS A SOCIAL CONSTRUCT. While basic biology sets limits on some aspects of sexual behavior, beyond these boundaries, every society has evolved a peculiar set of expectations and definitions of sexuality. In each society, deep-seated traditions, values, and formal and informal regulations have developed to govern most aspects of male and female interaction. In most modern societies, these traditions generally have limited acceptable sexual practices to the confines of monogamous heterosexual marriage and have defined sex as primarily for the purpose of reproduction. Pre- or extramarital intercourse, homosexuality and the use of contraceptives or abortion have been considered either taboo or, at various times, illegal. In other societies, different standards and expectations have evolved—in some, masturbation, multiple premarital sexual partners and/or homosexuality have been encouraged; in others, polygamy is still practiced (Gregersen, 1983).

AUTHORS' NOTE: The first author would like to thank the Gannett Center for Media Studies for providing time for writing, the assistance of Lia Nikopoulou, and the opportunity for interchange with fellow Fellows Paul Perry and Jim Kinsella. Thanks, too, to Chuck Salmon, Susan Newcomer and Ev Rogers for helpful comments on earlier drafts of the chapter.

Communication campaigns may be seen as one of the ways in which contemporary societies deal with the necessity of continually defining and redefining which specific sexual practices will be considered "appropriate or inappropriate, moral or immoral, healthy or perverted" (Weeks, 1986, p. 22). Interventions designed to change existing sexual norms and behaviors have included organized communication campaigns at least as far back as the beginning of the century, when pioneers such as Margaret Sanger fought to be allowed to distribute birth control information to poor women (Gordon, 1977). Today, communication campaigns are conducted to influence knowledge, beliefs, attitudes and behaviors on a number of topics relevant to sexuality. Campaigns have been conducted against pornography, against the censorship of pornography, against child sexual abuse, for rape awareness, for and against the right to have an abortion, for and against sex education in the schools, for sexual abstinence and for the use of condoms for the prevention of disease, etc.

In every case, the particular political, economic and social structures of the society in which these campaigns have been conducted have affected all aspects of these campaigns, including when they were conducted, who sponsored them, to whom they were directed, what they tried to accomplish and which channels of communication were (and could be) used. In almost all cases, the campaigns were met with some form of opposition. As we will demonstrate, feelings about sex and sexuality run deep, and dramatic shifts in cultural standards and norms are not accomplished quickly. These debates often are grounded in very fundamental notions about the procreative role of women. As a result, the effects of these campaigns often are felt disproportionately by women and are most severe for the most disenfranchised—the young, the poor, the racial minority.

All societies have both formal and informal regulations about sexual behavior (Weeks, 1981). In many societies these regulations are tied closely to religious beliefs and traditions that often have been codified in secular law. Historically, communication campaigns about various aspects of sexuality have been conducted for two purposes: (1) to persuade people to change patterns of sexual behavior within the boundaries of existing religious and political regulations, and/or (2) to persuade religious and/or political institutions to change regulations about sexual behavior. The first purpose is illustrated by the many family planning programs around the world that use communication campaigns as a central mechanism for persuading people to use contraceptives to limit family size and by efforts to promote "safe sex" in order to stem the AIDS epidemic. The use of communication campaigns to affect formal regulations is best illustrated currently by efforts in both the United States and Europe to change abortion laws (Lovenduski & Outshoorn, 1986).

In some political contexts, attempts to change aspects of sexuality through the mass media or interpersonal communication are buttressed with formal regulations. Recent examples include proposals that would allow the detention of people infected with the AIDS virus who knowingly engage in risky sexual behavior ("Florida considering locking up some carriers of the AIDS virus," 1988), attempts by antiabortion advocates to restrict U.S. government funding for domestic and foreign agencies that counsel clients about abortion (Roberts, 1987) and the regulations that undergird China's one-child family campaign.

In this chapter, we focus our attention on communication campaigns that satisfy Rogers and Storey's (1987) definition: an organized set of communication activities intended to generate specific effects in a relatively large number of people within a specified period of time. We concentrate on three broad topics around which definitions and norms of sexuality currently are being debated around the world: family planning, abortion and AIDS. We describe specific examples, whenever possible from countries other than the United States, in order to show the extent to which the political and regulatory climate and prevailing social norms affect the conduct of campaigns dealing with sexual topics.

FAMILY PLANNING CAMPAIGNS

For centuries, men and women have tried to control the timing of their children and the number of children they have. The birth control pill is, in fact, the only contraceptive device that does not have at least 150 years of history. Our ancestors knew about withdrawal (coitus interruptus) and the rhythm method; they used suppositories and diaphragms, intrauterine devices and condoms, sterilization, abortion and infanticide (Reed, 1978). Typically, women developed and passed on knowledge about birth control because they were the ones who suffered most directly from the burden of too many children. But the use of birth control always has been regulated in some way because it bears directly on two crucial social issues: population size and sexual activity (Gordon, 1977).

Today, in many developing countries around the world, ever-increasing populations have led to overcrowding, poverty and hunger, and governments, often assisted by foreign funding, have launched communication campaigns to encourage the use of birth control to limit population growth. Two examples of this kind of campaign are discussed here to show how, in different political and social climates, the similar objective of limiting population growth has been achieved with very different strategies. We then turn to the ways in which communication campaigns have been used to influence regulation of abortion in the United States. In many industrialized countries, contraceptives and abortion are no longer seen primarily as solutions to population problems but, rather, have become primary sites of controversy over modern definitions of women's sexuality and women's role in society and the family.

EVOLUTION OF FAMILY PLANNING CAMPAIGNS

Rogers (1973) has identified three distinct eras in the evolution of family-planning campaigns. In the first era, campaigns were centered on health clinics that dispensed contraceptives, and communication campaigns were designed to inform people about the existence of family-planning methods. Many of these campaigns were unsuccessful because couples were not motivated to use birth control, because the campaigns ignored traditional male dominance in family-planning decisions and because the countries couldn't afford adequate family-planning services.

The failure of the clinic-based approach led to the "field era," based on assumptions that the field staff were needed to motivate couples to adopt family planning. The mass media, heavily emphasized during this era, were used to increase public knowledge about family planning and to promote the small-family norm. Field workers soon discovered, however, that potential family-planning clients were more likely to be persuaded by people like themselves than by "experts." Thus, planners developed an incentive system to encourage those who already had adopted a family-planning method to bring in new adopters. The rates of acceptance of contraceptive methods increased, but reports of coercion of unwilling clients made the use of incentives very controversial (Vines, 1985). The one-child family campaign conducted in the People's Republic of China exemplifies this era.

In the third era, some countries have developed social marketing campaigns, in which contraceptives are sold rather than given away, and the mass media are used to advertise specific contraceptive products (Kotler & Zaltman, 1971; Solomon, 1981; Manoff, 1985). One of the earliest and most illustrative of these social marketing efforts was conducted in Bangladesh.

THE ONE-CHILD FAMILY CAMPAIGN IN CHINA

In 1981, the population count in the People's Republic of China (PRC) reached the one billion mark. Even if China meets the formidable goal of limiting growth to 1.2 billion by the year 2000, the population increase in two decades still will be nearly equal to that of the total U.S. population. The government's task is to convince the Chinese people, who for centuries have preferred large families and male children, that the ideal family is a mother, a father and one child of either gender (Freemon, 1987).

In the 1970s, China launched the "wan.xi.shao" or "later, fewer, longer" campaign, which sought to relieve population problems by encouraging late marriages and by promoting the norm of a two-child family. During this campaign, the government developed an infrastructure for administering the national program at the local level, giving study groups organized around factory work or residence in a commune the task of setting goals for planned births in their communities. In the late 1970s, when the new policy of one-child families was adopted, these groups continued their role as local monitors and, in the language of communication effects, served as sources of interpersonal communication and reinforcement of the mass media messages (Freemon, 1987; Liu, 1981; Greenhalgh and Bongaarts, 1986; Jacobsen, 1983).

The media campaign was designed to change the Chinese people's attitudes about the benefits of large families. All available mass media were used: billboards, posters, magazines, newspapers, radio and, most recently, television, which is becoming increasingly prevalent in the country. Other, more traditional communication channels, such as local theater, dance and music, also have been used.

The messages transmitted at the national level explicitly identified the locus of benefit as the Chinese nation, rather than the individual family. The messages called the standard of the one-child family a "strategic task" important for: "development of our national economy," "the Chinese nation's prosperity," "the speed and future of the four modernizations" and the "health and happiness of generations to come." In initiating the campaign, Vice Premier Chen Muhan told the Chinese people that individual interests must "voluntarily be subordinated" to the interests of the PRC (Population Reports, 1982).

Although the language of the messages focused on these national interests, the visual images suggested individual benefits, for example, happy, prosperous, one-child families. The audiences most frequently targeted were married couples of reproductive age and their parents, who might be pressuring them for grandchildren.

Interpersonal channels of communication and monetary incentives reinforced mass media persuasion attempts. Since peers and coworkers set birth goals for each group, the government hoped that couples would be less resentful about having to restrict the size of their families. This campaign, like others in China, stressed the roles of personal decision making and "active participation," which build on well-known principles of persuasion (Liu, 1981). Couples made public commitments to have only one child and were subject to severe peer pressure if they reneged. More tangible rewards and stringent punishments also were used in the interpersonal persuasion stage of the communication campaign—couples who made a commitment to having only one child received a certificate that entitled them and their son or daughter to certain health, education, housing and employment benefits. However, if the couple had a second child, they had to give up the certificate and pay the government for whatever benefits they already had received (Chen & Tian, 1982).

The campaign appears to be working, at least in terms of population control. The total fertility rate (number of children per woman) in China has declined from 5.9 in 1970 to 1.9 in 1984 (Greenhalgh and Bongaarts, 1986). There are some signs, however, that even in China, a society with a history of totalitarian governments and cultural norms of self-sacrifice for the collectivity, sexual traditions are not easily changed. What Weeks (1986) calls "cultures of resistance" apparently exist, especially in the rural areas of China, where communities have argued that more children are an economic necessity. Many couples in China still choose to have a second and sometimes even a third child, especially if the first children are girls (Greenhalgh and Bongaarts, 1986).

Western observers also have reported large numbers of dangerous second and third-trimester abortions and increasing incidence of female infanticide (Jacobsen, 1983). Because group leaders are responsible for attaining the birth planning goals, they put great pressure on and sometimes coerce wayward group members to have abortions, even very late in their pregnancies. Regrettably, female infanticide results when families still prefer sons and their only allowed child is a girl. While the Chinese government officially condemns infanticide and coerced abortion, it may unofficially view the abortions as necessary to prevent more catastrophic population consequences later.

SOCIAL MARKETING IN BANGLADESH

Bangladesh was formed after a civil war left it divided from Pakistan in 1971. As a new nation with a politically unstable, conservative Moslem population, it has little centralization of political control and little potential for community mobilization. It is a very small country with a very dense population. In 1981, 90 million people lived in Bangladesh; the population was expected to double in fewer than 30 years, given the fertility rate at that time. The infant mortality rate was one of the highest in the world at 130 per 1,000 live births (as compared, for example, with Sweden which had the lowest rate at 6 deaths per 1,000 live births) (UNICEF, 1987).

A social marketing program for contraceptives was begun in Bangladesh in 1973 with funding from the U.S. Agency for International Development (USAID). Formative research showed that, in the effort not to repel the Moslem population, the pilot messages were, in fact, too carefully worded. Subsequent messages more clearly advertised three kinds of contraceptives, which had been given brand names: Raja (condoms), Maya (oral contraceptives) and Joy (foaming vaginal tablets) (Family Planning Social Marketing Project, 1988).

In a controversial move, contraceptives were sold in public markets rather than distributed free in medical clinics in order to reduce suspicion of Western or governmental racism or coercion, and, in keeping with the marketing approach, to increase the value of the product in the eyes of the consumer. In contrast to previous campaigns, contraceptives were openly displayed; local merchants were provided with colorful dispensers. All available media were used: messages such as "Raja—the confident choice of the prudent man," and "Raja for a happy marriage" were heard on the radio and from bullhorns and were read in newspapers, on billboards, posters, leaflets, calendars, sunshades and boatsails.

The marketing of the condom was most successful, primarily because it was directed to men, who enjoy much more economic and social freedom than women in the society. The "female" contraceptive methods, however, were not adopted because Moslem traditions generally kept women out of the marketplaces and because women needed reassurance that the side effects they experienced from oral contraceptives were normal. The mass-media campaign alone was not successful in providing that reassurance.

A subsequent campaign beginning in 1982, again based on social marketing techniques, capitalized on the primarily male market in Bangladesh by producing a series of radio advertisements written specifically for men and designed to "confront the dramatic male prototype with doubts about his competence as a planner of his family." (Manoff, 1985, p. 245). The advertisements presented a mini-drama in which a man confesses that he used to be foolish, believing that family-planning methods were unsafe because he had "listened to tales told by ignorant people." He says he investigated the matter, however, and now he knows that family-planning methods such as condoms and the pill are safe. Every advertisement used specific key phrases: "Be a wise man—do the right thing." "Use condoms, pills and other safe methods" (Manoff, 1985).

The social marketers chose radio as the primary medium for this campaign because it was the most widely used medium, especially in rural areas where the need for population control was considered greatest. The program planners also hoped that women would have greater access to radio messages because they could hear them in the privacy of their homes, and they then might encourage their husbands to purchase the products. In 1982, enough condoms were sold to protect 970,000 couples for a year (Schellstede & Ciszewski, 1984).

SUMMARY

It is clear from the examples of China and Bangladesh that communication campaigns about sexual behavior, even those aimed at essentially the same goal, must be conducted differently, given the existing political, religious and social constraints of the time. In both of these countries, the political structure and control over the media system allowed leaders ubiquitous repetition of a consistent message, with little chance of a competing message. In China, strong, politically loyal interpersonal networks already were established and could be used to both support and pressure women to conform to the new standards in the interest of their emerging country. But, in both countries, conflicting religious and cultural traditions limited the success of the campaigns. In China, some rural community groups refused to cooperate; in Bangladesh, the entrenched religious and cultural restrictions that exclude women from public life necessitated directing communication to men and, in effect, limited the array of birth control options available in the marketplace, for the most part, to the condom.

ABORTION IN THE UNITED STATES

In the United States, recent campaigns about birth control and abortion have had more to do with concerns about sexuality than with population size,[1] but have, as in other countries, engendered controversy because of fundamental conflicts and shifts in the role and status of women and the political power of conceptions of morality based on religious beliefs.

In the United States and most other Western countries of Judeo-Christian heritage, the public debate over the use of contraceptives and abortion as methods of family planning has been long and rancorous (Lovenduski & Outshoorn, 1986). The contemporary phase of the battle is rooted in arguments intially raised a century earlier, primarily by feminists, who were concerned about the health and welfare of mothers and children, and by Victorian-era moralists who argued that birth control and abortion were immoral because they allowed sexual intercourse without procreation—the only religiously-sanctioned function of sexual intercourse for both conservative Christians and Jews.

In both Great Britain and the United States, early birth control advocates argued that information about contraceptive techniques should be available so that women could control the spacing and the number of their children. One of the best known advocates was Margaret Sanger, a public health nurse in New York City in the early 1900s. Disturbed by the number of women she saw who died in childbirth or who were chronically ill from having borne too many children in too few years, Sanger began a campaign to provide contraceptive information. Although her magazine, *The Woman Rebel,* did not provide advice about specific techniques, the U.S. Post Office declared it obscene in 1914 under the Comstock laws, which forbade the distribution of materials "for the prevention of conception."[2] Eventually, Sanger, who coined the term *birth control,* was instrumental in setting up a number of clinics that distributed contraceptive information and, in some cases, provided sex counseling (for married women only) through her organization, the American Birth Control League.

Over the next 50 years, questions of morality were muted somewhat as birth control and abortion (as well as other aspects of sexuality) became increasingly controlled by the scientific and medical communities (Gordon, 1977; Tiefer, 1987). The resurgence of feminism in the 1960s put the issue of reproductive freedom back on the public agenda. Feminists, in coalition with doctors who had been performing "therapeutic" abortions under the existing laws, began to pressure state legislatures for liberalized abortion statutes. By the early 1970s, one-third of the states had adopted more liberal laws. But in 1973, when the Supreme Court faced head-on the question of when life begins and ruled that abortions should be legal in the first trimester because the fetus was not yet viable, a new generation of moralists was galvanized to action.

The debate soon became consolidated and articulated as an issue of competing rights—those of the woman and those of the fetus. The protagonists have skillfully relabeled the primary stances on which they organize communication campaigns as "pro-choice"—rather than pro-abortion—and "pro-life"—rather than antiabortion (Jowett & O'Donnell, 1986). Although often obscured in the rhetoric, one of the primary underlying issues on both sides is the role of women in contemporary culture.

As sociologist Kristin Luker found from interviews with 200 activists on both sides of the abortion issue, opinions about abortion are only one aspect of very different and often diametrically opposed beliefs about gender, sex and parenthood. Pro-life activists tend to believe that any mechanical effort to control conception is threatening because it undermines the role of motherhood—viewed by them as woman's most natural and meaningful function in life. Pro-choice women, on the other hand, see sex primarily as a means of creating intimacy between people and believe that contraception allows people to develop this intimacy without being burdened with the fear of unwanted pregnancy. They see abortion not as a routine method of birth control, but rather as a sometimes-necessary measure when other birth control methods have failed (Luker, 1984 a, b).

The communication strategies employed by both sides in the past two decades have sought to capitalize on these underlying beliefs. Shortly after the Supreme Court decision, the National Conference of Catholic Bishops, Family Life Division, created the National Right to Life Committee. Over the next 15 years, the group grew into the largest of the anti-abortion organizations, with 2,500 local chapters in 50 states.

Their attempts to outlaw abortion with a "Human Life Amendment" to the U.S. Constitution failed, but they were successful in restricting the spending of federal money to fund abortions and in getting states to limit access to abortions, especially for adolescent girls. By 1987, more than one-fourth of the states required girls under 18 to notify or obtain consent from their parents before they could have an abortion, and a number of other states were debating such requirements (Glazer, 1987).

Toward the end of the 1970s, various pro-life groups shifted their energies to defeating congressmen who blocked passage of the anti-abortion constitutional amendment. Their political action committees (PACs), utilizing sophisticated direct mailings and mass leafletings to churchgoers, got pro-life voters to the polls. In 1980, four of the six targets lost their Senate races, and the new president was Ronald Reagan, who supported the Human Life Amendment. But elated pro-lifers soon were disillusioned as Reagan appointed an apparently unsympathetic Supreme Court justice, Sandra Day O'Connor, who was unanimously confirmed by the Senate (Hershey & West, 1983).

By the early 1980s, some of the more radical pro-lifers, frustrated by their lack of political success with traditional communication strategies, split off from the Right to Life Committee and formed organizations committed to "direct action." One such group, Americans Against Abortion, sponsored a "Walk Across America" by evangelical minister Norman Stone, who displayed an allegedly aborted fetus named "Baby Choice" at demonstrations outside abortion clinics. A professionally produced videotape, beginning with an endorsement by Reagan and featuring "Baby Choice" and other dead fetuses, was sent to all members of Congress.

In 1985, in a book called *CLOSED: 99 Ways to Stop Abortion*, Joseph Scheidler, the head of the Pro-Life Action League, described how antiabortion activists could use traditional communication-campaign and organizational and lobbying techniques, as well as more militant tactics, such as "counseling" pregnant women attempting to enter abortion clinics, picketing abortionists' homes and warning garbage men that they were "hauling corpses."

In contrast, the primary nationally organized adversaries of the Right to Life Committee have been the Planned Parenthood Federation of America (PPFA)—the descendant of Margaret Sanger's American Birth Control League—and the National Abortion Rights Action League (NARAL).

Another communication skirmish illustrates how important it is to both sides to control symbols and cultural definitions and the ways in which modern communication technologies have changed the ways in which communication campaigns can be conducted.

THE SILENT SCREAM

The Silent Scream, a 28-minute film released in early 1985 and dedicated to "the unborn children of America," was narrated by Dr. Bernard Nathanson, an obstetrician and gynecologist who, paradoxically, also was one of the founders of NARAL in 1973. In the film, Nathanson said that ultrasound techonology had convinced him, a former "abortionist," that abortions were wrong. He then showed computer-generated pictures based on ultrasound waves, of a fetus being aborted and pointed to what he claimed was the 12-week-old fetus' mouth open in a scream of fear or pain.

Despite much criticism from medical experts who claimed the fetus was not sufficiently neurologically developed to experience pain, video copies of the film were distributed to all members of Congress. During the next couple of weeks, the tape was shown on the Reverend Jerry Falwell's "Old Time Gospel Hour," broadcast across the country on superstation WTBS; parts of the video appeared on the nightly network news; and still photographs of the "key moment" were published in many newspapers and magazines. The text of the film was read into the *Congressional Record,* and President Reagan told more than 70,000 pro-life demonstrators in Washington, D.C., that "if every member of Congress could see this film, they would move quickly to end the tragedy of abortion" (Pesce & Levine, 1985). By summer that year, a Harris poll showed that 42% of Americans had seen, heard or read about the film. Of those who had seen the film, almost half (45%) said it made them more opposed to abortion (Harris, 1985).

The clearest effect of the video, however, was that it forced some pro-choice groups to reconsider their communication strategies. The PPFA, immediately after release of *The Silent Scream,* convened a panel of medical experts to review the film and distributed their critique in a booklet called *The Facts Speak Louder: Planned Parenthood's Critique of "The Silent Scream."*[3] In early 1986, PPFA launched a million dollar communication campaign that included a film called *Personal Decisions,* a technically high-quality portrait of seven women who had had abortions. The film and eight different full-page ads that ran in such national magazines as *Time, Esquire* and the *New York Review of Books* were designed to "divert discussion from the fetus to the women and families involved in abortions" (Schmich, 1986). Doug Gould, PPFA's vice president for communications, said the campaign was produced to debunk stereotypes about women who have abortions. "We wanted to make sure that the fetus was not seen as the primary focus" (Krause, 1986).[4]

SUMMARY

Despite these concerted communication efforts on both sides of the issue, public opinion polls since the mid-1970s have shown consistently strong support for the right to abortion if the woman's health is seriously endangered, if the pregnancy is the result of rape or if there is a strong chance of a serious defect in the baby. Few Americans (19%) believe that abortion ever will be outlawed totally again (Harris, 1985). On the other hand, large proportions (in 1987, about 60%) are less sure about the right of a woman to have an abortion for "lifestyle" reasons, e.g., because the family can't afford another child, because the woman is unmarried or if a married woman doesn't want another child (Glazer, 1987).

As Luker (1984b) argues, the abortion controversy in the United States probably will remain "heated, passionate and bitter," (p. 110) because it is fundamentally a debate over the role of women and motherhood in modern society. If the past is any indication, the communication campaigns designed to influence how the American public and their elected officials feel about these issues will continue to reflect both passion and bitterness as the society struggles to determine how much control women should be given over their sexuality.[5]

AIDS

Since late-1981, when the first reports of a rare pattern of "opportunistic infections associated with immunosuppression in homosexual men," appeared in American medical journals (Black, 1985, p. 49), the world has struggled to cope with a disease that has pushed issues of sexuality once again into the foreground of political, religious and medical debate.

By June 1988, more than 64,000 cases of AIDS (Acquired Immune Deficiency Syndrome) had been reported in the United States ("A new attack against AIDS," 1988); more than half of those infected had died. The segment of the population hardest hit by the disease was homosexual and bisexual men, but by 1988, others, especially intravenous drug users and their sexual partners—primarily lower class Blacks and Hispanics—also were dying. Public health officials estimated that there would be 270,000 cases in the United States by 1991 (Boffey, 1988). The World Health Organization (WHO) estimated that five million to ten million people were infected worldwide (Peracchio, 1988).

DISBELIEF GIVES WAY TO DENIAL AND PANIC

The early years of the AIDS epidemic were characterized by disbelief, confusion, fear, and increased stigmatization of homosexuals and members of other groups identified as being at high risk for contracting AIDS, (primarily Haitians, hemophiliacs and intravenous drug users). Few organized communication efforts were undertaken, except by activist gays in cities with large, openly homosexual populations, because the limited resources available were directed primarily at finding a cure for the disease (Institute of Medicine, 1986). Both the medical and scientific communities found it hard to believe that a new, untreatable epidemic was on the horizon just as scientific advances had virtually eliminated the old contagious diseases (Patton, 1985).

Initially, many homosexuals also were reluctant to believe that the disease was related in some way to their modern, sexually adventuresome lifestyle. Some gays in both New York and San Francisco fought to maintain their new-found sexual freedom and accused gays who advocated fewer sexual partners and the use of condoms (and later the closing of the bathhouses) of being homophobic and antierotic (Shilts, 1987).

Despite such criticism, a handful of gay activists began education campaigns, especially in New York and San Francisco, where the devastation wrought by the disease was most evident. Groups such as the Gay Men's Health Crisis (GMHC) in New York and the San Francisco AIDS Foundation developed explicit pamphlets, posters and advertisements[6] that described "safe(r) sex" techniques and urged gay men to have safe sex with fewer partners, at least until the cause of the disease was known.[7] These communication campaigns included extensive educational efforts in the bathhouses and backrooms of gay bars, where much of the dangerous sexual activity was taking place.[8] Advertisements were placed primarily in the gay press.

The mainstream media were remarkably slow in covering the spreading epidemic, even in cities with large gay populations. Gay critics of the media argue that the disease would have achieved much greater coverage if it had been affecting heterosexuals (Watney, 1987). Analyses of coverage do suggest that press coverage increased whenever events linked the disease to non-homosexuals (Schwartz, 1984; Dearing, Rogers, & Fei, 1988; Kain & Hart, 1987).

As the public began to learn more about the spreading epidemic, primarily through news reports in the mass media, disbelief gave way to panic. Some nurses refused to treat AIDS patients, paramedics donned elaborate protective gear, and the New York State Funeral Directors Association recommended that its members refuse to embalm AIDS victims (Shilts, 1987). In the same period, the first indications of the "moral panic" that the epidemic generated were published. One column by conservative Patrick Buchanan in the *New York Post* was headlined, "AIDS Disease: It's Nature Striking Back." Buchanan argued that homosexuals were a major public health threat and urged official restrictions, such as the closing of bathhouses (Schwartz, 1984).

Sporadic bursts of media coverage resulted in high levels of public awareness by 1986. By October 1986, more than half (55%) of a random national sample of adults polled by CBS cited AIDS as one of the "most serious diseases or medical problems facing the country today" (Singer, Rogers, & Corcoran, 1987, p. 584).

But awareness does not always equal understanding or tolerance. In the same CBS poll, about one-third of those sampled believed that they could get AIDS by using the same drinking glass as someone who had AIDS or by *donating* (rather than receiving) blood. In another poll, one-third said that they or people they knew had avoided certain places where homosexuals might be present to try to reduce the chances of contracting AIDS (Singer, Rogers, & Corcoran, 1987).

To the religious right, as well as much of the rest of American society, AIDS was seen as punishment for (homo)sexual sins. As late as spring 1987, almost 43% of a national sample of American voters and 60% of voters classified as "moralists" still considered AIDS "God's punishment for immoral sexual behavior" ("AIDS and the Real Electorate," 1988).

MOBILIZATION

Organized communication campaigns aimed at non-homosexual audiences were developed primarily in the third stage of public response, as it became clearer that it might take years to develop the technological solution or "magic bullet" (Brandt, 1987) vaccine necessary to stop the spread of the HIV virus (which both French and American scientists had identified in April 1984), and as fear increased that the disease would spread to the heterosexual population. Reports from Africa suggested such spread was likely, and AIDS cases were being identified in many other regions of the world.

In December 1986, Dr. Jonathan Mann, director of WHO's Special Programme on AIDS, summed up his perspective on the situation:

This is the first time we have all our eggs in one basket, and that basket is education. It is not a matter of education as a supplemental strategy, as a complementary approach, as an alternative. Education is all we have, and we must make it work. (1986, p. 8)

Just as was seen earlier with the issue of family planning and birth control, the approach any country took in developing its communication campaigns about AIDS depended, in large part, on the society's willingness to discuss sexual topics and on the political power of sexual moralists.

In the relatively sexually permissive Scandanavian countries, for example, television messages for AIDS prevention depicted sexual intercourse and demonstrated the use of condoms; the messages in Denmark included a bare-breasted woman and a man engaged in foreplay; in Sweden the government produced a poster in which teen males were encouraged to practice masturbating with a condom in place (Morfeldt, 1987). In more sexually repressed societies, such as Great Britain and Australia, strong fear appeals were used but messages were frank ("A man can carry the virus in his sperm, a woman in her vaginal fluid. . . . So don't sleep around . . . if in doubt, always use a condom.") In England, the government-sponsored campaign included the image of a tombstone with the word "AIDS" chiseled in. The themeline for the campaign was "AIDS: Don't Die of Ignorance." In Australia, the grim reaper bowled down people with AIDS, and viewers were warned, "If you have sex, have only one partner or always use condoms. Always."

In the United States, the earliest communication campaigns were conducted by and for homosexual men and often included very explicit descriptions and illustrations of safe-sex techniques.[9] One pamphlet published by the GMHC, for example, included color photographs of a condom being put on an erect penis. But campaigns developed for broader audiences were much less explicit and rarely mentioned either sexual transmission or the use of condoms.

TABOO COMMUNICATION

In the United States, discussion of contraceptive devices, including condoms, is a classic example of what Rogers (1973) has identified as taboo communication. Until AIDS, few people talked about condoms (or most other sexual topics) in polite company. Until 1987, when the San Francisco station KRON-TV accepted a 15-second spot for Trojan condoms, it was rare to see advertisements for condoms, except in the back pages of men's magazines. At this writing, the television networks still refuse to accept contraceptive advertising and have refused to run some public service announcements about AIDS that include mention of condoms.[10] Needless to say, these communication taboos made public discussion of AIDS transmission and prevention extremely difficult.

Other countries faced similar problems. In Haiti, AIDS communication efforts were stymied because messages in French—the official language—are distrusted, but in Creole, the language used most often in informal communication, the only word for sexual intercourse is the equivalent of "fucking." The word is reserved only for communication between close friends, "homophilous individuals," in Rogers' (1973) term. The Creole equivalent of "making love" means only kissing and hugging. Health authorities decided, therefore, that they would have to depend on health care providers in private settings rather than the mass media for spreading the word about how the disease is transmitted (E. Rains, personal interview, 1988).

Similar strategies evolved in the United States. Mass media campaigns aimed at heterosexuals were designed primarily to decrease the lingering fear of casual contamination and to encourage sympathy rather than discrimination toward persons with AIDS. The discussion of modes of transmission (such as anal intercourse or dirty needles) or methods for reducing risk (such as the use of condoms or clean needles) were rarely included. Perhaps appropriately, given research on the difficulty of inducing behavioral change through the mass media (Rogers and Storey, 1987), information about transmission and prevention has been provided primarily at the interpersonal communication level—either over the phone or at blood-testing sites.

By 1988, a number of campaigns aimed at heterosexuals in the United States had been or were being developed.[11] Most deliberately did not include explicit references to sex or condoms in order to get airtime and to avoid political fallout. Since the federal government was slow in developing a national educational strategy, in many cases, advertising agencies and media institutions worked with local AIDS organizations to develop educational campaigns.

One of the most impressive of these was initiated by San Francisco station KPIX, which began regular reports on AIDS in 1983. By 1987, the award-winning "AIDS Lifeline" campaign, produced in consultation with the San Francisco AIDS Foundation, included some 1,000 news reports on AIDS and sixty public-service announcements on AIDS prevention. Jim Bunn, the reporter behind much of the campaign, and others at the station, were convinced that continual coverage of AIDS would pay off as the community came to rely on the station for current and accurate AIDS information (Kinsella, 1988). In 1988, Metropolitan Life Insurance Company agreed to provide one million dollars to underwrite Group W Television's efforts to expand the campaign nationwide.[12] Although much of the campaign was geared toward the non-homosexual audience, many credit the sustained and even-handed coverage with helping to reduce the spread of AIDS among homosexuals in San Francisco.[13]

The federal government's national education campaign finally was launched in October 1987.[14] The campaign relied heavily on the mass media. In 10- and 30-second and 2-minute messages, slickly produced by the Ogilvy and Mather advertising firm and distributed to every commercial radio and television station in the country, a racial mixture of somber Americans, some with AIDS or with relatives with AIDS, encouraged people to learn the facts about the disease by calling a toll-free number. Although in one of the spots, an AIDS counselor is shown saying, "If you're going to talk about AIDS and how to prevent AIDS, there's no way you can avoid talking about sex," sexual transmission or the use of condoms as a preventive measure were mentioned in only one of the 25 spots.

People who called the hotline were given more explicit information in a three-minute tape-recorded phone message (in either Spanish or English) and were told that they could call another number if they wanted to talk with a counselor. In the first month of the campaign, 50,000 calls were made; campaign organizers expected an average of 10,000 a day by mid-1988 (Rains, 1988).

The U.S. Centers for Disease Control (CDC), the federally-funded agency which produced the campaign, supplemented the muted media messages by sponsoring leadership forums and discussion groups with community organization leaders from cities around the country. Three-day workshops in eight to ten cities also were planned to teach leaders the skills to develop AIDS campaigns and services in their own communities. The CDC also distributed transit posters and 45 million brochures targeted to specific groups, such as sexually active adults, Blacks, Hispanics and parents of teenagers. In May and June 1988, the CDC and the U.S. Public Health Service mailed out 107 million copies of an 8-page educational brochure, *Understanding AIDS;* the mailing was intended to reach virtually every household in the United States ("A new attack against AIDS," 1988).

According to campaign consultants, the innocuous campaign strategy stemmed primarily from realistic fear of political repercussions from the religious right. Just as the campaign was launched, the Senate voted 94 to 2 to bar the CDC from using federal funds for anti-AIDS campaigns that "promote or encourage, directly or indirectly, homosexual activities" (Cummings, 1988a,b). The conservative Republican Senator Jesse Helms who introduced the bill earlier had accused (inaccurately) the GMHC of using federal funds to produce comic books on AIDS prevention that promoted "sodomy and the homosexual lifestyle" (Rich, 1987).

In response to New York City Mayor Koch's accusation that the measure reflected Helms' callousness toward AIDS victims, Helms clearly articulated the religious right's perspective on AIDS prevention in a letter to the editor of the *New York Times:*

> The facts are self-evident: Abstinence from sex outside marriage, including abstinence from sodomy, is the most effective way to avoid contracting the AIDS virus.
>
> To admit that abstinence from homosexual activity—not sodomy with condoms—is the most effective way to avoid AIDS would force Mayor Koch to admit also that casual sex is a perilous vice. It would force him to turn his back on the "sexual revolution" which has ravaged this nation for the last quarter of a century.
>
> So let the word go out, clearly and unequivocally, that Americans who don't want to risk being killed by AIDS have a clear choice and a safe bet available: Reject sodomy and practice morality. If they are unwilling to do that, they should understand the consequences. (Nov. 12, 1987)

A number of conservatives believed that efforts to alert the heterosexual population to the possibility of infection actually were scare tactics to keep the issue alive. George Will, a conservative columnist, for example, argued in June 1987 that American journalists, "infused with liberal values," and afraid of being accused of discrimination against homosexuals, were unwilling to "clarify that the primary reason for the AIDS epidemic is that the rectum, with its delicate and absorptive lining, is not suited to homosexual uses" (Will, 1987).

These moral convictions affected communication campaigns around the country. In New York City, a campaign aimed at young heterosexuals and produced *pro-bono* for the city health department by Saatchi and Saatchi, an international advertising firm, was rejected by network affiliates because the spots promoted the use of condoms (Winters, 1987). An award-winning videotape called *Sex, Drugs and AIDS,* narrated by "Fame" star Rae Dawn Chong, produced for the New York City Health Department and designed for use in city high schools, had to be reshot after school officials complained that too little time was spent talking about abstaining from drugs and sex and too much time was spent on discussion of homophobia and condom use (Viadero, 1987). In Los Angeles, the State Department of Health Services halted distribution of a prevention brochure called *Mother's Handy Sex Guide,* which was aimed at gay men. Another brochure was attacked by a Los Angeles county supervisor as "hard-core pornographic trash totally unsuitable for the public" (Richardson, 1988).

SUMMARY

At this writing, the United States and other countries of the world are beginning to take a more rational approach to the problem of AIDS. Some of the panic of the first years of the epidemic has given way to the hard work of trying to prevent greater spread of the virus, especially in hard-to-reach populations who engage in high-risk behaviors. The World Health Organization (WHO) has taken responsibility for helping to develop strategies for education and prevention around the world. But WHO is faced with all the problems discussed here— cultural restrictions on discussion of sexual topics; resistance from gay rights groups who suspect homophobia or from conservatives who believe education efforts promote immoral sexual behavior. In many countries, WHO and others who are working to stop the spread of AIDS, are faced, too, with inadequate medical and public health infrastructures which will be hard pressed to provide the personal counseling (or the materials) that may be necessary for changing patterns of sexual behavior ("AIDS: A Global Challenge," 1987). It is a formidable task in which communication undoubtedly will continue to play a vital role.

CONCLUSION

Communication campaigns have been used to affect sexuality in many societies in the world. Some such campaigns have been generated by governments attempting to influence their populations' sexual behavior, while others have been conducted to affect the ways in which legal and political structures regulate sexuality. In many cases, sexual taboos have limited the form communication could take. In all cases, these campaigns have met with informal and often formal resistance.

If the past is any indication, both governments and special interest groups will continue to use communication campaigns to persuade individuals to adopt prevailing norms of "appropriate" and "healthy" sexual behavior and to affect how societies regulate sexuality. These campaigns will grow increasingly sophisticated as more is learned about how the persuasion process works and as modern methods of communication, such as the video cassette recorder and video tape, the computer and satellite receivers, become widely accessible.

But fundamental questions about the social construction of sexuality will remain. As Weeks (1986) and other social historians have shown, and as the authors' examples illustrate again, social control of sexuality often disproportionately affects the less powerful segments of society. Attempts to control and regulate sexuality often are aimed at youth, women, racial minorities and people in lower social classes—those who have the least opportunity to speak about their own needs and desires. At this writing, antiabortion forces have succeeded in limiting U.S. government funding for abortions and abortion counseling. Women who cannot pay are thus denied access to safe abortions (Holden, 1987). Antiabortion groups in many states also have won passage of laws requiring minors to obtain parental consent or to notify their parents before obtaining abortions (Bonavoglia, 1988).

By February 1988, 273 children (primarily Black and Hispanic) in New York City had been born with the HIV-virus, and public health officials increased availability of testing and counseling for women at risk of contracting the virus or of transmitting the virus to their unborn children. So far, women have been allowed to decide whether or not to abort babies who have a high likelihood of being born with the virus, but community leaders are concerned that the costs of caring for HIV-infected babies may lead to forced abortions in the future (Gross, 1988).

Communication campaigns about sexuality are only one way in which societies deal with often highly-charged sexual issues. The specific religious, political and economic climate of the time will affect all aspects of these campaigns. It is, however, most often governments and special interest groups who can afford to organize increasingly expensive communication campaigns; often those most affected by the campaigns have little to say about campaign goals. Too often, attempts to change sexual behavior in the name of moral or public health have meant less sexual or personal freedom for the society's underclass or for those considered sexually deviant. It is to be hoped that future campaigns will be sensitive to these issues and will serve to increase the possibility of liberating rather than repressive definitions of human sexuality.

NOTES

1. A population control movement gained popular support in the United States in the late 1960s and early 1970s with the publication of *The Population Bomb* by Paul Erlich. The "Stop at Two" campaigns organized by groups such as Zero Population Growth advocated the use of birth control and were the impetus for many family-planning programs in developing countries as well.

2. After Sanger fled to England to avoid prosecution, her husband was sent to jail when he gave a pamphlet called *Family Limitation* that did contain information about contraception to a plainclothes policeman (Gordon, 1977).

3. The Seattle Planned Parenthood affiliate also produced a video in which a panel of professionals explained what they considered inaccurate in *The Silent Scream*. *Ms.* magazine announced the availability of this video in August 1985.

4. The latest communication campaign counterpunch from the antiabortion forces is testimony from women who claim to have suffered "postabortion trauma." They have formed groups called "Women Exploited by Abortion."

5. Abortion activists on both sides of the issue began shifting their attention to state legislatures after the Supreme Court's July 3, 1989, decision to uphold a Missouri law that sharply restricted public funding of any kind of abortion services and required doctors to test for fetal viability before performing abortions during or after the twentieth week of pregnancy. Anti-abortion organizations announced plans to push state legislatures to adopt new restrictions, including one type—usually called "informed consent" requirements—that would amount to state-mandated communication campaigns designed to convince women considering abortions not to end their pregnancies (Salholz et al., 1989). Even before the *Webster* decision was announced, pro-choice leaders had begun lobbying Congressmembers for a federal law to protect abortion rights, and pro-choice groups had spent an estimated $2.5 million on print and broadcast advertising aimed at rallying public support for abortion rights (Holmes et al., 1989).

6. Beginning in 1984, the San Francisco AIDS Foundation based campaign strategies on a set of longitudinal and cross-sectional probability samples of the city's self-identified bisexual and homosexual men. Objectives of the interpersonal and media components of successive waves of the educational campaign were linked to current levels of awareness and behavior change in the target populations. The contracted agency's reports on these activities are classic examples of effective use of formative and evaluative research in communication campaign development (Research and Decisions Corporation, 1984, 1985, 1986 a, b; Communication Technologies, 1987).

7. Strategies differed between the east and west coasts. The New York gay commmunity was more concerned about civil rights issues than were activists in San Francisco. In New York, early educational materials stressed "informed choice," while the *Can We Talk* brochure being distributed in San Francisco explicitly told gay men what was safe and not safe under such headings as "Sucking" and "Fucking" (Shilts, 1987).

8. As a result of these campaigns, unsafe sexual practices became so socially unacceptable in San Francisco that by 1988, health officials were saying that the spread among uncloseted gay males in San Francisco was effectively stopped. Tragically, these efforts came too late; by 1988 it was estimated that one-half of the homosexual men in the United States already had been infected with the AIDS virus (Coates, Catania, Dolcini, & Hoff, 1987). Changes in risky sexual behavior also were not as evident in other cities and rural areas where educational efforts were less organized and peer pressure was not as strong.

9. Initial evaluations of some of these educational efforts reinforced lessons learned from previous communication campaigns. Evaluations of programs funded by the California Department of Health Services in 1986 and 1987 showed that didactic lectures resulted in knowledge gain; small-group, intense discussion groups were effective in changing behavioral intentions and were more effective if participants came from social situations which supported behavioral change. Programs were less effective when they were insensitive to the targeted audience's cultural situation (Harder, Wexler, Marotta, Murphy, & Houston-Hamilton, 1987).

10. A fall 1987 poll of radio and TV stations found that 86.5% were broadcasting PSAs on AIDS, but only one-third (35.3%) were accepting advertising for condoms (Hersch, 1987). Earlier in 1987, in testimony before a special congressional panel, television network representatives had argued that "while condoms may afford a measure of such protection against AIDS," condom advertising was unacceptable because "it is impossible to separate this product use from the original and long-standing use of the product, which is for birth-control purposes." (Committee on Energy and Commerce, 1987, p. 49).

11. This occurred even though by the end of 1987, other countries already were reconsidering their earlier decisions to aim education campaigns at mass audiences. Great Britain, for example, concluded from extensive evaluation of their $32 million year-long media campaign that it had needlessly raised general anxieties about AIDS and had missed those individuals in population groups at high risk (e.g., drug users) (Department of Health and Social Security and the Welsh Office, 1987; Reed, 1987).

12. Group W Television, the parent company of KPIX, licensed rights to the "Lifeline" campaign to local stations around the country in 1988. With underwriting from the Metropolitan Life Insurance Company, Group W planned to produce five new thirty- and sixty-minute educational programs for airing in primetime and two new sets of PSAs, one with celebrities and another with still pictures of "AIDS heroes"—

people who had made significant contributions to the fight against AIDS. Group W and each of more than fifty stations scheduled to use the campaign also agreed to donate any profits resulting from the airings to local AIDS organizations.

13. The campaign, at the least, helped to keep the issue of AIDS on the public agenda and therefore may have indirectly influenced the city's strong commitment to further education efforts (Dearing, Rogers and Fei, 1988). By 1988, San Francisco had provided more direct support to AIDS programs than any other city in the United States (Richardson, 1988).

14. The U.S. government did not sponsor a national AIDS communication campaign until well into the sixth year of the crisis, although U.S. Surgeon General Koop had published a report on AIDS in October 1986 in which he advocated early sex education in the schools and the use of condoms, much to the consternation of others in the Reagan administration (Rovner, 1987) and later, some factions in the Catholic church (Goldman, 1987). Koop reiterated his views in public service announcements produced by the Public Health Service. His report was widely distributed by individual congressmen to their constituents. Soon after Koop's report was published, the Institute of Medicine and the National Academy of Sciences released a detailed account of lack of direction and coordination in the federal government's efforts against AIDS. The report described attempts to educate the public as "woefully inadequate." (Bazell, 1986)

REFERENCES

"AIDS and the real electorate." (1988, January 24). *The New York Times.*

Academy for Educational Development. (1987). *Aids: A global challenge.* Washington, DC: Author.

A new attack against aids. (1988, June 13). *Newsweek.* pp, 66–7.

Bazell, R. (1986, November 24). Surviving AIDS. *The New Republic,* pp. 20–23.

Black, D. (1985). *The plague years.* New York: Simon and Schuster.

Boffey, P. M. (1988, February 14). Spread of AIDS abating, but deaths will still soar. *The New York Times,* pp. 1, 36.

Bonavoglia, A. (1988, April). Kathy's day in court. *Ms.,* pp. 46–52.

Brandt, A. M. (1987). *No magic bullet: A social history of veneral disease in the United States since 1880.* New York: Oxford University Press.

Chen, P., & Tian, X. (1982). 11m Chinese opt for 'only child glory' certificate. *People, 9(4),* pp. 12–15.

Coates, T. J., Catania, J. A., Dolcini, M. M., & Hoff, C. C. (1987). *Changes in sexual behavior with the advent of the AIDS epidemic.* Unpublished report prepared for the Hudson Institute.

Committee on Energy and Commerce. (1987). *Condom advertising and AIDS.* (Hearing before the U.S. House of Representatives Subcommittee on Health and Environment [Feb. 10]). Washington, DC: U.S. Government Printing Office.

Communication Technologies. (1987). *Designing an effective AIDS prevention campaign strategy.* Report prepared for The San Francisco AIDS Foundation.

Cummings, P. (1988a, January 19). Homophobic legislation threatens British gays. *The Advocate,* pp. 13, 17.

Cummings, P. (1988b, March 15). British gays step up protests of antigay bill. *The Advocate*, pp. 14–15.

Dawson, D. A. (1986). The effects of sex education on adolescent behavior. *Family Planning Perspectives*, (July/August), 162–170.

Dearing, J. W., Rogers, E. M., & Fei, X. (1988). *The agenda-setting process for the issue of AIDS.* Paper presented to the International Communication Association, New Orleans.

Department of Health and Social Security and the Welsh Office. (1987). *AIDS: Monitoring response to the public education campaign, Feb. 1986–Feb. 1987.* London: Her Majesty's Stationery Office.

Family Planning Social Marketing Project. (1988). *Diary 1988.* Dhaka, Bangladesh: Author.

Florida considering locking up some carriers of the AIDS virus. (1988, January 27). *The New York Times*, p. A-15.

Freemon, R. (1987). China's phenomenal fertility decline. Distinguished lecture, Carolina Population Center, Chapel Hill, NC.

Glazer, S. (1987). Abortion policy. *Editorial Research Reports, 2(14),* 534–547.

Goldman, A. L. (1987, December 14). Cardinal won't allow instruction on condoms in programs on AIDS: New York's Archbishop criticizes U.S. bishops over a policy paper. *The New York Times*, p. 1, 21.

Gordon, L. (1977). *Woman's body, woman's right: A social history of birth control in America.* New York: Penguin.

Greenhalgh, S., & Bongaarts, J. (1986). *Fertility policy in China: Future options.* (Center for Policy Studies Working Paper No. 127). Princeton, NJ: Princeton University Press.

Gregersen, E. (1983). *Sexual practices: The story of human sexuality.* New York: Franklin Watts.

Gross, J. (1988, March 6). New York's poorest women offered more AIDS services. *The New York Times*, pp. 1, 38.

Harder, P., Wexler, S., Marotta, T., Murphy S., & Houston-Hamilton, A. (1987). *Evaluation of California's AIDS community education program.* San Francisco, CA: URSA Institute.

Harris, L. (1985). Public attitudes about sex education, family planning and abortion in the United States. (Study No. 854005) New York: Louis Harris and Associates.

Hersch, P. (1987, November). AIDS and PSAs: Broadcasters are seizing the initiative locally. *Channels*, p. 6.

Hershey, M. J., & West, D. M. (1983). Single-issue politics: Prolife groups and the 1980 Senate campaign. In A. J. Cigler & B. A. Loomis (Eds.), *Interest Group Politics* (pp. 31–59). Washington, D.C.: CQ Press.

Holden, C. (1987). U.S. antiabortion policy may increase abortions. *Science, 238,* p. 1222.

Holmes, S., Mehta, N.S., & Taylor, E. (1989, May 1). Whose life is it? *Time*, pp. 20–24.

Institute of Medicine. (1986). *Mobilizing against AIDS: The unfinished story of a virus.* Cambridge, MA: Harvard University Press.

Jacobsen, J. (1983). Promoting population sterilization: Incentives for small families. (Worldwatch Paper 54).

Jowett, G. S., & O'Donnell V. (1986). *Propaganda and persuasion.* Beverly Hills, CA: Sage.

Kain, E. L., & Hart, S. (1987). *AIDS and the family: A content analysis of media coverage.* Paper presented to the National Council on Family Relations, Atlanta, GA.

Kinsella, J. (1988). *Mortal lessons for the media: What covering the plague years should teach us.* Paper presented to the American Association for the Advancement of Science, Boston, MA.

Kotler, P., & Zaltman, G. (1971). Social marketing: An approach to planned social change. *Journal of Marketing, 35,* 3–12.

Krause, A. (1986, March 24). Videos newest ammunition in abortion debate. *The Fresno Bee.*

Liu, A. P. L. (1981). Mass campaigns in the People's Republic of China. In R. E. Rice & W. J. Paisley (Eds.), *Public communication campaigns* (pp. 199–223). Beverly Hills, CA: Sage.

Lovenduski, J., & Outshoorn, J. (Eds.). (1986). *The new politics of abortion.* Beverly Hills, CA: Sage.

Luker, K. (1984a). *Abortion and the politics of motherhood.* Berkeley, CA: University of California Press.

Luker, K. (1984b). The war between the women. *Family Planning Perspectives, 16*(3) May/June, 105–110.

Mann, J. (1986). *AIDS: The global impact.* Washington, DC: Academy for Educational Development.

Manoff, R. K. (1985). *Social marketing.* New York: Praeger.

Marsigliano, W., & Mott, F. (1986). The impact of sex education on sexual activity, contraceptive use and premarital pregnancy among American teenagers. *Family Planning Perspectives,* (July/August), 151–162.

Morfeldt, J. (1987). *AIDS education for the general public.* Paper presented to the Third International Conference on AIDS, Washington, DC.

Patton, C. (1985). *Sex and germs: The politics of AIDS.* Boston: South End Press.

Peracchio, A. (1988, January 28). Global forum gauges AIDS' scope. *New York Newsday,* p. 22.

Pesce, C., & Levine, J. (1985, February 14). The *Silent Scream* outcry: Sides argue over what's fact and what's propaganda. *USA Today.*

Population Reports. (1982). China's one child policy. (Series J). Baltimore, MD: Johns Hopkins University Press.

Reed, J. D. (1987, June 15). At last the battle is joined. *Newsweek,* pp. 56–57.

Reed, J. (1978). *The birth control movement and American society: From private vice to public virtue.* Princeton, NJ: Princeton University Press.

Research & Decisions Corporation. (1984, 1985, 1986 a,b). *Designing an effective AIDS prevention campaign strategy for San Francisco.* Reports prepared for the San Francisco AIDS Foundation.

Rich, S. (1987, November 20). Anti-AIDS comics used no U.S. funds: HHS report agrees that N.Y. gay group is playing by the book. *Washington Post,* p. 17.

Richardson, D. (1988). *Women & AIDS.* New York: Methuen.

Roberts, S. B. (1987, July 31). Abortion counseling under fire. Reagan seeks cuts in federal funding. *The (Raleigh, NC) News and Observer,* p. 1.

Rogers, E. (1973). *Communication strategies for family planning.* New York: Free Press.

Rogers, E. M., & Storey, J. D. (1987). Communication campaigns. In C. Berger & S. H. Chaffee (Eds.), *Handbook of communication science* (pp. 817–842). Beverly Hills, CA: Sage.

Rovner, J. (1987). Fighting AIDS: Congress looks for a way to help. *Congressional Quarterly 45(7)*, 263–268

Salholz, E., McDaniel, A., King, P., Calonius, E., Gonzalez, D.L., & Joseph, N. (1989, July 17). Voting in curbs and confusion. *Newsweek,* pp. 16–20.

Schellstede, W., & Ciszewski, R. (1984). Social marketing of contraceptives in Bangladesh. *Studies in Family Planning, 15,* 30–39.

Schmich, M. T. (1986, February 10). A loud answer to *The Silent Scream. Chicago Tribune,* p. 5-1.

Schwartz, H. (1984). AIDS in the media. In *Science in the Streets* (pp. 87–97). (Report of the Twentieth Century Fund Task Force on the Communication of Scientific Risk). New York: Priority Press.

Shilts, R. (1987). *And the band played on: Politics, people and the AIDS epidemic.* New York: St. Martin's.

Singer, E., Rogers, T. F., Corcoran, M. (1987). The polls—A report: AIDS. *Public Opinion Quarterly, 51(4),* 580–595.

Solomon, D. S. (1981). A social marketing perspective on campaigns. In R. E. Rice & W. J. Paisley (Eds.), *Public communication campaigns* (pp. 281–292). Beverly Hills, CA: Sage.

Tiefer, L. (1987). Social constructionism and the study of human sexuality. In P. Shaver & C. Hendrick (Eds.), *Sex and gender* (pp. 70–94). Beverly Hills, CA: Sage.

UNICEF (1987). *The state of the world's children.* New York: Oxford University Press.

Viadero, D. (1987, March 4). Teaching guides, videotapes, films on AIDS flood the marketplace. *Education Week,* p. 21.

Vines, G. (1985, September 19). Bangladeshis coerced into sterilisation. *New Scientist,* pp. 20–21.

Watney, S. (1987). *Policing desire: Pornography, AIDS and the media.* Minneapolis: University of Minnesota Press.

Weeks, J. (1981). *Sex, politics, and society: The regulation of sexuality since 1800.* London: Longman.

Weeks, J. (1986). *Sexuality.* London: Tavistock.

Will, G. (1987, June 9). Concern for discrimination blurring truths about AIDS. *The (Madison, WI) Capital Times,* p. 11.

Winters, P. (1987, May 11). New York City tries AIDS ads, *Advertising Age,* p. 2, 106.

Chapter 4

THE KNOWLEDGE-BEHAVIOR GAP IN PUBLIC INFORMATION CAMPAIGNS: A DEVELOPMENT COMMUNICATION VIEW

Robert Hornik

INTRODUCTION

THE CENTRAL THEORETICAL problem in the field of purposive communication is explaining the gap between knowledge and behavior. There are practical problems in achieving widespread knowledge: It may be difficult to structure a message so that it can be understood; it may be expensive to reach the intended audience as frequently as required. However, by and large, a skilled communication professional with sufficient resources can help a mass audience to have *knowledge* about a new practice. Saying that problems are mainly practical is not to underestimate the talent and work required to realize widespread knowledge or to deny that there are many theoretically interesting issues associated with developing efficient strategies for achieving attention and knowledge retention. But the fundamental theoretical problem is at the next stage in the communication process, turning knowledge into behavior.

AUTHOR'S NOTE: This chapter presents an intellectual framework and a series of studies undertaken by students and colleagues of the author over the past decade, including Jeremiah O'Sullivan-Ryan, Eduardo Contreras-Budge, Jane Gould Torous, Judy McDivitt, Sikandra Spain, Jeff McDowell, Chien Lei, Nina Ferencic, and Karin Wilkins. They are thanked both for their research and their rather substantial effect on the underlying conceptual approach. In addition, P. Stanley Yoder, Susan Zimicki, and Nancy Morris, as well as McDivitt and Wilkins made insightful comments on a previous draft of this chapter.

In this chapter the knowledge-behavior gap issue is developed from the perspective of purposive communication programs in the Third World. This perspective provides more than a useful store of examples which may be fresh for some readers of this volume. Less-developed-country experience demands attention to different explanations for the gap than have been current in parallel studies in more developed countries, in particular with respect to U.S. domestic campaigns.

In the U.S. domestic literature, psychological explanations feature strongly, with social network explanations a secondary but still common focus (e.g., see Chapter 9 by Devine & Hirt in this volume). In contrast, many scholars concerned with development communication look first to "system" (or structural) explanations, secondarily to social network explanations and only reluctantly at individual psychological explanations.

In the United States, the archetypal example of the knowledge-behavior gap is smoking. Smokers know they shouldn't smoke, but they do it anyway. How is the gap explained? While there is a common reference to physical addiction, there is much emphasis on psychological needs, including describing smoking as habitual behavior responding to environmental cues. Some note the strong association of social class with smoking and suggest that social reference groups may play some role. However, many of the essential intervention strategies, such as behavior-modification or smoking-education programs, reflect an assumption that the decision to give up smoking must be made by an individual and, implicitly, that the decision is substantially within the control of the smoker.

In the developing country context, the archetypal example is the adoption of agricultural innovations, notably the use of fertilizer. Explanations for the failure to employ fertilizers point first to structural variables. Do the farmers have the money or credit needed to purchase fertilizers? Is there a market for increased yields? Is the risk associated with borrowing funds greater than farmers can afford? Secondary explanations point to the influence of social networks, that is, the practices of neighbors, demonstrated, for example, by the geographic concentration of adopters. Only as a residual and unfavored explanation will current scholarship admit to the possibility of a major influence of individual psychological characteristics such as innovativeness or fatalism, although those were favored explanations of an earlier generation of scholars.

The contrasting tendency to rely on systemic/structural rather than individual/psychological causes to explain knowledge-behavior gaps may reflect the different real circumstances of the First versus Third Worlds. The relative poverty of the Third World may place greater limits on individual choices with lives more affected by economic and other constraints beyond individual control.

The contrast may also reflect the particular intellectual traditions which have come to dominate scholarship in each field. Psychologists and some sociologists have been in the forefront of domestic scholarship. Developing-country scholarship has reflected the strong presence of economists and anthropologists with a tendency to seek explanations in economic or cultural systems, respectively. Also, there is a substantial presence of critical scholars for whom themes of class conflict are central.

Much of the rest of this volume focuses on the U.S. case; in this chapter, the focus will be on purposive communication in less-developed countries. In the following pages, a perspective derived from research in that environment is developed. It may be relevant in other arenas, also.

A PERSPECTIVE FROM DEVELOPMENT COMMUNICATION

Historically, many advocated a significant role for communication programs in bringing about rapid development. Some attributed slow development to the lack of knowledge and skills among developing-country populations. At the same time, they recognized that there was a shortage of trained educators and field extension agents to remedy knowledge deficits. They often turned optimistically to mass media as a promising alternative channel to reach mass audiences. However, in retrospect, communication should, perhaps, have been regarded as an odd intervention. The next paragraphs consider this oddness, incorporating some material slightly edited from a recently published book, *Development Communication* (Hornik, 1988).

Communication programs traffic in information. They throw words—ways of understanding, behaving and organizing—at development problems, problems that are substantially and contrarily defined by a lack of resources: low agricultural productivity, poor health or nutritional status, or unequal shares of society's goods.

An argument that information provision alone can resolve development problems makes the assumption that available resources are being inefficiently used. It says that substantially more benefit could be derived from what is already in place if only individuals or groups knew better how to organize the use of those resources: Enhanced agricultural yield can result from improved farming practices without the introduction of expensive fertilizers; infants' nutritional status can be improved with better feeding and health practices, although there is no additional income to permit the purchase of more calories and no new medical facilities are available in the community. In both of these examples, the assumption is that current behavior is poorly adapted to the existing environment, that this behavior does not produce the maximum benefit from available resources. People do not know, so they do not act optimally. Historically, this assumption of human ignorance was central to much of the practice of communication for development.

Yet most scholars who have looked closely at agricultural or nutritional practices, for example, claim that the assumption of poor adaptation is often inappropriate. Theodore Schultz (1964) argued that farmers were highly responsive to economic rewards and that they refused to adopt an innovation when the potential rewards did not counterbalance the risks. Jeremiah O'Sullivan (1980) found that farmers in the Guatemalan highlands who rejected no- or low-cost innovations (like compost piles and seed-spacing recommendations) did so reasonably. He could find no evidence that farmers who did adopt such agronomist-recommended innovations were more productive than those who did not. Carlos Benito (1976) found that farmers in Mexico who rejected a recommended planting package did so with good economic justification. While the package did produce greater yields and profits, it also required more labor, and that labor, it turned out, could be sold elsewhere at a higher return than if it had been used for farming.

Many more such examples could be supplied. Together they would point to the care one must take before assuming that the audiences of a communication program do not know what they are doing, before readily deciding that experts behind radio microphones know more about what is best for their audiences than do those audiences. Indeed, there are those who would take these results and reject use of communication altogether, at least for purposes of diffusing prodevelopment information. This position suggests that "failure" to make use of knowledge reflects system failure rather than individual failure; if farmers use less fertilizer than is ideal, it is to be explained by their poor access to credit or another explanation beyond their individual control. From this perspective, communication programs which seek to provide knowledge to individuals under the assumption that they are free to change practices are bound to fail.

If individual change is impossible because resource constraints permit only trivial improvements, the favored role for communication is one which enables the mass of the population to organize politically. Then they can demand their fair share of society's resources so that government funds go to increasing farm credit availability rather than to military expansion.

Yet, while it is tempting to say that access to resources is everthing and the only role for communication is the furthering of political ends, that has difficult policy implications. It also may not be true, or, at least, it may be untrue often enough to justify consideration of serious communication efforts.

Surely economic and other structural factors set upper limits on how much change is possible. But, knowing that failure to innovate is *sometimes* structurally explained is not evidence that it can *always* be explained structurally. There is counterevidence that supports the notion that worthwhile change is possible given fixed economic resources. The Amish in Pennsylvania, Japanese farmers in Brazil and kibbutz farmers in Israel have all been able to make more of their farms than others around them, and those differences cannot be explained by access to capital alone.

Lockheed, Jamison and Lau (1980) bring together studies supporting the effects of farmer schooling on productivity. When newer technologies were available, farmers with more than four years of schooling produced about 10% more than their neighbors with no education but equal resources. These studies only reinforce what any informal or formal study of farming communities suggests—that some farmers outperform others consistently, regardless of resources.

In practice, having seen evidence on both sides of the issue, one can decide that purposive communication (excluding that which serves as stimulus to political organization) is irrelevant and move to another field. One can also accept that not all knowledge gets turned into behavior but assume that some does and then ask when. Under what circumstances will an information intervention affect practice? Or, asking the same question from the point of view of the audience, when are individuals and their communities susceptible to the influence of communication programs?

As Yoder suggests (personal communication, 1988), "the issue is not so much a question of choosing between saying that systemic or individual factors explain the differential adoption of innovations, and thus choosing between trying to use purposive communication or not, but rather, trying to differentiate between situations in which these factors appear largely systemic and other situations."

It is this stance that is taken here. The remainder of this chapter elaborates this question, differentiates categories of explanation for rates at which knowledge turns into behavior and presents some methods for studying the issue. The discussion incorporates presentation of selected results from studies undertaken in the past ten to twelve years which illustrate both the conceptual approach and empirical methods.

FIVE TYPES OF HYPOTHESES

When will the knowledge-behavior link be tight, and when will it be loose? When will the knowledge-behavior relation look like line (A) in Figure 4.1, and when will it look like line (B)?

There are five classes of "susceptibility" hypotheses to be considered. Each class includes a set of propositions which suggest that individuals or communities which have more or less of a particular resource or characteristic are, therefore, more or less likely to adopt a behavior once they have knowledge of it. Each hypothesis suggests that some characteristic interacts with knowledge in affecting behavior. Many of the hypotheses will be familiar. The classes of hypotheses follow:

1. Structural characteristics of communities
2. Structural characteristics of individuals
3. Community social influences
4. Learned characteristics of individuals
5. Enduring characteristics of individuals

The rest of the chapter elaborates each of these classes of hypotheses one by one. However, before beginning with the first, a note on methodology is appropriate.

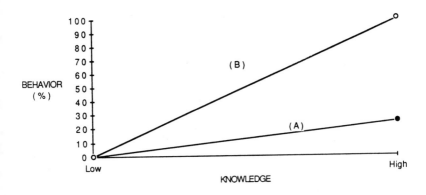

Figure 4.1 Basic Susceptibility Model

TESTING EXPLANATIONS FOR THE KNOWLEDGE-BEHAVIOR GAP

All of the hypotheses posit that change in practice results from an interaction between knowledge and some characteristic of an individual or a community. To take an example, one might hypothesize that knowledge about fertilizers would only turn into practice if an individual had access to credit. Assume that knowledge about fertilizers is measured on a ten-point interval scale and that practice is measured as a percentage of the ideal actually applied per acre. Access to credit is a dichotomy—indicating whether there is a local credit agency which would have provided credit to purchase the ideal amount of fertilizer to a particular farmer if he/she had applied.

It is useful to begin with a graphic presentation of the hypothesis (see Figure 4.2).

The hypothesis suggests that the slopes of the relationship between knowledge and practice are different for each access subgroup. For those without access to credit, the gap between knowledge and behavior is large; increased knowledge is slow to turn into increased practice. In contrast, among those who have access to credit, the knowledge-behavior gap is much smaller. Increased knowledge is much more readily turned into practice.[1]

Depending on the assumptions a particular data set allows (e.g. linearity, interval character of variables, dependent variable a dichotomy or not, need to eliminate the effects of other variables to avoid spurious inference, availability of time series or panel data, etc.) the

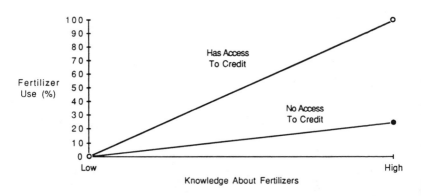

Figure 4.2 Hypothetical Model: Credit Access, Knowledge and Fertilizer Use

particular procedures to be employed will vary, but the logic doesn't. One always wants to know whether the joint effects of knowledge and the "susceptibility" variable explain variation in the practice variable better than the main effects of the two variables in isolation.

This basic method for displaying and testing the significance of explanations for specific knowledge-behavior gaps will be repeatedly used as the chapter turns to substantive results. The next section presents hypotheses relating to structural characteristics of communities.

STRUCTURAL CHARACTERISTICS OF COMMUNITIES

Hypotheses which involve structural characteristics of communities are of two types. One group points to specific aspects of community structure which must be present if knowledge is to be turned into behavior. An example in agriculture is access to credit; without it, few will be able to turn knowledge of better practices into innovation. A parallel example for health communication would be immunization programs. Even if parents hold quite sophisticated knowledge about the vaccinations required by a child, they will rarely obtain vaccination if there is no local clinic or other source for them.

A second group of hypotheses within this category focuses on the general prodevelopment situation in a community. If a community is advantaged in its development (it has a school, a paved road to a city, a health clinic, etc.), it may be a place where opportunity is greater and therefore knowledge is more readily turned into behavior. This may be true even though the specific behavior to be adopted doesn't require the presence of the particular institutions that allow a community to be classified as advantaged.

A useful example of this latter category comes from McDivitt (1985) and a study she completed in The Gambia. The Gambia was the site for a major intervention in health communication, in which, over several years, radio and other communication channels were used to encourage the use of a home-mixed rehydration formula (W-S-S, so called because it contains specific amounts of water, sugar and salt) to treat diarrheal disease. Diarrheal disease is a major cause of child mortality in The Gambia (as in many parts of the Third World). While there are no simple interventions available to reduce the incidence of diarrhea, in most cases deaths result not from the diarrhea per se but from the rapid dehydration that often accompanies it. The home-mixed W-S-S, if properly administered, is likely either to prevent such dehydration or to remedy at least milder forms of dehydration.

The evaluators of the program (Foote et al., 1985) had interviewed mothers regularly over a two-year period in 16 villages around the country. They found the program produced widespread knowledge and substantial use of the solution. McDivitt undertook additional analyses, examining a large number of hypotheses considering which factors conditioned the relation between knowledge and practice. Among her analyses was one which asked whether the level of general community development was such a factor. She used survey data collected two-thirds of the way through the program implementation.

Knowledge of W-S-S was coded as a dichotomy; respondents were classified as either knowing something about W-S-S preparation as well as having heard about it, or not knowing anything about how to prepare it. (About 85% of 549 interviewed mothers knew something.) W-S-S practice reflected a woman's report as to whether she had used W-S-S for the last case she treated or not. (About 61% used W-S-S the last time they treated a case of diarrhea.) General community development was a reliable scale (alpha=.71) which reflected the presence or absence in a community of a health center, a paved road, a school, and foreign-sponsored development projects. The community development scale was used in dichotomous form, with about 50% of respondents classified as high and 50% as low.

The essential result appears in Figure 4.3.

Among those who lived in communities with lower levels of community development and who had some knowledge of W-S-S, about 58% used it for the last case they treated. In higher development communities, more than 80% of those who had some knowledge used W-S-S. This interaction was statistically significant at $p < .02$.[2] While the exact causal mechanism isn't clear, this is a case where the evidence supports the hypothesis that community-level structural variables condition the transition from knowledge to behavior. It appears that it was easier to use W-S-S if one lived in a community where there was complementary prodevelopment activity than if one lived elsewhere.

STRUCTURAL CHARACTERISTICS OF INDIVIDUALS

The McDivitt analyses are evidence about how community-level structural variables interact with knowledge in affecting behavior. An analogous set of hypotheses can be generated at the individual level. These hypotheses suggest that for some people turning knowledge into behavior is impossible because they lack the personal resources to undertake the practice.

A mother may not have the time required to provide a child the large quantity of fluids needed to replace the fluids lost during diarrhea. Her workday is already too long, and, unless the child appears quite ill, she simply cannot give up other tasks to undertake this new one. Implementing new health practices may be constrained by time available, by facilities in the home like clean water supplies or adequate sanitary facilities, and by disposable income available to purchase the prescribed medicines or the extra food needed by a malnourished child.

In agriculture, the issues are quite similar. New planting practices may demand more time from the farmer; they may demand more resources than can be mustered; or they may demand that the farmer take more financial risk than is tolerable, if the terms of a credit arrangement mean that a bad year entails the loss of income required to subsist or the loss of one's landholding. If a farmer is but a tenant, the terms of his agreement with a landlord may allow him only a

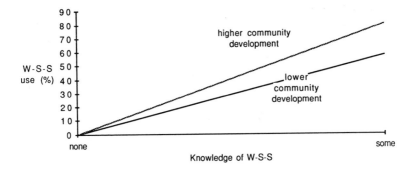

Figure 4.3 Community Development, Knowledge and Behavior in The Gambia

partial return on an increase in crop yield. All of these are individual structural characteristics which limit the utility of knowledge and thus its likelihood of being turned into behavior.

A convincing example comes from a study by O'Sullivan in Guatemala (1980). O'Sullivan undertook a survey of 600 farmers in the highlands of Guatemala, examining the relationships among farm productivity, innovations adopted, characteristics of the farm and the farmer, and access to extension services. Among the analyses presented was one which examined the effect of access to an extension service (and thus knowledge about appropriate practices) on farming practice, depending on whether the farmer owned a smaller or a larger farm.

The results of the study are of great interest; they bear so strongly on the theme of this subsection that they are presented, although the use of involvement with an extension agent as a measure of knowledge is clearly tenuous. Indeed, O'Sullivan doesn't claim that extension contact is a measure of knowledge. However, a strong case can be made that the effects described below occur because of the knowledge transmitted by the agent, and thus agent contact is a rough indicator of knowledge.

About 42% of the sample had contact with extension agents; they are classified as higher-knowledge farmers. Farming practices adopted are estimated from the expenditures per unit of land. O'Sullivan found a very strong relationship between farm expenditures per unit of land

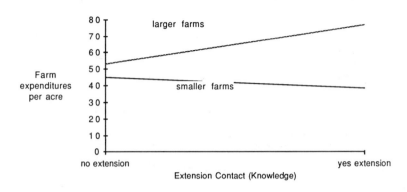

Figure 4.4 Size of Farm, Extension Contact and Farm Expenditures in Guatemala

and yield (r=.85); the costs were largely expended on the purchase of agricultural inputs (fertilizer, seed, and so on), so they represent a reasonable measure of effective practices adopted. Farm costs averaged about $52 per acre. The size of farms varied from one-half acre to more than thirty acres. Approximately 60% of the farmers worked less than two acres of land; their farms are classified as small; the rest are classified as larger farms.

Again the results are clear[3]. Among farmers who worked less than two acres, contact with an extension agent (and the presumed knowledge that provided) had little effect on actual practice. In contrast, among those farmers who worked from two to thirty or more acres, the effects of extension-agent contact were salutary. O'Sullivan suggests that the information the extension agents had to offer was of minimal value to the farmers with little land. They were already implementing what they could; adding to their information store was of little relevance. In contrast, farmers with more acres were able to take advantage of the information; they seemed less constrained by their individual structural circumstances in making changes and could turn knowledge into behavior.

COMMUNITY SOCIAL INFLUENCES

Public information programs often accept, implicitly, an *individual* cognitive and/or affective model of behavior change. They assume that if people learn something that is to their advantage and it is painted with the appropriate emotional colors, they will decide on their own to change practice in response. The televised ad says "Vaccinations protect, you can get them on the first Friday of the month at your local clinic," and the message is delivered over an image of a child unprotected by immunization, crippled with the aftereffects of a bout of polio. The ad delivers both information and motivation to encourage an individual decision to take action. However, there is a contrasting view which may be worth considering and which may lead to a different communication strategy.

A *social* view of the process of behavior change says that behavior doesn't belong only to individuals but also belongs to social groupings. For example, there is evidence that smoking is substantially a social behavior. Smoking is correlated with educational level and class in both the United States and in many Third World countries. However in the United States, better education and less smoking go hand in hand, while the reverse is true in many developing countries, where smoking in university classrooms can be nonstop. Similarly, breast-feeding has been (re)adopted among many better educated, middle-class women in the United States; it is more common among them than among women from working-class backgrounds. Again, in developing countries the association is in the opposite direction.

A consistent positive correlation between education and "good" health behaviors might lead to a conclusion that it is the cognitions associated with education which count: Better educated people don't smoke because they know better as individuals, as the result of their education. However, the reversal of those associations in the Third World suggests that another mechanism is operating in both places. It may be that these behaviors are substantially the result of social pressures within reference networks. That social hypothesis explains the contrasting results in a way that an individual cognitive hypothesis does not. Social explanations for the response to public information campaigns carry a strong intellectual tradition. However, that tradition has been stronger on theory than on evidence.

From the time of the landmark studies by Columbia University's Bureau of Applied Social Research (summarized and extended by Katz and Lazarsfeld in *Personal Influence*), the idea that social networks act as mediator of the effects of mass-communicated information has been widely accepted. The best evidence has come from studies of neighborhood influences (e.g. Festinger, Schachter, & Back

1950) and the geographic pattern of innovation diffusion (Brown, 1981). These studies are strong as evidence that social relationships play a major part in diffusion of information and practice. However, they do not show, in any direct way, that those networks mediate the effects of mass communication. The conclusions of Katz and Lazarsfeld are more widely accepted for their sensibleness than for the evidence that supports them.

In order to show that the effects of mass communication are different depending on the social networks in which an individual is embedded, one has to be able to contrast networks that vary in their support of the message transmitted through public information channels. One needs to show that if a network is supportive, knowledge (garnered from a public information campaign) turns into behavior and that if the network is unsupportive, individuals are less likely to turn knowledge into behavior. Wilkins (1987) did such a study in Ecuador based on a methodology introduced by McDivitt (1985) and Ferencic (1985).

Wilkins examined the effects of a national public information campaign advocating the use of an oral rehydration solution (ORS) for the treatment of fluid loss during diarrhea.[4] In contrast to The Gambia, which recommended a home-mixed solution, Ecuador based its program on the use of a prepackaged dry mixture which needed only to be added to a liter of water to make the required rehydration solution. Recognition of the solution (the measure of knowledge used in this study) was estimated through answers to three questions concerning whether a respondent had heard about ORS, could recognize the ORS packet, and could recognize the mixing bag distributed with the packet. About 73% of the respondents were able to recognize all three items. They were classified as high on knowledge, while the remaining 27% were classified as low.

ORS practice was estimated through the self-reported use of the solution to treat a child's case of diarrhea in the two weeks previous to the interview. Of the 580 women whose child had diarrhea in those two weeks, 23% claimed to have used ORS.

Social network support was measured indirectly. The sample had been selected from 60 clusters which were drawn randomly from almost all of Ecuador. Each cluster included about nine or ten women with a child who had a recent case of diarrhea. Since the clusters were defined by geographically concentrated census areas, it was assumed that these women who represented the community also represented the type of social pressures present in the community. It was further assumed that if the women in the community were behaving in a particular way (that is making use of ORS or not), their behavior would be reflected in the social communication about that behavior that was being exchanged in the community. Specifically, the study assumed that a good measure of the messages that a woman was likely to hear from her social network about ORS practice was the actual ORS practice of the other women interviewed in the cluster.

The social support measure was the proportion of other women in the cluster (excluding the respondent in each case) who used ORS for the last case. About 37% of the women lived in clusters where at least 30% of the other mothers reported using ORS. These women were classified as living in communities with higher social support. The remaining women were classified as living in communities providing lower social support.

The interaction between social support and knowledge in their effects on practice is presented in Figure 4.5.

Wilkins performed an analysis of variance with ORS practice as the dependent variable and social support and knowledge as predictors. The analysis established that the main effects of each variable as well as the interaction between them were strongly statistically significant. The hypothesis that social support conditioned the turning of knowledge into behavior was supported. Mothers with high commu-

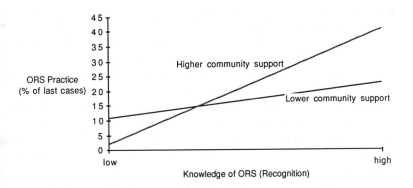

Figure 4.5 Social Network Support, Knowledge and ORS Practice in Ecuador

nity support were more likely to turn knowledge into behavior than those with low community support.

LEARNED CHARACTERISTICS OF INDIVIDUALS

The two remaining categories involve hypotheses which address intrinsic characteristics of individuals. The boundary between the categories is ill-defined, but the hypotheses in the category of learned characteristics of individuals is meant to include factors such as prior knowledge and learned skills, which may be relatively open to shorter-term changes, and contrast with the last category, which involves hypotheses about personality or fundamental values, which are assumed to reflect more enduring characteristics of individuals.

Within the first category, one would include prior beliefs about a problem and its solutions and previous experience trying to solve it, as well as factors like education, language skill, visual literacy and experience with particular communication channels. These are the types of variables which have most often been used in "knowledge gap" studies which seek to explain why the socially advantaged sometimes gain new knowledge more readily than the less advantaged in the presence of an increasing flow of relevant communication (Tichenor, Donohue, & Olien, 1970, 1980).

The hypotheses suggest that experience affects the ease with which one handles the concepts transmitted in a public information campaign. If one is more comfortable with the concepts, if one can fit them into preexisting cognitive schema, one can act on them more readily. An individual who knows that the great risk from diarrheal disease is dehydration may be ready to make use of information about a rehydration solution which solves that problem. Someone who is concerned about the quantity of diarrhea may be less open to a message emphasizing further intake of liquids.

Conceptually, this category of hypotheses is somewhat different from the previous examples. These "learned characteristic" hypotheses do address the issue of the conditioning effect of prior skills on the turning of knowledge into behavior. However, their underlying causal mechanism assumes that prior skills ease the process of turning exposure to an information source into sophisticated (and actionable) knowledge, which, in turn, leads to practice. The study by S.

Spain used to illustrate this explores how the relation of access to information with knowledge is conditioned by the prior skills of an individual.

Spain (1983), like McDivitt, gathered data in The Gambia as part of the evaluation of that country's campaign for the use of a water-sugar-salt formula for the treatment of diarrheal disease. She was interested in how visual literacy interacted with exposure to a flyer in affecting an individual's ability to interpret the flyer. The flyer described how to mix the W-S-S solution and was designed for a nonreading population. It presented the amounts of each ingredient to be mixed and other information through pictures which Spain describes as "representing a moderate level of complexity of interpretation."

Flyer comprehension was measured through an instrument which assessed recognition of objects and details in the flyer and accuracy of interpretations of actions to be taken. Scores varied from 0 to 17 on the highly reliable (alpha=.87) scale, with a mean of 12. Visual ability was measured through an instrument based on the types of recognition and interpretation tasks typical in such tests. It included ability to recognize objects, understand perspective, and make inferences as to ongoing actions. The resulting scale varied from 0 to 8, with a mean of 4 and acceptable reliability (alpha=.64). Of the 388 women included in the analysis, about one-third were classified as low (0–2 points), one-third as moderate (3–4) and one-third as high (5–7).

Exposure to the flyer was classified either high or low: High exposure included those people who had seen the flyer and still had a copy they could show the interviewer. Low exposure included those women who said they had seen the flyer but did not have a copy in their homes.

As Figure 4.6 illustrates, Spain found that visual ability affects the influence of flyer exposure on flyer comprehension. The interaction of the two predictors was highly significant when added to a multiple regression equation already including the main effects of visual ability and flyer exposure. The interaction, clearly enough, is negative. Those who had relatively greater visual ability learned to interpret the flyer with little exposure and weren't much helped by repeated exposure to it. Those who were less visually able comprehended it far better if they had repeated exposure to it.

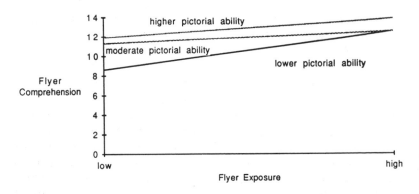

Figure 4.6 Pictorial Ability, Flyer Exposure and Comprehension in The Gambia

ENDURING CHARACTERISTICS OF INDIVIDUALS

In an earlier period, there was a great deal of emphasis on personality and strongly held values as explanations for failures to adopt innovation. The concepts of innovativeness, of fatalism, of entrepreneurial spirit, of the need for achievement all played important roles in early theories of development. For some scholars, these traits might be modified as individuals became exposed to "modern" institutions like the factory or the mass media (Inkeles and Smith, 1974; Lerner, 1958); for others they were fixed at an early age (McClelland, 1961). However, for all, they were seen as major determinants of the pace of development. These scholars assumed that there were many possibilities for change awaiting individuals if only they were willing to grasp them, but it was their own reluctance to change which held them back.

These individual personality explanations lost favor in the skeptical intellectual tides of the late 1960s, when explanations emphasizing the failures of systems rather than of individuals came to the fore. This change reflected a variety of forces. There was some evidence that indeed structural barriers held individuals back from change. There was also some preference from a policy perspective for system-blame explanations, recognizing that systems might be more open to intervention than were personalities. Finally, there was a sincere political preference among the people who worked on developing country problems to see those problems as systemic rather than individual in character. These forces led to a rejection of the enduring characteristics of individuals as a favored explanation for slow development. However they are not evidence that such variables do not matter.

Enduring characteristics are, indeed, the residual explanation: If nothing else explains the knowledge-behavior gap, it must be personality. However, establishing that positively, rather than merely claiming it to be the residual explanation, is a difficult matter.

There are two different versions of enduring-characteristics hypotheses worth discussion. One version recognizes that there is variation in behavior not predictable from available measures of likely variables. The unexplained variance is partly to be seen as the product of unmeasured variables, partly seen as the product of poor measurement of available variables, and partly the product of idiosyncratic factors. Some may see such idiosyncratic variance as representing irreducible individual differences which reflect the operation of fundamental personality traits. There may be no claim that a particular trait is operating; rather, unexplained variation in behavior is credited to the complex mix of traits which define individual character but whose measurement is beyond available technology.

This version of the enduring-characteristics hypothesis may be a fair and accurate way to explain residual variance in behavior. But, by definition, it is empirically untestable. Thus, for all practical purposes, it does little to move the argument forward; one might as well take the extreme opposite view and declare unexplained variance in behavior random.

The second version of the enduring-characteristics hypothesis makes more direct claims. Assume that, for example, an openness to innovation was a personality characteristic rather than a description of behavior. In parallel with the model used for the previous categories, one could hypothesize that those who, by dint of personality, were more open to innovation would be more likely to turn achieved knowledge into behavior.

The set of research studies from which examples were drawn for the rest of this chapter do not contain any good illustrations of this type of study. This is partly a reflection of the less favored status of this category of hypothesis; it is also a statement about the sheer difficulty of doing satisfactory measurement of personality characteristics like innovativeness. Then, in contrast to the previous sections which presented illustrations of tests of hypotheses, this section focuses on the difficulty of measuring enduring characteristics in field studies.

The difficulty of assigning individuals scores as to their degree of innovative personality, for example, seems daunting. One way is to use a paper-and-pencil measure in which individuals describe their openness to new ideas or practices. Robertson uses a measure of attitude toward innovation relevant to U.S. consumption studies, "How willing are you to buy new products—very willing to very unwilling?" and finds that responses to that question are associated with the number of new products purchased (1971, p. 89).

However the difficulty of relying on such abstract measures can be illustrated by imagining that the research had shown no association. Would the author have rejected the hypothesis that innovativeness is related to innovative behavior? That seems unlikely; rather, the tendency would have been to reject the abstract measure on the assumption that any measure of innovativeness had better predict behavior if it is to be useful. The criterion for describing someone as more or less innovative is their behavior, with abstract measures serving as a surrogate for that measure. That is another way of saying that the obvious best measure of innovativeness is the actual innovative behavior individuals undertake.

If innovative behavior is the best measure, then one is in a bind, since specific innovative behavior is also the dependent variable in any study of the interaction of personality with knowledge in producing behavior. One cannot use innovative behavior as a predictor (representing innovative personality) and also as an outcome (representing behavior) without risk of tautology. Alternatively, one might use an abstract measure of innovativeness and a measure of behavior only for the dependent variable. But then the measure of the dependent variable is a better indicator of innovativeness than is the putative measure of innovativeness, an impossible situation. Surely this problem reoccurs with many personality characteristics said to be related to changes in practice (like openness to risk and venturesomeness, which are often considered predictors of innovative behavior). The best evidence for the presence or absence of the personality trait is often the behavior it is meant to explain.

An additional problem in the use of abstract measures for personality traits is that they require introspection by respondents and thus depend on respondents' articulateness. Particularly in parts of developing countries where the survey interview is an unusual activity, people may be unused to answering the types of questions required to assign them scores on personality traits. Surely the articulateness of respondents will be a function of their education, their comfort with the research context and other factors unrelated to the trait being measured. Apparent variation in personality traits may just be a stand-in for variation in social class and educational background. Unlike the fairly concrete measurement tasks associated with the previous categories of explanation for the knowledge-behavior gap, measuring personality may be a morass.

SOME CLOSING COMMENTS

The previous pages have described elements of a particular approach to organizing explanations for the gap between knowledge and behavior. Examples from public information programs studied in developing countries accompanied each category of explanation. However it should be understood that the purpose of the discussion was to present the underlying approach. Neither are these studies a census nor are they a representative sample of all studies which fit in these categories. They are a purposive sample, designed to make the case for the approach, not to lead to any definitive conclusions about the substantive hypotheses they examine. Some other related work includes many analyses in the McDivitt and Wilkins studies, and studies by Contreras-Budge (1979) and Ferencic (1985). Lei (1984) and Gould (1982) have done related studies using data gathered in the United States. Not all of them found the interactions they were looking for.

The fact is that we as researchers are more at the point of believing that these are important ways of looking at the issue than of knowing what the eventual answers will be. We do not know whether the knowledge-behavior gap will have different predominant explanations depending on the behavior, depending on the public information approach taken or depending on the context in which the program operates. We do not know whether eventually we will be able to classify behaviors and contexts in a parsimonious way. We do not know whether we will be able to suggest that for this behavior, in this context, the best class of predictors for the failure to turn knowledge into behavior tend to be this type of characteristic.

In these closing pages it will be useful to address a number of miscellaneous concerns which may help put the previous discussion in context. These concerns include: the importance of this focus on knowledge and behavior gaps with regard to overall study of public information programs; the meaning of "knowledge"; the possibility of refocusing the discussion from the point of view of the system to that of the audience and the possible application of the categories of explanation to explain other gaps, including those between exposure to communication and knowledge or practice.

Research studying knowledge-behavior gaps may play only a secondary role if one were faced with the task of evaluating public information programs and explaining why they had or had not achieved their goals. The best explanations for relative success or failure of programs probably have to do with how many people were reached by messages, how often they were reached and how clearly the messages provided information that would help the recipient solve a problem that was already recognized. Most projects, in developing countries as least, founder because these tasks are not done very well (Hornik, 1988). While explaining the knowledge-behavior gap is of substantial theoretical interest, it is possible to remain agnostic as to its practical utility. That decision will await evidence that these types of hypotheses explain very much of the variation in practice and have implications for intervention design.

In each of the illustrative examples, a case was made for the relevance of different measures of knowledge, without much explicit consideration of the notion that they represented the type of knowledge which should lead to behavior. Expressing concern about a knowledge-behavior gap assumes that the knowledge was sufficient to serve as the foundation for behavior. If one accepts that assumption, then it is reasonable to wonder why there was no "practice" house constructed on the "knowledge" foundation. However, if the knowledge was inadequate, that in itself may be sufficient explanation for the lack of behavior, without need to turn to susceptibility explanations.

This emphasizes the need to consider carefully what type of knowledge is being measured in a particular study. One wants to be sure not to confuse mere recognition of a solution (like recognizing a packet of rehydration salts) with sufficient knowledge of how it is used and what problem it solves, if this latter knowledge is what is required if knowledge is to lead to practice. Weaker measures of knowledge (like the recognition measure) may be useful indicators of a more developed level of knowledge, but they are not the same thing. Their use is likely to dilute any effects of a susceptibility variable, since they will only permit an imprecise estimate of the true knowlege-behavior relation.

A related issue is the care one must take in making inferences about causal direction. The susceptibility studies reported here depend on cross-sectional data; that is, data gathered at a single point in time. Any observed knowledge-practice relation might be explained as easily by the effects of practice on knowledge and vice-versa. Unless one can sort out temporal order among variables, one only may be able to make an inference that a susceptibility variable is associated with a greater or lesser correlation of knowledge with behavior.

The organization of this discussion examined the issues from the point of view of the audience. What individual, community and system characteristics condition the individual's response to knowledge? However many of these hypotheses can also be regarded from the perspective of the system that generates new practices and tries to diffuse them. For example, one can ask whether the tendency to use fertilizers, given knowledge of them, reflects individual disposable income. Or one can express the same issue differently. Why is it that agricultural agencies produce recommendations that fit with the financial resources of better-off farmers but not poorer ones? The original version focuses on the lack of resources of the individual; the second, looking at the same problem, addresses the failure of the system to respond to that situation. Conceptually, the two views are quite similar; from a policy view, they may lead down quite different paths.

Similarly, one may note that the lack of a prior intellectual framework makes it difficult for someone to make use of knowledge—for example, knowledge about rehydration fluids may not fit with an individual's notion of the problem of diarrhea and therefore may only be accepted reluctantly as a diarrhea treatment. However, that view can be turned around. One can ask why the information communicated about the rehydration fluid wasn't better adapted to the conceptual framework common in the audience? In the first view, the emphasis is on the individual's "failure" to have a receptive conceptual framework; in the second, the emphasis is on the "failure" of the message-delivery system.

The focus of this chapter has been on the knowledge-behavior gap and how it is to be explained. However, one can easily extend most of the logic to other gaps within the field of purposive communication. One can ask why exposure to information doesn't always turn into knowledge. In Figure 1, knowledge was on the horizontal axis and practice on the vertical axis. The exposure-knowledge gap hypotheses would move knowledge to the vertical axis and exposure to the horizontal axis. Again one might search for variables within the five categories which predict stronger or weaker relationships between exposure and knowledge. One might also extend the model to the direct relation between exposure and practice, ignoring the intervening knowledge variable.

NOTES

1. The graphic display of the interaction can be presented in equation form, which also permits a straightforward statistical test of the presence of an interaction. If one can assume linearity in the relationships among the variables, and satisfaction of other assumptions of multiple regression procedures, the interaction can be tested in the comparison of the power of two equations.

1) $P = b_1 K + b_2 A + a_1$
2) $P = b'_1 K + b'_2 A + b'_3 K^*A + a'_1$

where P: Practice; K: knowledge; A: Access and K*A is a multiplicative interaction term.

If the variation in P accounted for when only the main effects of knowledge and access are present (equation 1) is significantly less than the variation accounted for when the interaction term is added (equation 2), there is a significant interaction. Standard statistical programs provide tests of this interaction through examination of the change in R-squared between steps of regression equations. If the b'_3 coefficient is positive, the interaction is positive, such that (in this case) those with greater access to credit are more likely to turn increased knowledge into practice.

2. McDivitt used analysis of variance to examine this effect, with a modified form of the practice variable (a residual version with the effects of certain control variables eliminated) predicted from community development, knowledge and their interaction.

3. Figure 2 is a reworking of material found in O'Sullivan-Ryan (1978). The picture in Figure 4 is entirely consistent with the intent of Graph 3 in that document, although some numbers could only be approximated.

4. Wilkins made use of data gathered for the Ecuadoran government agency INNFA by a social research firm (CEPLAES) as part of an evaluation under the supervision of Eduardo Contreras-Budge. The project was funded by USAID through its Communication for Child Survival Program (Academy for Educational Develop-

ment) and a subcontract with the Annenberg School of Communications at the University of Pennsylvania.

REFERENCES

Benito, C. A. (1976). Peasants' response to modernization projects in minifundia economies. *American Journal of Agricultural Economics, 58,* 143–151.

Brown, L. A. (1981). *Innovation diffusion.* London: Methuen.

Contreras-Budge, E. (1979). *Communication, rural modernity and structural constraints.* Unpublished doctoral dissertation Stanford University, Stanford, CA.

Ferencic, N. (1985). Factors affecting the knowledge and adoption of new health practices: Results of a survey preceding a communication and development campaign in Swaziland. Unpublished masters thesis University of Pennsylvania, Philadelphia.

Festinger, L., Schachter, S., & Back, K. (1950). *Social pressures in informal groups.* Stanford, CA: Stanford University Press.

Foote, D. R., Martorell, R., McDivitt, J. A., Snyder, L., Spain, P. L., Stone, S. M., & Storey, J. D. (1985). *The mass media and health practices evaluation in The Gambia: The final report of major findings.* (A report from Stanford University to the United States Agency for International Development.) Menlo Park, CA: Applied Communication Technology.

Gould, J. E. (1982). A theoretical development and empirical tests of a theory of susceptibility to media effects. Unpublished doctoral dissertation. University of Pennsylvania, Philadelphia.

Hornik, R. C. (1988). *Development communication: Information, agriculture and nutrition in the Third World.* New York: Longman.

Inkeles, A., and Smith, D. H. (1974). *Becoming modern: Individual change in six developing countries.* Cambridge, MA: Harvard University Press.

Katz, E., & Lazarsfeld, P. F. (1955). *Personal influence: The part played by people in the flow of mass communications.* New York: Free Press.

Lei, C. J. (1984). Communication behavior and beliefs about American social norms: An acculturation study of Southeast Asian refugees in West Philadelphia. Unpublished masters thesis. University of Pennsylvania, Philadelphia.

Lerner, D. (1958). *The passing of traditional society.* Glencoe, IL: Free Press.

Lockheed, M. E., Jamison, D. T., & Lau, L. J. (1980). Farmer education and farm efficiency: A survey. *Economic Development and Cultural Change, 29,* 37–76.

McClelland, D. (1961). *The achieving society.* New York: Van Nostrand.

McDivitt, J. A. (1985). Constraints to knowledge gain and behavior change in response to a multi-media health education project in The Gambia, West Africa. Unpublished doctoral dissertation. University of Pennsylvania, Philadelphia.

O'Sullivan, J. (1980). Guatemala: Marginality and information in the Western Highlands. In E. McAnany (Ed.), *Communications in the rural Third World,* (pp. 71–106). New York: Praeger.

O'Sullivan-Ryan, J. (1978). Rural development programs and the problems of marginality and the Western Highlands of Guatemala. [Microfilm]. Ann Arbor, MI: University Microfilms International.

Robertson, T. S. (1971). *Innovative behavior and communication.* New York: Holt, Rinehart and Winston.

Schultz, T. W. (1964). *Transforming traditional agriculture.* New Haven: Yale University Press.

Spain, S. (1983). Factors affecting pictorial comprehension in non-literates: Results of a survey in The Gambia, West Africa. Unpublished masters thesis. University of Pennsylvania, Philadelphia.

Tichenor, P., Donohue, G., & Olien, C. (1970). Mass media flow and differential growth in knowledge. *Public Opinion Quarterly, 34,* 159–170.

Tichenor, P., Donohue, G., & Olien, C. (1980). Community conflict and the press. Beverly Hills, CA: Sage.

Wilkins, K. (1987). The role of community support in mothers' decisions about health practices: A study of oral rehydration solution use and knowledge in Ecuador. Unpublished masters thesis. University of Pennsylvania, Philadelphia.

Yoder, P. S. (1988). Personal communication.

Chapter 5

MEDIA COVERAGE AND SOCIAL MOVEMENTS

Clarice N. Olien, Phillip J. Tichenor and George A. Donohue

THERE IS A STRONG BELIEF, rooted in populism and the traditional ideology of journalism, that reporting social problems is a prime role, if not *the* role, of media. If media perform such a role, one might expect media reporting to trigger, if not create, social movements. This belief would seem to follow from the "Fourth Estate" view, tracing to seventeenth and eighteenth century European views, that the press is a necessary and independent channel for reporting social strains. In this perspective, the press is an alternative source of information that government and other institutions either do not possess or refuse to divulge (Carlyle, 1841; Boyce, 1978).

While there is little doubt that mass media coverage may have substantial impact in a particular movement, there is considerable question about where such coverage appears in the life of a social movement and what its consequences are. Do media initiate movements? Does media reporting provide the perspective of the originators of a movement? Does media attention to a movement make it more likely to succeed?

What makes this media role in social movements so salient for analysis is that in a modern, pluralistic and interdependent world, mass media are relied upon increasingly to let members of concerned groups know what others are thinking and doing and what, in particular, the opposition is doing and thinking. Much of what the general public knows about social movements reaches them through the printed pages and airwaves. This does not rule out the role of family, work place and other institutions, but it emphasizes mass media as primary sources of new information.

MASS MEDIA AND SOCIAL CONTROL

Media reporting of any movement may be seen as part of the process of social control and conflict management. A prime need of any social system is regulation of individual and collective behavior to maintain group stability, adapt to changing conditions, and reach group goals. Social controls are enforced through the normative order and through specific agents in all institutional realms, including the family, government, the economic sector, religion and education. Mass media, given their deference to mainstream values, are highly visible agents of social control (Janowitz, 1952; Breed, 1958; Donohue, Tichenor, & Olien, 1973).

While social control is often viewed primarily as an effort of established authority to prevent deviance (e.g., Oberschall, 1973), the position here is that social control is basic to all aspects of collective behavior, ranging from constraints on individual behavior to constraints on established authority. The Ten Commandments and the first ten amendments to the U.S. Constitution are both prescriptions for social control. While each one provides guidelines for social conduct, the first states what *individuals* "shalt not" do in their daily lives and the second what *government* shall not do regarding matters of religion, speech, and other civil rights. It might be noted that "shalt not" control is more permissive, and that the shift, in many movements, is to obligatory "thou shalt" statements that specify a much narrower range of conduct than would be allowed by, say, the Bill of Rights.

Social conflict invariably centers around questions of social control. Conflicts generally imply questions about (1) the behavior of some individual, group, or agency, (2) the socially-derived rules governing such behavior and (3) the consequences of (1) and (2). A televised protest of the plight of homeless persons draws attention to the cultural belief that all persons should be entitled to shelter, while implying that welfare agency policies may be a hindrance to providing these basic needs. A newspaper report about a strike at an automobile factory describes negotiations over rules for salary and work conditions. An attempt before TV cameras to block a train carrying nuclear materials draws attention to the behavior of protesters, the response by the governmental agency operating the train, and regulations for disposal of such waste. Media reports center on the established rules which are being protested and on whether the protesters are following socially accepted rules for expressing grievances. Which of these two questions of "rules" is emphasized by the dominant institutions will have ramifications for media reporting and, ultimately, for public perceptions of the protest. All of these issues are matters of social contract relationships, and all are, for that reason, issues of social control.

SOCIAL CONFLICT AND SOCIAL MOVEMENTS

There are sharply differing perspectives on how social control should be conceptualized. One view, which no longer holds the prominence that it did a few decades ago, is that conflict is primarily disorder, while consensus is primary and necessary for social survival (La Piere, 1965, p. 480). Emphasis upon "social pathologies" and "social disorganization" often reflects a view of conflict as a social abnormality.

A different view, the one adopted here, is that conflict is not only a basic social condition but is functional for a variety of outcomes which may be viewed as negative *or* positive at a given point in time. Such a view has been propounded by Marx, Simmel, Coser, Dahrendorf, and other observers of social change. A central point in these writings is that conflict may generate new norms and serve as a stimulus to political thought, economic activity and technological development (Coser, 1954; 1967, p. 20). Laski (1943) noted that civil conflict opens up "an immense reservoir of new talent" which would have been unexpressed otherwise (p. 45). Oberschall (1973) emphasizes the "dynamic aspects" of group conflict, seeing it as having crucial functions in the management and allocation of resources (pp. 24–28). Marx's analysis of dialectical processes, as illustrated by the extensive discussions of these processes in subsequent literature, stands as a classical statement of how contradictory social forces lead to new intellectual perspectives and to social change (Bottomore, 1983, pp. 122–129). Evidence indicates that news media coverage tends to be greatest at periods of high intensity of controversies and that coverage and intensity are interactive processes. (Tichenor, Donohue and Olien, 1980).

ORIGIN OF MOVEMENTS

Social movements arise from basic discrepancies within the system. These discrepancies reflect a gap between what is valued by the group and what is seen as occurring. A classic statement of such a discrepancy is the "American Dilemma" as described by Gunnar Myrdal (1944): the creed of equality in America alongside the widespread and widely rationalized unequal treatment afforded Black citizens. Compared to other countries, Myrdal noted, America has the most explicitly expressed system of general ideals for human interaction (p. 3), as illustrated by slogans about the "Land of the Free" and the "Mission of America" in righting social injustices in the world. Myrdal saw that much is permitted in practice while much is forbidden in law, a condition generally undermining respect for law. The Second World War—ostensibly against Fascism, prejudice and enslavement of whole populations—left without any intellectual merit the traditional rationalizations for the low status accorded Blacks.

Social movements seem to arise when the system can tolerate them, when the time is opportune. The civil rights movement occurred at a time when a coalescence of factors produced a need to redefine the status of Black people. Several authors (e.g., Zald & Ash, 1966; Gamson, 1975; Jenkins, 1983; Staggenborg, 1988) have emphasized such factors as resource mobilization, formalized organizations and the role of professionals in determining degrees of success attained by protest movements.

Conflicts invariably raise questions of power allocation. While power may be a source of conflict, it does not by itself explain all conflicts. In all systems, there is a tendency for power centers to work out their respective positions so as to maintain the status quo. This is particularly the case in homogenous structures, in which communication takes place largely on a primary, interpersonal basis and decisions are made by consensus and with minimal public interaction. In a more urbanized, diversifying structure, however, there is a plurality of power centers and potential power centers, more interaction in all institutional areas and, therefore, more conflict. This conflict is a continuing condition, which gives rise to the establishment of formalized bureaucracies to manage it at a safe level and thereby maintain stability. Bureaucracies are designed not to resist change but to control the way change occurs and to mitigate consequences which are considered undesirable.

Such fluid, dynamic systems are characteristic of industrializing nations. Proponents of equilibrium models see social modification as a response to different parts of an industrial system changing at unequal rates and falling out of a state of adjustment which previously existed. Among these observers are Smelser and Ogburn, whose approaches to social change are considered here as fruitful to understanding the basis of social movements.

Smelser (1959), though criticized by some for not explicitly noting human conflict (Oberschall, 1973), gives central attention to the "disturbances" in social change accompanying the industrial revolution. The system for producing cotton yarn, left over from medieval days, led to considerable dissatisfaction in eighteenth century England. There was a shortage of cotton yarn for textile production, friction between spinners and weavers, and brow-beating and scapegoating of poor people for not resolving the yarn shortage by working harder. Aminzade (1981) found similar processes on the European continent during the nineteenth century. One of the first responses to such strains, which Smelser finds common in industrializing nations, is an attempt to control the disturbances among the textile workers.

These control procedures, whether called "crowd control," "riot control" or "antiterrorism," may themselves be sources of controversy, as they were in the U.S. student protests of the early 1970s (Gitlin, 1980), in the American Agriculture Movement's protests of farm auctions (Cigler and Hansen, 1983) or in the recent Israeli army actions in the West Bank. These "disturbance control" actions are typically followed by legitimation of new ideas and social experiments and open encouragement of new inventions, such as the Spinning Jenny, which revolutionized cotton-yarn production as well as the household industry that had produced yarn up to that time (Aminzade, 1981). An outcome, Smelser finds, was a substitution of competition for the earlier medieval regulations controlling production and distribution of wealth.

Whereas Smelser concentrated on change within a given industrial sector, Ogburn (1964) introduced the "cultural lag" hypothesis, which conceives of disjunctions which may occur across institutional areas. Cultural lag occurs when one of two correlated elements in a culture changes before or in greater degree than the other part, leaving less adjustment than existed previously. An illustration is the highway system and automobiles, which were in good adjustment in 1910 but out of adjustment by the 1930s when high-speed cars rendered the narrow and often unpaved existing roads obsolete. While Ogburn noted that the independent variable could be economic, political, ideological or anything else, he emphasized technology and science as the "great prime movers of social change" in modern times. The shift of populations from farms to cities and of political power from rural to urban centers are seen by Ogburn as resting heavily upon inventions. These include inventions of machinery and crop and animal production systems that increased agricultural efficiency and transportation systems, starting with the railroads, which encouraged population movement to cities and made possible urban domination of trade in surrounding areas.

The cultural-lag hypothesis has been sharply criticized for its emphasis upon technological determinism. A countering position is that change in the normative belief structure is primary in bringing about both technological developments and their organized use (e.g., La Piere, 1965). The idea for new modes of personal travel must have been present in the system before automobile technology was developed in the first place.

INITIATION AND ACCOMMODATION OF MOVEMENTS

A question often debated is whether and how social disparities become translated into social movements. The organized phases of concerted movements typically begin with small but highly involved sets of concerned people, particularly intellectuals, seeking to identify and articulate a problem. Initiation as a stage may occur over a period of months, years or decades, and it may be largely invisible to the public. Marx's early intellectual statements about the plight of workers in industrializing and capitalistic structures was a major problem definition for the later mobilizing efforts of Lenin in the Bolshevik movement and Eugene Debs. W. E. B. DuBois may be seen as having a problem definition role in the civil rights movement, predating the speeches and mobilization strategies of Martin Luther King. Still earlier was the statement by Alexis de Tocqueville, early in the nineteenth century, about the social condition of American Blacks and Native Americans (de Tocqueville, 1947). Myrdal's documentation of the consequences of racial segregation in the 1940s was part of a mobilization process rather than initial problem definition. In the feminist movement, the writings of Simone de Beauvoir offered a sharp insight into the cultural institution of marriage as it bears on the female role in modern society. This definition was known in the inner circles of the movement at an early stage and was later applied by popular writers, such as Betty Friedan, to home-economics education and other forms of maintaining the traditional female role.

Publicity may not be sought at the initiating stage and may be actively avoided, particularly if initiating groups have not articulated the problem to their satisfaction. A group may fear that premature media attention would leave them in disarray and further behind than ever. When and how to "go public" is often a major point of contention among newly organized groups.

Definitions of social problems ultimately emanate not from initiating groups, however, but from interactions within the dominant power-and-influence structures that often take over the movement. Any movement on a major scale poses a potential threat to established institutions and power centers. In the case of the environmental movement, *Silent Spring* appeared as a frontal challenge to the agricultural and chemical industries, the U. S. Department of Agriculture, and agricultural colleges. All had advocated usage of chemical products for pest and plant control and all were criticized by the ecologists for advocating practices deemed harmful to wildlife and human health. An initial response was to view *Silent Spring* as an insurgent uprising to be quelled quickly in the interest of protecting existing food production methods. At the same time, the environmentalist movement established a political power base which included support for legislation putting certain controls on usage of chemicals and additives and release of various pollutants into the water, air and soil. By the mid-1960s, the agricultural and industrial groups had shifted from summary rejection of the movement to accommodation and cooptation.

The civil rights movement, following the 1954 *Brown v. Board of Education* decision, centered initially on the Birmingham bus boycott and school desegregation (Oberschall, 1973, pp. 221ff). As in other cases, established groups moved to accommodate the movement because of its potential threat to the stability of the entire power and influence structure in the nation. Several laws were passed, ostensibly to create equal opportunity in education, housing and employment. In spite of changes made, neither the environmental nor civil rights movements reached the objectives articulated by either Rachel Carson or Martin Luther King. An environmentalist bureaucracy with voluminous rules developed, and the chemical approach to pest control remained as basic social policy. In civil rights, neither desegregation nor enforced school busing equalized the educational experiences for Blacks and Whites, and a Black-dominated underclass with high unemployment remains as an unsolved problem in the urban core. In both cases, the movements led to accommodations but few of the structural changes sought by the movement's advocates. Generally, the regulatory agencies of government are established by, and serve the interests of, the businesses that are regulated rather than the consuming public, a point observed by Harold Ickes (1943) following a career in New Deal regulatory agencies and the Roosevelt cabinet.

THE MYTH OF A FOURTH ESTATE

The view of media as Fourth Estate has had wide appeal not only for journalism but also for popular government, since it reinforces the notion that each member of the public gathers information and makes an independent decision. Realistic or not, this meshes with the myth of the press as a sentinel and monitor for the "little people" in guiding public policy (Lippmann, 1925; Leonard, 1986).

Along with other myths, belief in a watchdog role has certain social functions, such as providing a standard for judging performance of media. The Hutchins Commission (1947) used this standard in contending that to maintain their First Amendment protection, the media needed to more actively seek divergent views on issues. This watchdog ideal is invoked repeatedly as justification for protection of press and speech rights under the First Amendment. It may also be argued that existence of the watchdog belief in journalism literature (Shoemaker, 1987) serves to temper the structural tendency of the media to support authority (Tichenor, Olien, Harrison, & Donohue, 1970) while reinforcing reporter enthusiasm for investigative journalism.

Deference of media to economic and other powerful interests has been amply documented in academic research since the Hutchins Commission critique was published. Some of the early work demonstrating press deference to economic and political powers was by Janowitz (1952), Breed (1958), and Edelstein and Schulz (1963).

More recent studies indicate that the more pluralistic the structure, the more the tendency for conflict to be a routine part of public life and the greater the structural need for it to be reported to the community at large (Olien, Donohue, & Tichenor, 1968). Additional evidence on how media content supports public authority has been reported by Paletz and Entman, (1981), Paletz, Reichert and McIntyre (1971), Molotch and Lester (1975), Morley (1976), Tuchman (1978), Lemert and Larkin (1979) and Gitlin (1980).

Conflict management, as a prime role of mass media, might be called "damage control." This is especially apparent in an urbanized, highly differentiated and pluralistic system, in which there are multiple power centers with multiple bureaucracies and multiple formalized mechanisms for dealing with and managing conflicts. Major crises affecting power centers are necessary for others to know, but "damage control" reporting from the authority's perspective may prevent injury to that authority. Media reports of industrial strikes are often found not to be surrogates for picket lines. To the contrary, such reports often portray picket lines through the eyes of management, the police and the national guard (Morley, 1976; Murdoch, 1973) and thereby marginalize the protest. When the American Agriculture Movement sent a tractorcade to Washington, D.C., several newspapers concentrated on the scars the tractors left in Washington D.C. boulevards rather than on issues as defined by the protesters. Herman (1985) notes that U.S. media, in selectively covering Third World countries, favor governments friendly to the U.S. while marginalizing groups critical of U.S. foreign policy. This gives attention to the problem but defines it as one for solution by the existing leadership structure.

The damage-control interpretation is further supported by findings from several Minnesota studies that leaders of established agencies and more powerful groups tend to perceive mass media as more helpful to their organizations than do leaders of less established groups. Among 91 leaders of such established groups as city government and state agricultural agencies, 61% viewed the media as helpful to their own organizations. This compares with only 35% of leaders representing less established interests, such as citizen or student groups. At the same time, 18% of the established leaders viewed one medium or more as harmful to their interests, compared with fully 58% of the leaders of less established groups (Donohue, Olien and Tichenor, 1984).

MEDIA AND PHASES OF MOVEMENTS

At what point in social movements does media coverage generally occur? Media do not generally possess independent knowledge-generating resources and are, as a whole, structurally dependent upon dominant power institutions both for definitions of problems and for information. A research team studying news magazine attention to fuel supplies prior to the "gasoline crunch" of 1973–74 found them performing "more like a thermometer than a barometer" in anticipating the crisis. In spite of various advance warnings, the "fuel crisis" was not defined as such until President Nixon's speech on the subject (Dangerfield, McCartney and Starcher, 1975), an event that signifies the responsiveness of media to power centers. Allocation of space and time by media to power centers such as Washington, D.C., New York and London is testimony of this dependence syndrome.

As integral parts of the process of accommodating and ameliorating social protest, media are reinforcers of established bureaucratic authority structures. In any crisis, they will be constrained to seek the definitions of established authorities, definitions which can be expected to color the reporting and commentary in the media. When there is a nuclear power plant disaster, media seek out the definitions of reactor safety and radiation fallout which were established before the crisis occurred (Friedman, 1981). In the marijuana issue, the administrators of health agencies are sought (Shepherd, 1981), which would be expected as well in the current AIDS controversy. In an oil spill, oil company and federal agency spokespersons are the predominant sources. (Molotch and Lester, 1975). This tendency is supported by journalistic procedures and views. The MacNeil-Lehrer or Ted Koppel programs, when reporting on crises, typically concentrate on interviews with the official spokespersons for the agencies and established organizations involved. One group investigating coverage of earthquakes concluded that media representatives wanted an "information czar" with official status to convey the most authoritative information available. The research team stressed the importance of a central information center to reduce the possibility of panic and, as they put it, "facilitate communication among those who need to know" (Sood, Stockdale, & Rogers, 1987).

Because of growing pluralism and vying for power, the American system, as well as others, has seen the bureaucracy become the major pattern of social networking. Bureaucratic agencies are accommodative structures for containing and "cooling out" movements. In response to civil rights, environmental, feminist and consumer concerns, agencies have been created to set the rules which supposedly guide progress toward the stated goals of the movement. Typically, as with rules for employment and training of minorities and disposal of industrial wastes, the outcome is a structural accommodation which controls the movement and its representatives so as to minimize the damage.

LEGITIMATION AND MEDIA COVERAGE

Bureaucratic agencies and procedures serve as legitimizing agents for the media. Strodthoff, Hawkins and Schoenfeld found that the most prominent clustering of federal environmental policy decisions occurred between 1968 and 1972. Before these agencies were developed, there was increasing environmental content in special-interest magazines, while the increase in general-audience magazines occurred primarily after the major developments in environmental agencies. The investigators (1985) interpreted this finding as supporting an earlier postulate that environmental issues were initiated by professional interest groups, followed by specialized publication and attention in government and then by general mass media attention and public concern (Strodthoff, Hawkins, & Schoenfeld, 1985; Tichenor, Donohue, Olien, & Bowers, 1971).

As a rule, media coverage of an emerging social movement is either highly restrained or nonexistent until the movement has been legitimized in the system. Kessler (1980) noted long periods in the suffrage movement of the nineteenth century when the movement was either ignored or treated derisively. In a study of coverage of this movement in the Portland *Oregonian* from 1870–1905, Kessler concluded that legitimation was crucial. Not until the last few years of this period, following comments by public officials and other legitimizers, did the *Oregonian* treat the suffrage movement as worthy for discussion and debate. Similarly, Morris (1973) found that Los Angeles newspaper coverage of the feminist movement was extremely limited in the 1968–1969 period, chosen as a time before the movement had received external legitimation. She interpreted this finding as supporting Breed's conclusion (1958) that media "blackouts" can serve social control purposes.

While legitimation typically comes from leadership in established institutions, crisis events may legitimize a definition or redefinition of a problem. The current coverage of Acquired Immune Deficiency Syndrome (AIDS) is illustrative. AIDS was first reported primarily as a problem of the gay community, then as one of the restricted groups of heterosexuals and now is being viewed as a concern for the perpetuation of the human species. These redefinitions grew primarily from announcements of new findings of transmission in different groups.

MOBILIZATION AND PROTEST TACTICS

Mobilization of a protest movement leans heavily upon mass media. Whether a given tactic involves immediate publicity or not, the planners must keep an eye on how it would fare if picked up by the media. It is not easy to catalogue the tactics employed in collective action, as is evident both in the classical writings of Machiavelli and in such prescriptive works as *Rules for Radicals* (1971) by Saul Alinsky or summaries of tactics by others (Oppenheimer and Lakey, 1971; Stewart, Smith, & Denton, 1984; Simons, 1970). Even though Alinsky calls his book a "Primer for Realistic Radicals," he concentrates on rules of organization rather than specific steps for action.

The principles of protest tactics may be summarized under the headings of (1) legitimization and delegitimization; (2) the critical importance of drama; (3) capitalizing on unforeseen events; (4) anticipating reaction of adversaries and (5) creating a protest-controlled medium or media system.

LEGITIMATION AND DELEGITIMATION

Weber's analysis of the role of legitimacy in modern social organization (Gerth & Mills, 1946) has fundamental importance for protest strategy. A group seeks to strengthen its own claim to legitimacy by challenging the legitimacy of an established power group or its actions (Ball-Rokeach, 1972; Oberschall, 1973; Anderson, 1969). Legitimation for a protest group may stem from its own organized strength, as when a protest group demonstrates that it can draw huge crowds or capture the following of thousands of shipyard workers. Such success indicates that the protest group is a power to be reckoned with.

To ridicule the established agency, such as a University's sponsoring of CIA recruiting, is not enough. To be effective, the group doing the ridiculing must somehow establish itself as worthy of respect while facing established groups' efforts to *de*legitimize the protest. Student activists of the 1960s were often portrayed by police and media as scruffy, window-breaking brats needing old-fashioned discipline (Gitlin, 1980).

Protest groups may gain legitimacy through association, as when an established group or powerful public official speaks on behalf of the cause being protested. Lyndon Johnson's strong speech supporting the Selma and Birmingham protests against civil rights abuses is a case in point (Garrow, 1978). Fraternizing with security forces is a related tactic for gaining some legitimacy and repectability (Oppenheimer & Lakey, 1971).

THE CRITICAL IMPORTANCE OF DRAMA

Protest is a highly creative and interactive enterprise, in which participants engage in a constant "struggle for novelty" (Hilgartner & Bosk, 1988). A spectacular incident, such as publicly burning a draft card, owes its impact to the way it shocks when first encountered. Farmers shooting calves or driving tractors to Washington, D.C. in protest of low prices; students symbolizing police as pigs; a police chief's spouse getting arrested for trespass in protesting against weapons-industry policies, people placing their bodies in front of bulldozers in protest of a building project—all depend upon dramatic appeal of a first-seen or first-heard-of event which is "outside the experience" of the established groups who have difficulty figuring out how to respond (Alinsky, 1971). The effectiveness of a tactic may well decline with routine use, when the tactic becomes predictable and security forces develop countermeasures that either prevent it or strip it of its drama.

Drama comes not only also from the sudden spectacle but from the extended artwork as well—the book, theatre, the novel, or music (Leith, 1968). Major speeches and popular books such as those by McWilliams and Steinbeck are often part of the mobilization phase of a movement. The powerful oratory of Eugene Debs, Robert LaFollette and Martin Luther King are cases in point. Betty Friedan's *Feminine Mystique*, James Baldwin's *The Fire Next Time*, Rachel Carson's *Silent Spring* and Ralph Nader's *Unsafe at Any Speed* were all critical and dramatizing public statements in the early mobilization periods of the feminist, civil rights, environmental and consumer movements. Theatrical productions such as *Cry Freedom* protesting South African apartheid and novels such as *Grapes of Wrath* on the plight of dust bowl emigrants of Oklahoma may be central to the strategies of a movement. They are not new devices, as can be seen by the extensive employment of theatre or music in the French Revolution, for example. Labor union songs by Pete Seeger and civil rights messages in tunes popularized by Woody Guthrie, Bob Dylan, and Peter, Paul and Mary illustrate the role of music in popularizing protest slogans. "We Shall Overcome" dramatized the plight of minorities seeking to be treated as dignified human beings, and "Blowin' in the Wind" tied that dilemma to general worry about war.

A problem with dramatic tactics is their potential for backfire through delegitimization. In the powerline protest, some groups smeared themselves with animal feces and then encountered police and workers before TV cameras. The tactic did command media attention but may have also contributed to popular revulsion at a time when the protest had already been defeated by the courts, public agencies and utilities.

CAPITALIZING ON UNFORESEEN EVENTS

Machiavelli (1952) noted the importance of "fortune," or the unexpected event, in a maintenance of political power by the Prince, while Alinsky (1971) makes a similar point from the perspective of protest groups. The propaganda windfall to one side when the other side stumbles is well known, as when environmentalists spoke out quickly against the insensitive statements of then-Secretary of the Interior James Watt. "Tactics," according to Alinsky "require that you move with the action." He recalls a convention of representatives of poor Chicago neighborhoods on July 14, 1939 when a reporter suggested it was "too revolutionary" to hold the event on the anniversary of the French Revolution. The organizers seized upon this idea and called it the "Bastille Day" of the movement. The "proxy tactic" for shareholder voting was initiated against the employment practices of Eastman Kodak when it appeared evident that boycotts against the mammoth photographic company would not be feasible (Alinsky, 1971).

ANTICIPATING REACTION OF ADVERSARIES

Protest tactics occur not in isolation but as part of interaction with other groups whose actions must be anticipated and who will similarly be analyzing what the protest group is up to (Alinsky, 1971; Johnson, 1966; Schelling, 1966). It appears that some of the major civil rights activities in the American South—such as the Birmingham demonstrations and the march on Selma—were undertaken in the anticipation of repressive police action which media would report (Garrow, 1978). At the same time, miscalculations about responses of established groups may lead to failure of a protest. A National Guard escort of non-union workers into a Minnesota meat packing plant was apparently an unforeseen strike-breaking tactic ordered by a governor whom some protesters had expected to symphathize with the union.

A PROTEST-CONTROLLED MEDIUM OR MEDIA SYSTEM

Anticipated hostility of the established media has often led protest groups to create their own newspapers, radio stations, magazines, pamphlets or other channels (Leith, 1968; Morlan, 1955; Kessler, 1984). This time-honored strategy was employed extensively during the French Revolution, the American Revolution, Polish worker protests, union movements and farm protest groups, such as the Nonpartisan League early in the twentieth century. *Ramparts* and *Rollingstone* and *Ms.* are associated with the civil rights, student, and women's rights movements, and *Modern Maturity* speaks to the interests of senior citizens. Such media often require extensive organization and member recruitment, even though they may well be instruments of further recruitment and control. They may be radical initially but moderate considerably as the movement becomes larger, socially accepted and part of the mainstream.

Media created by protest groups represent the media of the time. Newspapers, magazines and playhouse art forms were used widely by French Revolutionaries (Leith, 1968). In recent times, radio, TV, documentary films and other media have been employed in various ways, including use of a regular time slot as in the TV church ministry. The National Farmers' Organization for several years had its own weekly radio hour. At the international level, various political groups have created clandestine broadcast stations for beaming messages to larger audiences, often across borders (Soley and Nichols, 1986).

It appears that "muckracking" journalism occurred when populist concerns about the railroads, industrial workers, and inequities in farm commodity pricing had been widely legitimized. The muckraking writers without question played a part in drawing public attention to turn-of-the-century problems, but it seems unlikely that muckrakers created initial problem definitions. Upton Sinclair's *The Jungle* drew attention to worker conditions in the meat packing industry, a problem that had been long debated in industrial cities. McWilliams' *Factories in the Field* and Steinbeck's *Grapes of Wrath*, both about the plight of workers in the California fruit industry in the 1930s, are primarily syntheses of problem definitions rather than initiators. They were written when resources could be mobilized by the respective groups and public responsiveness to the respective problems was possible (Staggenborg, 1988).

The role of major figures in journalism is relevant in this synthesis role. Walter Winchell, Drew Pearson, Paul Harvey, Father Coughlin, H. V. Kaltenborn, Edward R. Murrow and H. L. Mencken were all identified with countervailing social philosophies, many of them conservative. Almost without exception, these commentators spoke to stabilization rather than destabilization of the system and called for a return to previously established values and norms when crises occurred. This may be apparent with Coughlin, Harvey and Mencken, but it applies as well to Murrow who, in his famous commentary on Senator McCarthy, clearly appealed to traditional democratic values of fair play and free speech, which he contended must be supported if the system is to survive.

SIMULTANEOUS ACCELERATION AND "DAMAGE CONTROL"

Media strategies of protest groups may succeed in acceleration of issues, placing them on the public agenda and giving them a measure of legitimacy as items for priority attention. Such coverage may be simultaneously instrumental to organizational goals of protesting groups and to cooptation goals of established centers of political and economic power. Established powers have considerable control over the nature of attention given to issues as well as the means of resolution in ways that maintain the stability of their own positions. Airing of the conflict gives the appearance of acknowledging, while not validating, the position of social protesters. Such "damage-control" reporting exists alongside other damage-control structures in the system, such as wage arbitration and mediation between bankrupt farmers and lenders. Press councils were advocated as "safety valves," allowing citizens to air grievances against the media without resort to legal action, which is often seen as far more destabilizing to the existing pattern of reporting.

MEDIA AND PHASES OF CONTROVERSY

Media coverage of a controversy over a three-year period involving a high voltage powerline in Minnesota provides some insights into media reporting of social movements. The assumption is that a protest on a specific issue may be seen as a microcosm of a movement. A coordinated protest has the phases of initiatory activity, problem definition, legitimation and mobilization that characterize movements over the long term.

This controversy arose from the introduction of a radically different organization of technology for providing electrical energy to large areas, primarily metropolitan. A 400-kilovolt, direct-current line was proposed to cross 400 miles of rural area, to transmit electrical power from the coal fields of North Dakota to users in Minnesota. The line was proposed initially as preferable to hauling coal 400 miles.

The powerline was regarded by a wide range of small town groups as (1) usurpation of local rights through improper application of the principle of eminent domain and (2) threatening to human and animal health because of the use of a new transmission technology that was untested in the U.S. (Olien, Donohue and Tichenor, 1984). This issue illustrates how a movement derives much of its energy from basic values. Defining the conflict in terms of usurpation of rights of local communities raised anew a long-standing question of rural groups bearing a heavy burden for changes seen as benefiting primarily urban populations. As in most rural areas, Minnesota had witnessed a long period of economic and political power gravitating to the metropolitan areas, and the historically accumulated resentments were basic to the rural outrage against the powerline. This resentment was pointedly expressed by a picket sign at a hearing which pictured a 100-foot-high tower and the words "stick it in Minneapolis."

Patterns of media coverage of this controversy in many ways paralleled those often seen in large-scale movements. These patterns were studied through analysis of content in a metropolitan daily newspaper and the daily newspaper of a regional city during the 1975–1978 period.

There was initiating action and a problem definition phase from mid-1974 to late summer 1975, when the power utility sought but failed to get landowners to sign individual easements for the line across their land. While the initiating activity was largely in small groups, early organizational efforts received coverage from weekly newspapers and regional dailies in the affected areas. This early coverage portrayed the issues of rural hardship for urban benefit, usurpation of rights, and use of eminent domain in ways instrumental for the organizational ends of objecting groups. A newspaper in one community would reprint letters to the editor and news items from a neighboring community, including organizational details about protest groups. Several mayors, local governmental officials, bankers, clergymen and other public leaders expressed views which were often nonspecific but did lend legitimacy to the issue *as* an issue.

Metropolitan newspapers began extensive coverage during a bureaucratic confrontation phase, which included hearings and court-type action for adjudicating questions of line location and need. These hearings illustrated the way media coverage is patterned after bureaucratic procedures, which, in this case, had utilities and countervailing groups in adversarial postures. A state environmental agency served as a "neutral" party, holding the hearings but ostensibly not favoring either side. Media coverage at this point was geared almost exclusively to reports about hearings rather than to other related events.

Metropolitan television stations increased their visual coverage of this controversy after the hearings ended with decisions favoring line construction. In summer of 1976, a series of confrontations occurred between construction crews and protest groups, and the controversy went into a new phase. Television coverage then remained high throughout the controversy, winding down in early 1978 after line construction was completed.

There was also heavy media coverage of various mediation efforts which were attempted, without success, in late 1976 and early 1977. There was then a "cooling off" period, which ended abruptly in September 1977, when the Supreme Court ruled that the line could be built. Opposition groups, the Court said, had not met the burden of proving that the line would be hazardous to human or animal health. This marked the beginning of the final phase of the controversy. Various editorials called for the protesting groups to now let the project proceed, since they had had "their day in court." A variety of media event strategies occurred during this final phase. These included picketing, blocking the movement of construction equipment, flag waving, singing, spraying ammonia gas at a construction site and giving flowers to highway patrolmen. There were a few altercations; several protesters were arrested; some damage to property; and a utility association guard was shot and injured slightly.

MEDIA COVERAGE AND SOCIAL INTEGRATION

Throughout a period of social controversy, media coverage is part of a process of integration, which consists of working through, interpreting and redefining tensions in ways that make the issue amenable to accomodations that appear to be resolutions. Media reports often, if not usually, appeal to universal views about participation and the rights of groups to be heard. Just as hearings create the impression of concerned citizens having their "day in court," newspaper and TV coverage may be seen as giving the protest its "day in the media."

The powerline controversy highlighted the role of public-opinion polling in issue legitimation. A Minneapolis newspaper at a later point conducted a statewide poll, asking "Which side do you think is right—the farmers or the power associations?" In both rural and urban areas, more said "farmers" than "power associations," and this widely reported gauge of popular feeling lent considerable credence to the issue.

Content analysis produced several conclusions. One is that protest groups indeed can succeed in gaining extensive media attention to their views through the employment of media strategies. A count of attribution of statements indicated that protest group sources were mentioned more frequently during the high coverage periods than were the utilities, state agencies, or law enforcement agencies.

Throughout the entire period, the statements attributed to the protest groups in the newspapers totalled about 40% of all such attributions, with 18% attributed to the utilities and 42% to state agencies and law enforcement agencies combined.

While the protest groups received extensive media attention, the coverage does not constitute what might be called watchdog-type surveillance. In a midwestern state, the cultural value placed on survival of small-town institutions and values is high, in spite of a general preference for the amenities of metropolitan areas as places to reside. Once groups had organized to raise issues based on these values and institutions, media response was to be expected. It was the initiating phase of the controversy, ahead of media coverage, that produced the basic definition of the issue as one of abrogation of property rights and small towns bearing an unfair burden of social progress. The implication was that if unwanted structures of this type could be forced on a small town, they could be forced in anywhere. The media coverage drew attention to this definition of the problem but also to the definitions offered by the utilities, the hearing examiner, the sheriff departments, the state governor and a religious leader who offered his "good offices" to try to work out a solution. At no point was there a media editorial position suggesting that the procedure established for locating powerlines or other such technology was inappropriate. The state siting law had been seen as a political innovation and the media editorial posture was generally one of how to get the powerline and yet acknowledge the protesters' concerns.

The media image, at the point of the heaviest coverage in late 1977 and early 1978, was of a protest group suffering a massive defeat rather than winning its point. The highest court in the state had sanctioned construction, and protests after that point were presented by the media as a last-ditch struggle that was bound to lose. While earlier media coverage had contributed to protest group legitimacy, this coverage gave a definition of *illegitimacy*. The regional and metropolitan daily newspapers editorialized during the peak coverage period that the protest groups had had a chance to be heard and should now allow the line construction to go ahead. This was "cooling out" of the protest.

By March 1978, which was after most construction was completed, coverage dropped off dramatically. It is also important to note that after the line was built, further activity included downing of some line towers and breaking of line insulators. These actions were referred to in media reports in March and later as "vandalism," which was a major delegitimating reference.

Media coverage may be thought to determine who wins and who loses in a protest. In the case of the powerline issue, in spite of all the media events, coverage and attention, the final outcome was, with few modifications, exactly what the utilities had advocated at the outset. The entire complex of public agencies and the bureaucratized hearings were structured to put the burden of proof on the protesters to indicate why the line should *not* be built, and not on the proponents to show why it *should* be built. The procedures set up by the state were on the side of the status quo, and this is the side that eventually prevailed in the media, in spite of heavy coverage and the fact that a well-known, former campus protester helped lead the protest group during the "last ditch" demonstrations. As in the anti-war demonstrations of nearly a decade earlier, media coverage of the powerline controversy produced an image of an intense, dedicated group fighting a lost cause (Gitlin, 1980).

This outcome can be contrasted with other situations in which protest groups appear to win in an arena of intense media coverage. Following the powerline episode, a Twin Cities planning agency attempted to establish a hazardous waste facility in the metropolitan area and get several million dollars of federal funds for doing so. Suburban groups, dominated by affluent and powerful professionals, packed the auditoriums and told TV crews, "this is our powerline." After a few such hearings, the waste site proposal was abandoned. Similarly, a protest group appeared to succeed in blocking establishment of a new airport at Toronto by facing down bulldozers at the construction site. This controversy was similar to the powerline controversy in involving exercise of the principle of eminent domain and its implications for loss of private property. There were crucial differences, one being that the Toronto airport project involved inter-province issues (Montreal vs. Toronto competition for air service) and opposition to the project from a key legitimizer—Air Canada (Milch, 1984).

CONCLUSION

This review of the literature and examination of a particular controversy suggests several generalizations about the role of media in social movements.

(1) *Media serve not as watchdogs for a general public, but primarily as guard dogs for powerful interests and mainstream values.* Initial reporting of a counter movement in the system will generally be skeptical, if not hostile, and the problem will be defined according to its ramifications for the existing power relationships.

(2) *Media play accelerating rather than initiating roles in social movements.* While not structured so as to initiate individual protests or major movements, media are major information resources and will be sought by all parties to an issue for information purposes.

(3) *In addition to accelerating roles, media play decelerating or "cooling out"roles.* A characteristic of protests and social movements is what seems to be a finite life or attention span. The issue will not stay alive forever, and the length of its life depends upon major acts or events that define where the balance of power rests. When Theodore Roosevelt put a pejorative label on the investigative journalists of his time, the tone of their coverage and the general reaction to it changed (Reaves, 1984). When all state agencies say a powerline can and will be built, the opposition is marginalized in print and on the airwaves as a last-ditch stand. While there is no denying that mass media play a vital role in system maintenance and stability, this stability comes at a cost, which includes suppression of dissent and stifling of innovation and full expression of diverse views.

(4) *While media coverage of issues tends to reinforce established authority, the flow of information does increase in intense periods, as expected by social-conflict theory.* The populist, union, women's rights and civil rights movements were intense periods and the various media-event strategies and confrontations were associated with heavy periods of coverage. While the outcome of the muckrakers coverage has been debated, there is no question that it was a period of high information flow about social issues. The same can be said for the environmental movement and the powerline protest.

While they are not independent Fourth Estate watchdogs, mass media do have a vital information role in social movements. This role promises to be more important than ever in an increasingly pluralistic society for public perceptions of social movements and what they portend for the human condition.

REFERENCES

Alinsky, S. (1971). *Rules for radicals: A pragmatic primer for realistic radicals.* New York: Random House.

Aminzade, R. R. (1981). *Class, politics, and early industrial capitalism: A study of mid-19th century Toulouse, France.* Albany, NY: State University of New York Press.

Anderson, W. (1969). *The Age of protest.* Pacific Palisades, CA: Goodyear Publishing.

Ball-Rokeach, S. J. (1972). The legitimation of violence. In J. E. Short, Jr., & M. E. Wolfgang (Eds.), *Collective violence.* Chicago & New York: Aldine-Atherton.

Bottomore, T., Harris, L., Kiernan, V. G., & Miliband, R. (1983). *A dictionary of Marxist thought.* Cambridge, MA: Harvard University Press.

Boyce, G. (1978). The fourth estate: The reappraisal of a concept. In G. Boyce, J. Curran, & P. Wingate (Eds.), *Newspaper history: From the 17th century to the present day.* London & New York: Constable/Sage.

Breed, W. (1958). Mass communication and sociocultural integration. *Social Forces, 37,* 109–116.

Carlyle, T. (1841, 1963). *On heroes and hero worship.* London: Oxford University Press.

Cigler, A. J., & Hansen, J. M. (1983). Group formation through protest: The American agriculture movement. In A. J. Cigler (Ed.), *Interest group politics.* Washington, DC: Congressional Quarterly Press.

Coser, L. (1954). *The functions of social conflict.* New York: Macmillan.

Coser, L. (1967). *Continuities in the study of social conflict.* New York: Macmillan.

Dahrendorf, R. (1959). *Class and class conflict in industrial society.* Stanford, CA: Stanford University Press.

Dangerfield, L. A., McCartney, H. P., & Starcher, A. T. (1975). How did mass communication, as sentry, perform in the gasoline "crunch?" *Journalism Quarterly, 52,* 316–320.

Donohue, G. A., Olien, C. N., & Tichenor, P. J. (1985). Leader and editor views of role of press in community development. *Journalism Quarterly, 62,* 367–372.

Donohue, G. A., Tichenor, P. J., & Olien, C. N. (1973). Mass media functions, knowledge and social control. *Journalism Quarterly, 50,* 652–659.

Donohue, G. A., Tichenor, P. J., & Olien, C. N. (1984). Media evaluations and group power. In A. Arno & W. Dissanayake (Eds.), *The news media in national and international conflict* (pp. 203–215). Boulder, CO & London: Westview Press.

Edelstein, A., & Schulz, J. B. (1963). The weekly newspaper's leadership role as seen by community leaders. *Journalism Quarterly, 40,* 565–574.

Friedman, S. (1981). Blueprint for breakdown: Three Mile Island and the media before the accident. *Journal of Communication, 31 (2),* 116–128.

Gamson, W. A. (1975). *The strategy of social protest.* Homewood, IL: Dorsey

Garrow, D. J. (1978). *Protest at Selma: Martin Luther King and the voting rights act of 1965.* New Haven, CT: Yale University Press.

Gerth, H. H., & Mills, C. W. (1946). *From Max Weber.* New York: Oxford University Press.

Gitlin, T. (1980). *The whole world is watching.* Berkeley: University of California Press.

Herman, E. S. (1985). Diversity of news: Marginalizing the opposition. *Journal of Communication, 35(3),* 135–146.

Hilgartner, S., & Bosk, C. L. (1988). The rise and fall of social problems: A public arenas model. *American Journal of Sociology, 94,* 53–78.

Hutchins, R. M. (1947). *A free and responsible press: A general report on mass communication.* Chicago: University of Chicago Press.

Ickes, H. (1943). *Autobiography of a curmudgeon.* New York: Reynal and Hitchcock.

Janowitz, M. (1952). *The community press in an urban setting.* New York: Free Press.

Jenkins, J. C. (1983). Resource mobilization theory and the study of social movements. *Annual Review of Sociology, 9,* 527–553.

Johnson, C. (1966). *Revolutionary change.* Boston: Little, Brown.

Kessler, L. (1980). The ideas of woman suffragists and the Portland *Oregonian. Journalism Quarterly, 57,* 597–605.

Kessler, L. (1984). *The dissident press: Alternative journalism in American history.* Beverly Hills, CA: Sage.

La Piere, R. T. (1965). *Social change.* New York: McGraw-Hill.

Laski, H. (1943). *Reflections on the revolution of our time.* New York: Viking Press.

Leith, J. A. (1968). *Media and revolution.* Toronto: CBC Publications.

Lemert, J. B., & Larkin, J. P. (1979). Some reasons why mobilizing information fails to be in letters to the editor. *Journalism Quarterly, 56,* 504–512.

Leonard, T. C. (1986). *The power of the press: The birth of American political reporting.* New York: Oxford.

Lippmann, W. (1925). *The phantom public.* New York: Harcourt, Brace.

Machiavelli, N. (1952). *The prince.* New York: New American Library.

McCarthy, J. D., & Zald, M. N. (1977). Resource mobilization and social movements: A partial theory. *American Journal of Sociology, 82,* 1212–41.

Milch, J. (1984). The Toronto airport controversy. In D. Nelkin (Ed.), *Controversy: Politics of technical decisions* (2nd ed., pp. 27–49). Beverly Hills, CA: Sage.

Molotch H., & Lester, M. (1975). Accidental news: The great oil spill as local occurrence and national event. *American Journal of Sociology, 81,* 235–260.

Morlan, R. (1955) *Political prairie fire.* Minneapolis: University of Minnesota Press.

Morley, D. (1976). Industrial conflict and the mass media. *The Sociological Review, New Series,* (May), 245–268.

Morris, M. B. (1973). Newspapers and the new feminists: Black out as social control? *Journalism Quarterly, 50,* 37–42.

Murdock, G. (1973). Political deviance: The press presentation of a mass demonstration. In S. Cohen and J. Young (Eds.), *The manufacture of news* (pp. 206–225). Beverly Hills, CA: Sage.

Myrdal, G. (1944). *An American dilemma.* New York: Harper.

Oberschall, A. (1973). *Social conflict and social movements.* Englewood Cliffs, NJ: Prentice-Hall.

Ogburn, W. F. (1964). *On culture and social change.* (O. D. Duncan, Ed.). Chicago: University of Chicago Press.

Olien, C. N., Donohue, G. A., & Tichenor, P. J. (1968). The community editor's power and the reporting of conflict. *Journalism Quarterly, 37,* 442–478.

Olien, C. N., Donohue, G. A., & Tichenor, P. J. (1984). Media and stages of social conflict. *Journalism Monographs, 90* (November).

Oppenheimer, M., & Lakey, G. (1971). Direct action tactics, In H. A. Hornstein (Ed.), *Social intervention* (pp. 558–565). New York: Free Press

Paletz, D., & Entman, R. M. (1981). *Media power politics.* New York: Free Press.

Paletz, D. L., Reichert, P., & McIntyre, B. (1971). How the media support local government authority. *Public Opinion Quarterly, 35,* 808–92.

Reaves, S. (1984). How radical were the muckrakers? Socialist press views, 1902–1906. *Journalism Quarterly, 61,* 763–770.

Schelling, T. C. (1966). *The strategy of conflict.* Cambridge, MA: Harvard University Press.

Shepherd, R. G. (1981). Selectivity of sources: Reporting the marijuana controversy. *Journal of Communication, 31(2),* 129–137.

Shoemaker, P. (1984). Media treatment of deviant groups. *Journalism Quarterly, 61,* 66–75.

Shoemaker, P. (1987). Mass communication by the book: A review of 31 texts. *Journal of Communication, 37(3),* 109–131.

Simons, H. W. (1970). Requirements, problems, and strategies: A theory of persuasion for social movements. *The Quarterly Journal of Speech, 56,* 1–11.

Smelser, N. J. (1959). *Social change in the industrial revolution: An application of theory to the British cotton industry, 1770–1840.* Chicago: University of Chicago Press.

Smelser, N. J. (1962). *Theory of collective behavior.* New York: Free Press.

Soley, L. C. and Nichols, J. S. (1986). *Clandestine radio broadcasting.* New York: Praeger.

Sood, R., Stockdale, G., & Rogers, E, M. (1987). How the news media operate in natural disasters. *Journal of Communication, 37(3),* 27–41.

Staggenborg, S. (1988). The consequences of professionalization and formalization in the pro-choice movement. *American Sociological Review, 88,* 585–606.

Stewart, C., Smith, C., & Denton, R. E. (1984). *Persuasion and social movements.* Prospect Heights, IL: Waveland.

Strodthoff, G. G., Hawkins, R. P., & Schoenfeld, A. C. (1985). Media roles in a social movement: A model of ideology diffusion. *Journal of Communication, 35(2),* 135–153.

Tichenor, P. J., Donohue, G. A., Olien, C. N., & Bowers, J. K. (1971). Environment and opinion. *The Journal of Environmental Education, 2(4),* 38–42.

Tichenor, P. J., Donohue, G. A., & Olien, C. N. (1980). *Community conflict and the press.* Beverly Hills, CA: Sage.

Tichenor, P. J., Olien, C. N., Harrison, A., & Donohue, G. A. (1970). Mass communication systems and communication accuracy in science news reporting. *Journalism Quarterly, 47,* 673–683.

Tocqueville, A. de (1947). *Democracy in America.* (Henry Reeve, trans.). New York: Oxford University Press.

Tuchman, G. (1978). *Making news.* News York: Free Press.

Zald, M. N., & Ash, R. (1966). Social movement organizations: Growth, decay and change. *Social Forces, 44,* 327–41.

Chapter 6

INFORMATION AND POWER: TOWARD A CRITICAL THEORY OF INFORMATION CAMPAIGNS

Lana F. Rakow

MANY SOCIAL SCIENTISTS are interested in information campaigns from the standpoint of campaign effectiveness.[1] Operating in the fields of advertising, public relations, psychology, organizational communication, interpersonal communication, political communication, and mass communication, they have looked at how and to what extent individual attitudes or behaviors are changed or could be changed through the strategic use of messages.[2] Did this market recall the brand name of the product? Did this public believe the company acted in the public interest? Did this group of clients learn where to go for help with their problem? Was the audience of the message moved to action? If not, how could they be?

That such campaigns exist and are on the increase in this country as well as world wide is taken by the social scientist as a given. This article will argue, however, that campaigns should be considered an issue of contemporary life, not a fact of it.[3] Why do we live in a world of information campaigns, and whose interests are served by them? By taking a sociological perspective on the production of information rather than a psychological perspective on the reception of information it will be seen that information campaigns arise out of a particular configuration of social relations in this country which gives institutions power over individuals. Social scientists reproduce these power relations when they fail to account for their own underlying assumptions about both the nature of information and the role of information campaigns. A critical theory of information campaigns is a necessary corrective; that is, the social scientist must stand outside of the paradigm of researchers and practitioners who are interested in improving the effectiveness of information campaigns in order to see them from a different perspective.

THE NATURE OF INFORMATION

To construct a critical theory of information campaigns, one must first look at the notion of information that underlies them. Even the very choice of the word *information* is strategic, since, as Brenda Dervin (1976) has observed, *information* is now a "go" word. Of course, not all campaign planners resort to the word *information,* instead referring to their efforts as *persuasion*. But *persuasion* is a word increasingly out of fashion. It is too close to *propaganda* and suspicions of manipulation.[4] Hence one can understand the history of public relations practitioners being called "public information officers" and the contemporary attention to "information processing," stemming in part from an increased perception of individuals as active and rational rather than irrational and persuadable.[5] Consult almost any advertising textbook for a justification of the system of advertising on the basis of its "information" function in the economy.

The implication is that information is raw material about the world, untainted by party interests or special pleading. From such a perspective, to provide information is to perform at the least, a neutral task, at the best, a socially commendable one. This view of information is what Dervin (1981) calls the "information as thing" notion, an understanding of information as something that can be dumped into the heads of individuals, that corresponds directly to "reality," independent of the observer. Such a notion is not a new one. It stems from the Cartesian legacy that mind and matter are separate, that language merely names a world that already exists, that, as human beings, our mental perceptions of things are only approximations of that world that is independent of us. Walter Lippmann, in *Public Opinion* (1922), crystalized the notion for contemporary researchers and practitioners. Lippmann surveyed with pessimism the capacity for humans to develop an accurate mental representation of the world; individuals operate on the basis of "pseudo-environments" in their heads which are inaccurate approximations of reality, he surmised. Lippmann is still widely quoted in articles and textbooks, and the idea for which he served as spokesperson is widely accepted. For example, the classic public relations textbook, *Effective Public Relations*, (Cutlip, Center, & Broom, 1985) cites Lippmann's barriers to communication and his characterization of individuals' operating on the basis of stereotypes rather than fact. William McGuire, a recognized theorist on persuasion, states that knowledge is:

> a representation of reality in terms sufficiently simplified and adapted to human cognitive capacities so that we can deal with it. Knowledge thus has at best an imperfect accuracy, representing reality correctly enough to guide our adapting to it but inevitably over-simplifying and distorting the thing in itself by transforming it to the kind of cognitive representation with which we can cope. Knowledge is not a perfect map of the thing known but without it one has to move through the environment with no map at all. (McGuire, 1981, pp. 41–42)

The Cartesian notion of information stands in contrast to a critical theory of knowledge, for which one must look outside of the dominant paradigm.[6] Here knowledge is seen as the product of human activity resulting from the human act of naming, which *creates* the world in which we live. To "name" the world is to create it, Paulo Freire (1970) tells us. No knowledge is divorced from human interest, according to Jürgen Habermas (1971); the positivistic belief in facts conceals the a priori human construction of the world which scientists believe they are merely describing. Dorothy Smith (1978) points out that men have put themselves in the position to produce the forms of thought and symbols that express and order the world we live in, depriving women of participation in creating the general currency of thought. Stuart Hall (1984) traces a history of the "sociology of knowledge" in an attempt to rescue a politics in which the roots of ideas can be seen in relation to material production.

These examples from the critical literature suggest that information must be thought of in relation to its production because information is always a particular account. One must know, then, who produces information for what purposes. Smith (1978) points out that the forms of thought and images that comprise our culture do not arise out of people's everyday lived relations; rather, they are "manufactured" by the "ideological apparatus" of society. David Altheide and John Johnson (1980) use the related concept of bureaucratic organizations, asserting that such organizations, through official accounts of themselves ("propaganda"), create a world that explains and justifies their existence and actions and provides the common-sense basis for the social order. James Coleman (1974, 1982) uses the term *corporate actor* to refer to legal entities whose values and purposes have come to dominate society and who control most of the information surrounding any transaction with individuals. Herbert Schiller (1981, 1984) argues that the government and the corporate sector have become the main producers of information, producing that which is most useful to their military and economic purposes.

It might be argued in response that surely not all information is self-serving and partial; there are sectors of society that have the best interest of the public at heart rather than their own. Yet even in these cases, the ideological basis underlying the information created and acted upon can be uncovered. For example, the medical profession and scientists have, over time, given varying accounts of women's biological and social nature, ranging from pronouncements that women are defective to pronouncements that they are incomplete, neurotic, superfluous or dangerous (see Ehrenreich & English, 1979). Ostensibly acting in women's best interest, these scientists were doing anything but. Such examples remind us of the danger of any institution's taking it upon itself to determine the best interest of the rest of society, no matter how well-meaning that institution's intentions.

As a consequence of the general currency of the culture being created by only certain segments of society, knowledge from other sources is "senseless," has no meaning, because what is considered information or knowledge makes sense within the logic of the very system that created it. Other knowledge falls outside that logic. In fact, Kathy Ferguson (1984, p. 44) argues that "the very definition of knowledge has come to serve the interests of other organizations in the technical society," which coincides with Altheide and Johnson's (1980) description of how bureaucracies draw on and reaffirm the socially constructed reality by using the logic of "official" information—statistics, annual reports, and so on—in a chicken-and-egg process. "Subjugated knowledges" (Foucault's term, 1981) are those from other groups and other contexts that are disqualified as inadequate because they fall outside the dominant definition of reality.

It is a self-perpetuating cycle, then. Information produced by organizations in a position to produce information justifies those organizations' right and ability to do so. Perhaps the "knowledge-gap" hypothesis which has received so much attention from media researchers should be reformulated. The hypothesis suggests that the more information is disseminated through the mass media, the greater becomes the relative disparity of knowledge possessed by various groups (Olien, Donohue, & Tichenor, 1983).[7] Instead, one might hypothesize a "knowledge-production gap": the more information certain bureaucratic organizations have come to produce, the greater becomes the relative disparity of knowledge produced by them as compared to others in society. This is an argument made by Schiller (1984, p. 34), who observes that the more information has come to be a privatized commodity, a process aided by the government, the less legitimate information function traditional producers and preservers of knowledge—universities and libraries, for example—are seen to have. The information that is produced is not simply bought and sold, however; it is also put into the public-policy process (by providing ready-made information to journalists, for example), as Oscar Gandy (1982) has investigated. Both uses of information constitute an exercise in power. The important point to be grasped is that not only is the possession of knowledge unequally distributed, but perhaps more importantly, its production is unequally distributed.[8]

There is yet another twist one might offer to the familiar "knowledge gap" hypothesis. Instead of comparing the knowledge possessed by groups of individuals of varying socioeconomic backgrounds, what if one compares the knowledge possessed by bureaucratic organizations with that of individuals? Under what conditions does that gap widen? If there is any group that does not suffer from a lack of information, for example, it is business, for business can create information, buy it, get it from the government, sell it, and extract it from individuals. Yet business does not have the same obligation to give *out* information that individuals do, on the justification that a business's information is "proprietary," that is, privately owned, and that it is necessary to the particular business's competitive strategy. In contrast, ask any individual who has ever applied for a bank loan, for a job, or for welfare benefits how much information about himself or herself he or she is "allowed" to consider "proprietary," despite the fact that its divulgence might interfere with his or her ability to compete in that particular "marketplace."[9] Furthermore, organizations put tremendous effort into acquiring other kinds of information about individuals—their purchase patterns and personality traits, for example—in order to better predict their behavior.

It is staggering to consider what it might be like to live in a society in which the effort and financial resources put into prying out of individuals how they behave and why they behave that way were instead devoted to forcing such information out of bureaucratic organizations.[10] If one were to investigate this "information disclosure gap," one would have to account for the role of social scientists. If we ceased prying information out of individuals, many social scientists would be out of a job, including, of course, those interested in the effectiveness of information campaigns.

Bureaucratic organizations are, then, selective about the information they provide, which exposes the myth that simply providing information is a commendable activity. Organizations control which information will be made available to whom because their goal is not really to inform but rather to control (see Phelan, 1977 and Gandy, 1982 for more discussion of this point). If the intent were strictly to inform, there would be no concern on the part of researchers and practitioners about attitude or behavior change, which is why so much effort is put into tailoring the messages created for individuals in order that the "desired effect" (desired by the sponsoring organization, not the individual) can be produced. That one can presume to have even the *right* to persuade someone else, let alone the *responsibility* to do so is never questioned, yet Sally Miller Gearhart (1979) raises the possibility that our cultural preoccupation with persuasion reflects a conquest mentality that justifies the "violence" (invasiveness) of strategies to change others, reflecting a larger cultural—masculine—propensity to dominate and conquer.

As a consequence of these selective strategies, other information will not be created or provided. What information is a consumer in a target market going to be given about a product? Its possible health hazards? The affirmative action record of the corporation producing it? The number of product liability claims pending against the manufacturer? What information is a potential client of a social service agency going to be given? How to beat the system that put her in the situation in the first place? Who benefits from a system that puts her at the bottom? Why behaviors such as drug use or teenage pregnancy are portrayed as the country's most important problems and not militarism, violence against women, or homelessness? Why is the medical profession targeting individuals with health messages such as restriction of cholesterol intake rather than targeting government and industry who are responsible for the actions and policies that put carcinogens in our food, pollute our planet, determine whose health problems get research attention, and the like?

Information, then, cannot be thought of as innocent or some "pure good." It is the product of social relations, and, at this particular point in time, it is by and large produced by institutions to suit their own purposes.

THE ROLE OF INFORMATION CAMPAIGNS

Having analyzed the assumptions behind the notion of information, one can turn to the larger problem of information campaigns. It is not surprising that we should be seeing the convergence of what has generally been discrete areas of research—advertising, public relations, and public information campaigns (generally "educational" campaigns by social welfare organizations)—under a general umbrella called information campaigns.[11] The strategies and assumptions of these research areas are remarkably similar, as shall be seen.

Underlying all of these information campaigns is a social theory that is seldom made explicit but is nonetheless accepted as inevitable and acceptable. The social theory has three components which will be examined here: the metaphor of the marketplace, pluralism, and progressivism. The metaphor of the marketplace to describe how society can and should work was articulated by Adam Smith in the eighteenth century and John Stuart Mill in the nineteenth century. From this metaphor has come the justification and model for the operation of our U.S. economy as well as our political system. Individuals competing in the free economic marketplace were presumed by Smith to produce the smoothly functioning society. Ideas competing in the free marketplace, Mill said, borrowing the metaphor, would produce a smoothly functioning and just democratic society. Both formulations rest on the notion of individuals "voting" in the ballot box and marketplace, choosing the best products and the best ideas among the unlimited (because of open competition) variety available to them. The classic formulation of how democracy supposedly works is described by C. Wright Mills (1956, pp. 299–300):

> The people are presented with problems. They discuss them. They decide on them. They formulate viewpoints. These viewpoints are orga-

nized, and they compete. One viewpoint 'wins out.' Then the people act out this view, or their representatives are instructed to act it out, and this they promptly do.

Few people probably believe that this is an accurate description of U.S. democracy at work (despite what high-school civics textbooks might say), though they may disagree over why the system does not work in this way. Bernard Berelson (1952), in a critique echoing Lippmann thirty years earlier, blamed the electorate for not having the appropriate personality structures; for being uninterested, apathetic, uninformed and unprincipled; for its unwillingness to engage in discussion, and for its inability to make rational judgments and consider the community interest. In contrast, critical scholars lay the blame not on the public, but on structures of power that prevent the public from carrying out the democratic process. These structures of power rest on a relationship that makes institutions subjects and people objects, a relationship that underlies information campaigns.

Mills (1956) and John Phelan (1977) both make an incisive critique of the myth of democratic theory and of the myth of the recalcitrant, deficient public. Mills argues that structural transformations (such as the enlargement of the size of the public and a shift from community association to groups of organized power) along with the rise of the mass media have prevented a true "public society" from forming; instead a form of "mass society" has been created.[12] The two are distinguished by such characteristics as the ratio of speakers to receivers (in a public society, everyone has equal opportunity to speak, but in a mass society, a spokesperson addresses million), sanctions against answering back (a mass society has rules about who can speak, when, and for how long), the relation of opinion to action (in a public society, there is a direct relationship) and the degree of autonomy from instituted authority (less in a mass society). The most important distinction, however, follows:

> The public and the mass may be most readily distinguished by their dominant modes of communication: in a community of publics, discussion is the ascendant means of communication, and the mass media, if they exist, simply enlarge and animate discussion, linking one *primary public* with the discussions of another. In a mass society, the dominant type of communication is the formal media, and the publics become mere *media markets*: all those exposed to the contents of given mass media. (Mills, 1956, p. 304)

Because the myth of the classic democratic model still prevails, however, despite a structure which prevents its operation, powerful and large-scale interest groups compete to capture public opinion, Mills argues, which is still believed to be the source of democratic power.[13]

Phelan (1977), too, contrasts two models of society: the traditional forum of public opinion, characterized by shared values and groups who participate in debate and compromise, and the transitional forum of public opinion, characterized by a loss of the legitimation and shared values that allow all issues to be debatable. Though neither model exists in a pure state, U.S. society is closer to the transitional forum, where genuine, debatable issues no longer exist.[14] Instead, issues have been converted into commodities. In fact, Phelan says, John Stuart Mill's marketplace of ideas is no longer a metaphor; issues are not *like* products, they *are* products, packaged and mass marketed. The media, government, and corporations are all "devoted to controlling publics by turning them into nothing but paying (or voting) customers in a passive audience" (1977, p. 28). All three spend huge sums of money to process and shape information, but the purpose is not to inform but rather to control.

Despite such critiques as these, researchers and practitioners rely on the marketplace metaphor to justify the necessity and ethics of engaging in information campaigns. If one accepts the metaphor, it is possible to justify the role of organizations in providing information to the public and competing for public favor. But such an acceptance belies the unequal distribution of the power to produce and control information and the structural relations of power that consign the public to a passive political role. Researchers and campaign planners who accept the marketplace metaphor do not acknowledge, nor are they likely to believe, that power lies in the hands of the organizations which they represent. After all, the reason that campaign effectiveness is a pursued research area is that the power of an organization to change attitudes and behaviors is so elusive and difficult to predict. Advertisers, public relations practitioners, and others would be delighted if they could be assured of the kind of power to persuade that critics suggest they already have. The discrepancy between assessments of power held by campaigners and the critics lies in the difference between a microscopic view of the psychological processes of the individual (who happily continues to resist the prediction and control that campaigners would like to have over her/him) and a macroscopic view of the sociological processes of a culture.

Rather than locating power in their own hands, then, campaigners locate it in the aggregate opinions of individuals, a common definition of public opinion.[15] Advertising and marketing textbooks assert that a business or industry only succeeds by the approval of the buying public. Public relations textbooks state that public opinion is the raison d'être for the existence of public relations. For example, the authors of *Effective Public Relations* (Cutlip, Center, & Broom, 1985, p. 151) claim, "The power of public opinion must be faced, understood, and dealt with. It provides the psychological environment in which organizations prosper or perish." This power of public opinion has grown steadily since the U.S. won its freedom and forged a system of government that rests on public opinion, they go on. Curiously, the authors see no contradiction between this view of public opinion as powerful and their accompanying statements that the goal of public relations is to manage it, a contradiction summed up concisely in this sentence: "Public opinion gets its power through individuals, who must be persuaded and organized." If individuals can, must and should be persuaded, where does the power actually lie? In the individuals? Or in the hands of those who do the persuading?[16]

Rather than locating public opinion as the *source* of power, it is more accurate to locate public opinion as a *site* of power, described (again unwittingly) by the authors of the same text:

> Because what people see, hear or read is recognized as a primary force influencing their opinions, there is an inevitable struggle as to what the public shall or shall not see, hear, or read. *This competition for individuals' minds* becomes a battle of communication and censorship, waged with slogans, symbols, and stereotypes in all media of communication, in our schools, plants, stores, and offices. Communication and censorship, or the lack of them, tend to regulate one's opinions and the rate of change. (Cutlip, Center, & Broom, 1985, p. 175) (Emphasis added)

Despite this admission that public opinion is the *result* of information campaigns, the same chapter locates the source of opinions held by individuals in such places as personality, environment, culture, the family, religion, school, economic and social class, race, and age, without any awareness that these factors are also products of the social production of knowledge. But the passage does reveal clearly that public opinion can be considered powerful if it is thought of as the "prize" that winning organizations acquire; that is, the winners are those organizations that can get their interpretation of what the public "really" thinks to stick (i.e., be accepted in the news media and by public policy makers). Altheide and Johnson make the same point:

> It is the strategy of the organizational propagandist wittingly or unwittingly to cultivate the assumptions and 'knowledge' of these targets for personal gain. . . . The public belief in consensus government and the concomitant symbolic necessity to achieve legitimacy when possible urge practitioners of information control to obtain public approval. Such approval is seldom given, but is inferred from the lack of massive protest. . . . [T]he public may be used as part of a strategy to support an individual or program . . . [C]laims [are] made that the public is 'behind me'. . . . (Altheide & Johnson, 1980, p. 15)

In sum, the marketplace metaphor provides a justification for the competition of organizations for public opinion under the guise that the public, not the organizations themselves, is the powerful actor in and arbiter of public affairs. Along with this justification is a belief that all groups and organizations are free and equally able to compete for resources and favor in the marketplace, which is a belief in pluralism. The power of any one organization or kind of organization is denied by making this claim of "equal opportunity to compete." "Fortunately," Cutlip, Center, and Broom (1985, p. 174) say, "this country is too large and too diverse for any single group, class, or ideological view to prevail." Society really is nothing but a neutral backdrop against which ideas can play themselves out and organizations accomplish their socially useful ends, from this perspective.

With this pluralistic notion of equal groups moving about on this neutral field comes further justification for information campaigns. Such campaigns oil the movement of these groups and keep the various elements of society working harmoniously, if competitively. As the official statement of the Public Relations Society of American claims:

> Public relations helps our complex, pluralistic society to reach decisions and function more effectively by contributing to mutual understanding among groups and institutions. It serves to bring public and public policies into harmony. (published in Cutlip, Center, & Broom, 1985, p. 5)

A less flattering characterization of the same process calls the conflict between organizations for recognition, support and symbolic legitimacy "democratic feudalism" and "seething pluralism" (Altheide & Johnson, 1980, p. 34).

Leaving aside the question of whether or not a pluralistic society is a desirable social order, there is little evidence to suggest that we now have one. The ability of particular organizations to define reality and make it stick has already been pointed out here and documented elsewhere. Other perspectives and other groups lack the resources and legitimacy to make any substantial inroads into this cycle, though they do make the attempt. But to suggest that any group can simply join in the foray, plan and execute an information campaign, and stand back to see whether the public votes it a winner is naive.[17] This is particularly true for a group that is bent on changing the social system, which would mean changing the underlying subject-object relation that constitutes information campaigns. As David Shugarman (1974, p. 12) says:

> Reformers tend to play by the rules of the system in order to bring about changes in sub-systems. . . . Revolutionaries tend to challenge the rules. The rules (laws, norms, conventions) of a system *are* functional—they maintain the system. Thus, from a revolutionary perspective it may be argued that if you play by the rules you will either lose, since the rules are stacked against change on the side of those with vested interests, or if successful you will merely *improve* the functioning of the system. Ergo, the following strategy: to bring about systemic change it is necessary to play by rules which negate and contradict those in practice.

With this insight, it is possible to see why the reform arms of social movements rather than the revolutionary arms have more "success"; that is, they may accomplish limited objectives, such as increased opportunities for members (e.g., Black women and men, and white women), which can be granted without any substantial change in either the social structure or its system of justification. It can even be seen that it is in the best interest of powerful organizations to advocate that marginalized social groups advocate their cause in the "court of public opinion," because for them to do so presents no real threat. Hence, one can understand those in the field of public relations claiming that public relations is really a neutral tool that *any* group or organization can use for its own purposes, but then defining public relations to make this claim logically impossible. The official statement of PRSA demonstrates that public relations is clearly not intended to be a tool for *any* organization to use:

> Public relations serves a wide variety of *institutions* in society such as businesses, trade unions, government agencies, voluntary associations, foundations, hospitals and educational and religious institutions. To achieve their goals, these institutions must develop effective relationships with many different audiences or publics such as employees, members, customers, local communities, shareholders and other institutions, and with society at large. (published in Cutlip, Center, & Broom, 1985, p. 5) (Emphasis added)

Of course, there is a purpose served here by using the term *institution* rather than *ideological apparatus* or *bureaucratic organization*. But, more importantly, this passage demonstrates that those organizations that *carry out* the present society are to use public relations while other groups are to be the *object* of it. This overriding objective—to preserve the status quo—comes through loudly in all the attempts at definition in which practitioners engage (which run along the lines of "a management function of an organization to earn public understanding and acceptance"). Imagine what the definition of public relations would look like if it described the activities of those groups normally its object, who "targeted" those same institutions for *their* purposes.[18] Pluralism obviously works only for particular organizations.[19]

A final component of the social theory underlying information campaigns is a notion of progressivism, a legacy of early twentieth century ideas that intervention in society in the shape of reform efforts contributes to the progressive, evolutionary improvement of society (see Hofstadter, 1955, and Wiebe, 1966, for more discussion). In the face of obvious problems caused by unfettered industrial capitalism and of the real and perceived threat of the "lower orders," progressives sought to both improve and solidify the social order and its structure of social relations. Distrust of "the masses" and their ability to govern ("In the baldest sense, [men in power] came to fear that in a democratic society the people might rule," observes Wiebe [1966, p. 77]) and a fear of losing power led to increased government regulation to ameliorate the worst conditions of industrialism.

By this time, the classical liberal public of rational decision makers, upon which the country's notion of democracy rested, was no longer a tenable one, as the ruling power had become alienated from the kinds of people demanding to be let into it (the uneducated, new immigrants, Black women and men, white women, and so forth). The newly constituted "public" was more rhetorical than real, no longer the subject of society but its object, depoliticized and removed from decision making (Splichal, 1987, pp. 250–251), leading to John Dewey's indictment that the Public had been "eclipsed" (Dewey, 1927).

Instead of the public getting the business of the society done, then, as democratic theory would lead one to believe should occur, "experts" (scientists and other authorities) were envisioned as necessary accomplices to government and industry. Lippmann's *Public Opinion* (1922, p. 31) reflected this belief that since the masses of individuals could not be trusted to govern, a representative government must be aided by an "independent expert organization for making the unseen facts intelligible to those who have to make the decisions." Given his view that individuals were inadequate to the task of accurately representing reality mentally, experts specially trained at gathering facts about the independent world would be used to improve the process.

Not surprisingly, this is the role that scientists have come to take and this is the belief that is commonly held about the ability of only science to capture the "objective truth" about the world. The legacy has been passed on in a field such as public relations from Lippmann to Hadley Cantril to Cutlip, Center, and Broom, who quote Cantril's 1947 book *Gauging Public Opinion* approvingly:

> By and large, if people in a democracy are provided educational opportunities and ready access to information, public opinion reveals a hardheaded common sense. The more enlightened people are to the implications of events and proposals for their own self-interest, *the more likely they are to agree with the more objective opinions of realistic experts.* (Cutlip, Center, & Broom, 1985, p. 178) (Emphasis added)

Cantril reflects the increasing reassurance of society's managers that people are not as irrational and volatile as had been feared; in fact, they are increasingly likely to take up the world as defined for them under the guise of objectivity. Social scientists are expected to aid the efforts of campaign practitioners of both public and private institutions to steer the course of society through strategic impact on individuals, on public opinion and on public policy making. The social change that can be expected to occur will *not* be a change *of* the system, but changes *in* the system, preserving and solidifying it.[20]

IMPLICATIONS

The problems of which information campaigns are both a cause and an effect can be solved, but the solutions do not lie simply in more access to information by the public nor in more groups producing a greater diversity of information for the public, perhaps subsidized in their efforts in some manner to make up for inequities. The possibility for *genuine* change lies with our ability to reconceptualize the structure of relationships and the model of communication underlying information campaigns. What has been described so far is a structure of particular organizations in the position to generate and distribute information to individuals divided into segments that suit the purposes of the particular organization—publics, markets, clients, audiences. (See Figure 6.1.)

The organizations are interested in the attitudes and behaviors of the individuals. But what "information" do the individuals receive? They get the definitions of reality, the particular conceptions of the world, that the organizations are willing to provide them. And what is "information" without the ability to act? Note what happens when an interest in individual "behavior" is replaced with an interest in collective action. Collective action is only possible when the public has the means to discuss and reflect and *exert* decision-making authority, not simply acquiesce to it. To divide individuals into publics, markets, targets, clients, or audiences is to maintain the flow of communication from the institution *to* people, preserving the institution's position of authority over them and preventing collective discussion and decision making *among* those groups.

This is just the kind of structural disassociation John Dewey (1927) identified when he warned us that the public had been eclipsed. He was concerned that in moving from a culture of genuine community life in the nineteenth century we had moved into a mechanical society, held together by channels of information and transportation but lacking the capacity for a genuine public life of discussion, consensus, and decision making. The public needs to find its voice, he argued.

If we are to take Dewey's critique seriously, we might envision the public at the center of activity, *directing* the actions of institutions, which become its object and not the other way around. (See Figure 6.2.)

With this reconceptualization, we have the possibility of envisioning an active public (not simply an active receiver, a less insulting

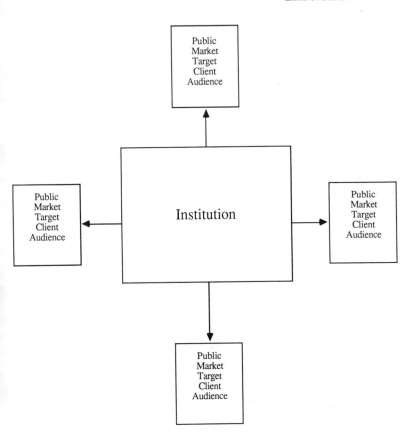

Figure 6.1 The Current Communication Model for Information Campaigns

characterization of individuals but nonetheless consigning them to object status). From this new position, *people*—not institutions—are in a position to "name the world" in consort with each other. The possibility of dialogue rather than monologue is introduced. Here is the possibility of Mills's "public society." Ferguson (1984) calls for just such a revisioning, which she believes is suggested by the feminist call for a nonbureaucratic collective life, anti-hierarchical and participatory:

Active, participatory citizenship is a process through which individuals create themselves with others through the shared processes of speaking, deliberating, and judging, ordering their collective lives through

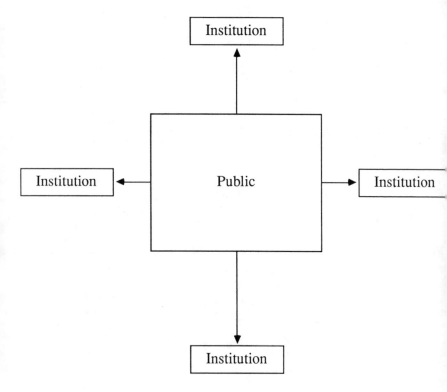

Figure 6.2 A New Communication Model to Recover Public Participation

institutions they have designed and in a language they have made their own. (p. 174)

This is not the same as calling for a reciprocity of interaction between institutions and individuals or publics, however, as implied by James E. Grunig and Todd Hunt's (1984) two-way symmetric model of public relations and Ron Pearson's (1988) ethic of dialogue in public relations. It is one step to say that, contrary to the amount of power typically exercised by institutions, individuals or publics should have equal power in an interaction with an institution. It is quite another to suggest, as is being suggested here, that institutions should not have a right to as much power as people, that is, that institutions have no right of dialogue, but that people do *with other people*. Only when institutions are subordinated to the public can we entertain the possibility of authentic discussion, the necessary basis for genuine democracy.

Such a vision calls into question the very logic of information campaigns, which presuppose a reality ready-made to be bought and sold by an otherwise politically inactive society of discrete individuals. It is not easy to conceptualize this new public and how it might function, but then, it is never easy to imagine what has never been imagined before.[21] Only if we turn our present model on its head can we begin to envision our way out of this dilemma, but it will take a critical theory of information campaigns to do so. We must take ourselves out of the logic of their paradigm to see them for what they are.

NOTES

1. The following discussion has been enriched by the ideas and comments of Brenda Dervin, Susan Herbst, and Ron Pearson.

2. Most of the remainder who have an interest in information campaigns are concerned about "effects" rather than effectiveness. Both camps stand in the paradigm described here. (See Chapter 1 by Salmon in this volume.)

3. This distinction is made by Kathy Ferguson (1984, p. 6) about bureaucracy.

4. Not all shy away from the term *persuasion*. Jowett and O'Donnell (1986) would like to insist on a clear distinction between propaganda (which is bad) and persuasion (which is good).

5. This is in addition to pressures to avoid the term *public relations* because of negative connotations, reflected in several Congressional acts restricting expenditures of funds for such purposes.

6. Dervin (1981) is one of the few information scientists to consider an alternative to the Cartesian notion of information. She argues that information should be seen as a subjective production of human observing. However, she retains the notion that perfect knowledge is constrained by human limitation, suggesting there is a world "out there" existing apart from the human act of creation.

7. The author is in agreement with Dervin's (1980) critique of this hypothesis that it "blames the victim" by claiming deficits in the receiver when he or she does not meet some standard of knowledge acquisition set by the researcher.

8. This is not to disagree with Dervin (1981) that audiences are active creators of information, not simply receptacles. However, to insist on seeing audience members as active members of the process is not the same as making them producers of the general currency of thought circulating in society.

9. James Coleman (1974) gives a very useful account of the imbalance of power between what he calls "corporate actors" and "natural persons," a distinction that is applicable here. He suggests one way to balance the power between the two is to guarantee "information rights" of individuals, requiring corporate actors to provide them with information.

10. The concern of Americans about invasions of their privacy is well-founded, but it should be directed at the role of American businesses in collecting information about them as well as at the government.

11. This text is an active attempt to draw these areas of research together and highlight their similarities. While this may be an innovation, that it makes sense to do so suggests that the movement was already started in this direction.

12. Given how the "mass-society debates" have been characterized in the dominant social science research tradition (for example in De Fleur and Ball-Rokeach, 1975), the author should caution readers against applying that characterization to the points Mills makes and to her own argument. The "mass-society" argument made here is not that there is a problem with "the masses" but with a social structure that makes them masses, that is, unable to act collectively to direct the political processes of their own society.

13. Susan Herbst (1988) demonstrates that despite the democratic assumptions of public opinion polling, which has been designed to give voice to people, current communication technologies and polling techniques have limited or replaced the open political debate necessary for democracy. Or, as Slavko Splichal (1987, p. 259) puts it, public opinion research has become a substitute for the opinion of the public, making public opinion research a form of repression in itself.

14. The author does not agree with Phelan that all cultural rules are now debatable in U.S. society. This may have seemed the case in the 1970s when he was writing, but we are not so fortunate in the 1980s.

15. This definition is often qualified by observing that public opinion consists of the opinions of active individuals, who may vary from issue to issue.

16. The author doesn't mean to imply that she agrees that individuals should be seen as easily manipulatable, an insulting characterization. She is, however, pointing out the underlying social theory of public relations and its view of human nature. The history of how public opinion came to be seen this way—as the aggregate opinions of either volatile or manipulatable individuals—is an interesting one. See L. John Martin (1984), Pierre Bourdieu (1979), Herbert Blumer (1966), and Slavko Splichal (1987).

17. Phelan (1977, p. 25) describes the attempts of alternative groups to reach audiences as just another "bicentennial moment." Given our structure of communication, the public is unable to make a coherent picture out of and act upon all of the disconnected messages presented to them, of which the messages of alternative groups are simply a part.

18. Of course, some groups do target institutions for change, and they do on occasion have success in changing particular institutions. These exceptions should not be taken lightly. However, until a profound change occurs in the existing and legitimated structure of institutions acting upon individuals, groups such as these remain out of the normal system of the way things get done and will continue to be exceptions.

19. The same critique is made by non-Western countries on an international level. "Freedom of information becomes the euphemism for trade and commercial expansion of Western powers, basking in technological mastery, while international organizations provide a moral umbrella for their actions," comments Arnold Gibbons (1985, p. 15). The "Right to Communicate" is a philosophy that must replace the doctrine of the "Free Flow of Information," he argues, because the flow of information is only one way. Note how the same model of communication underlies U.S. information campaigns and the information role of U.S. organizations worldwide.

20. Shugarman (1974), as have others, make the important distinction of a change *within* a structure versus change *of* a structure. As a radical, Shugarman cautions us from thinking that all change is good. Unlike so many other commentators on social change, he insists we look at who benefits from a proposed change.

21. The sheer size of our country in terms of geography and popuation makes it difficult to envision people working collectively in a directly participatory fashion. Dewey (1927) suggests the public would be amorphous, going in and out of existence and comprised of different people at different times, given the issue at hand. It is apparent we must give thought to how this could occur while resisting the temptation to fall back on the concept of "publics," a term too haunted by the present practice of putting a possessive in front of it.

REFERENCES

Altheide, D., & Johnson, J. (1980). *Bureaucratic propaganda*. Boston: Allyn & Bacon.

Berelson, B. (1952). Democratic theory and public opinion. *Public Opinion Quarterly, 16*, 313–330.

Blumer, H. (1966). The mass, the public, and public opinion. In B. Berelson & M. Janowitz (Eds.), *Reader in public opinion and communication* (2nd ed.) (pp. 43–53). New York: Free Press.

Bourdieu, P. (1979). Public opinion does not exist. In A. Mattelart & S. Siegelaub (Eds.), *Communication and class struggle* (pp. 124–130). New York: International General.

Coleman, J. S. (1974). *Power and the structure of society*. New York: W. W. Norton.

Coleman, J. S. (1982). *The asymmetric society*. Syracuse, NY: Syracuse University Press.

Cutlip, S. M., Center, A. H., & Broom, G. M. (1985). *Effective public relations* (6th ed.). Englewood Cliffs, NJ: Prentice-Hall.

De Fleur, M. L., & Ball-Rokeach, S. (1975). *Theories of mass communication* (3rd ed.). New York: Longman.

Dervin, B. (1976). Strategies for dealing with human information needs: Information or communication? *Journal of Broadcasting, 20*, 324–353.

Dervin, B. (1980). Communication gaps and inequities: Moving toward a reconceptualization. In B. Dervin & M. Voigt (Eds.), *Progress in communication sciences* (Vol. 2) (pp. 73–112). Norwood, NJ: Ablex.

Dervin, B. (1981). Mass communicating: Changing conceptions of the audience. In R. E. Rice & W. E. Paisley (Eds.), *Public communication campaigns* (pp. 71–81). Beverly Hills, CA: Sage.

Dewey, J. (1927). *The public and its problems*. Athens, OH: Swallow Press.

Ehrenreich, B. & English, D. (1979). *For her own good: 150 years of the experts' advice to women*. Garden City, NY: Anchor.

Ferguson, K. E. (1984). *The feminist case against bureaucracy*. Philadelphia: Temple University Press.

Foucault, M. (1981). *Power/knowledge: Selected interviews and other writings*. New York: Pantheon.

Freire. P. (1970). *Pedagogy of the oppressed* (M. B. Ramos, Trans.) New York: Herder and Herder.

Gandy, O. H., Jr. (1982). *Beyond agenda setting: Information subsidies and public policy.* Norwood, NJ: Ablex.

Gearhart, S. M. (1979). The womanization of rhetoric. *Women's Studies International Quarterly, 2,* 195–201.

Gibbons, A. (1985). *Information, ideology and communication: The new nations' perspectives on an intellectual revolution.* Lanham, MD: University Press of America.

Grunig, J. E., & Hunt, T. (1984). *Managing public relations.* New York: Holt, Rinehart and Winston.

Habermas, J. (1971). *Knowledge and human interests.* (J. J. Shapiro, Trans.) Boston: Beacon Press.

Hall, S. (1984). The hinterland of science: Ideology and the "sociology of knowledge." In the Centre for Contemporary Cultural Studies, *On ideology* (pp. 9–31). Wolfsboro, NH: Longwood.

Herbst, S. (1988, May). *Effects of public opinion technologies on political expression: Putting polls in historical context.* Paper presented to the annual conference of the American Association for Public Opinion Research, Toronto.

Hofstadter, R. (1955). *The age of reform: From Bryan to FDR.* New York: Alfred A. Knopf.

Jowett, G. S., & O'Donnell, V. (1986). *Propaganda and persuasion.* Beverly Hills, CA: Sage.

Lippmann, W. (1922). *Public opinion.* New York: Macmillan.

Martin, L. J. (1984). The genealogy of public opinion polling. *Annals of the American Academy of Political and Social Science, 472,* 12–33.

McGuire, W. J. (1981). Theoretical foundations of campaigns. In R. E. Rice & W. E. Paisley (Eds.), *Public communication campaigns* (pp. 41–70). Beverly Hills, CA: Sage.

Mills, C. W. (1956). *The power elite.* New York: Oxford University Press.

Olien, C. N., Donohue, G. A., & Tichenor, P. J. (1983). Structure, communication and social power: Evolution of the knowledge gap hypothesis. In E. Wartella & D. C. Whitney (Eds.), *Mass communication review yearbook* (Vol. 4, pp. 455–461). Beverly Hills, CA: Sage.

Pearson, R. (1988, May). *Beyond ethical relativism in public relations: Coorientation, rules and the idea of communication symmetry.* Paper presented to the annual conference of the International Communication Association, New Orleans.

Phelan, J. A. (1977). *Mediaworld: Programming the public.* New York: Seabury Press.

Schiller, H. I. (1981). *Who knows: Information in the age of the Fortune 500.* Norwood, NJ: Ablex.

Schiller, H. I. (1984). *Information and the crisis economy.* Norwood, NJ: Ablex.

Shugarman, D. P. (Ed.). (1974). *Thinking about change.* Toronto: University of Toronto Press.

Smith, D. E. (1978). A peculiar eclipsing: Women's exclusion from man's culture. *Women's Studies International Quarterly, 1,* 281–295.

Splichal, S. (1987). "Public opinion" and the controversies in communication science. *Media, Culture and Society, 9,* 237–61.

Wiebe, R. (1966). *The search for order, 1877–1920.* New York: Hill & Wang.

Chapter 7

CAMPAIGNS, CHANGE AND CULTURE: ON THE POLLUTING POTENTIAL OF PERSUASION

Richard W. Pollay

ADVERTISING, THE MOST COMMON FORM of persuasive campaign, is typically treated with contempt, cynicism and grave misgivings about its corruptive role in shaping our children, characters and culture. That this attitude is widely held by academics and practitioners in allied fields, such as those contributing to this volume, is understandable. Critical attitudes toward advertising, as will be detailed below, are not only widely held but also constitute the prevailing conventional wisdom about advertising among most scholars.

But is advertising to be judged as immoral while "information campaigns" go ethically unjudged? In practice, the distinctions between private sector advertising and information campaigns are often subtle and/or irrelevant to ethical considerations. Yet the bias and hope of information campaign planners to escape serious ethical reflections is manifest in the very language they commonly use, that is, substituting the term *information campaign* for *propaganda* or *persuasion,* and speaking of "managing social change" rather than "manipulating public opinion."

Increasingly in the public sector, campaign planners use not only the language but also the technologies of marketing and advertising. They address carefully constructed and complex efforts at multiple target audiences. Research and polling, elaborate theories of sociological and psychological processes, and empirical experience all shape campaigns to induce and accelerate change. Finnegan, Bracht,

Viswanath (this volume) discusses the wide variety of research activities instrumental in shaping lifestyle campaigns. Other chapters in this book outline the often well-thought-out and highly developed efforts by politicians (O'Keefe), those concerned with birth control, AIDS and abortion (Brown, Waszak, & Childers) and other agents of change. Elsewhere, detailed strategic analysis and tactical executions that rival those of the biggest consumer packaged-goods firms can be seen for public health programs (McGuire, 1984; Lovelock & Weinberg 1984, pp. 408–417).

The latter describes cluster analysis to identify psychographic segments for a government fitness campaign. Psychological insights in this, like other campaigns, led to fine tuning of objectives, media strategies, timing of efforts, development of targeted messages and programs implemented through mass media, schools, employers and other intermediaries. Results were carefully assessed by program evaluation research. Efforts in many full-bore campaigns often involve mass-media public-service announcements, public relations, agents in the field (salespersons), correspondence (direct mail), and events, such as contests or celebrations; going from majestic goals to mundane gimmicks and gadgets as tactics to realize the strategic goals.

The ethical responsibilities that accompany this technocratic sophistication are considerable. They are certainly no less weighty than those borne by commercial advertisers. Indeed, they may be even more substantial, for many *information campaigns* are directly addressed to people's politics, religious convictions, social values, sexuality, lifestyles and moral choices as citizens. They almost invariably involve far more than simple transmission of data or information but, rather seek to induce behavioral change of a more profound nature than the choice of a specific brand of a packaged good that the advertiser seeks. This deeper social change can take the form of inculcation of values, adoption of symbol systems and altered norms as well as alterations of lifestyles and personal outlooks.

It is the purpose of this paper to introduce and briefly discuss (1) the domains of ethics in communication, (2) the critical concerns about the cultural consequences of professional persuasion, and (3) the research that could, and should, be undertaken in response to these concerns. This will draw upon the analogous analysis of advertising, with examples illustrating the application of these ideas to information campaigns more generally.

DOMAINS OF COMMUNICATIONS ETHICS

There are three domains of judgment particularly relevant to the ethical evaluation of persuasive communications: the what, how, and with-what-effects of the communication. These focus on the nature of the product (service, idea) that is the subject of the communication, the process of the communication itself, and the by-products or aftermath of the communication. Of these, the first two typically have received the greatest attention because they are obvious and immediate, but it is the latter which may be the most important and enduring effect.

THE PRODUCTS

In advertising, dimensions of ethical concern often focus on product importance and safety. Promoting the trivial is criticized as wasteful or indulgent, distracting resources from more substantial needs. In the case of personal products, for example deodorants and hemorrhoid ointments, product promotion has been criticized as embarrassing or in poor taste. Promoting the dangerous has more serious ethical implications, and criticism can occur for products which potentially threaten many or only a few. Unsafe products range from addictive and destructive drugs, such as the nicotine in cigarettes, to more mundane products such as ladders requiring use-instructions and warnings.

In contrast, public information campaigns can sell tangible goods, but more often they sell a service, idea or attitude, as in campaigns to sell people on the idea of registering to vote, quitting smoking, staying in school, using condoms for safe sex, supporting foreign aid programs, or understanding the elements of nutritious diets. As a result of the gravity of many of these topics, the criticism of triviality is less germane than in the case of product advertising. As Rothschild (1979) has noted, the range of personal involvement elicited by promoted products is far narrower than by promoted issues, and such possible campaign topics as the military draft, school integration, and political races can be of great social significance.

On the other hand, the criticism of promoting danger is equally applicable to public information campaigns, although the danger is likely to be manifest in a different form then it is for advertising. It is rare, for example, for a public information campaigner to be criticized for promoting products which potentially induce physical danger; on the contrary, many public information campaigns are dedicated to public safety and welfare and to reducing the risk of physical harm. Instead, the danger posed by public information campaigns is more likely to be described in terms of "dangerous ideas," "revolutionary rhetoric," or threats to morals, convention and the status quo. This is a different kind of danger, but it is no less threatening to a potential victim than is physical danger.

Most organizations have substantial conviction, if not evangelical zeal, about the goodness of their products. This is often true for firms selling trinkets, but even more so for public and nonprofit organizations with a purpose or mission that transcends financial feasibility. Yet this conviction, like the communication itself, is ideologically grounded in a system of values, for both the product and the bare facts about it are inevitably meaningless without contextual perspective. The value basis for assessing product goodness can be seen most easily by considering the differences of opinion about campaigns promoting birth control, abortion or sexuality. Campaigns offering information in street language about AIDS transmission, for example, are seen in some eyes as pornographic, encouraging of sexual deviance.

THE PROCESS

Advertising communications are criticized for being manipulative, misleading or deceptive because they include either (1) false information; (2) incomplete disclosures; (3) appeals with excessive emotionality (vs. informativeness); (4) irrelevant associations and production values; or (5) exaggerated promises of benefits or satisfactions. Unfairness of process can be compounded when communications are addressed to target audiences vulnerable because of age or experience, skills or knowledge. Political campaigns, for example, are notorious for their reliance on style over substance, presentation of partial information, use of simplistic stereotypes, and emotional appeals to "motherhood" issues.

The courts typically measure communication acceptability by testing for the literal truthfulness or falsity of assertions, with some allowance for sellers' puffery and associated consumer cynicism. The real ethical test, however, is not the literalness of the words alone but rather the validity of the impression received from the totality of the campaign, including source effects, visual imagery, media context, and so on. The core issue is how reliable are the expectations created? Does the product live up to the implied promise? Thus, cigarette advertising which shows bold and lively behavior and/or pure and pristine environments, presenting the very pictures of health in contiguous association with the product, is clearly ethically suspect, even if no verbal claims are made about the healthfulness of cigarettes.

Public information campaigners face similar concerns and criticisms regarding their efforts. In some cases, organizations disseminate false information to further their cases, and thus there are distinctions between "white" and "grey" propaganda, corresponding to the degree to which information has been falsified or misrepresented. In other cases, particularly in the arena of public health, information is disseminated that eventually is proven false but which at the time was considered truthful. These cases clearly need to be differentiated in ethical considerations of the topic.

More compelling ethical arguments can be made regarding incomplete disclosures and exaggerated promises. A habit is developed through years of conditioning and is not easily changed. Do public information campaigns always inform individuals of the physical and emotional pain that must be endured when altering a lifestyle? Are the stated benefits of weight reduction, a new federal tax, or a foreign aid progam actually those accrued? In some cases, they are not.

THE BY-PRODUCTS

Often communications, like seeds tossed into the winds, have impacts far beyond the immediate pragmatic goals of the sender. The term *unintended consequences* has been used (Pollay, 1986a) to describe those impacts often unexpected and ignored by advertisers. Fortunately, the topic has not gone unnoticed among advertising critics and academics, and there exists a substantial body of thought readily transferable to all sorts of campaigns. For example, a campaign that cites the substantial fraction of people needing treatment for mental illness may be intended to produce sympathy and financial support, but when seen in a crowded metropolitan subway it may produce anxiety and alienation in viewers. Nutritional and health programs encouraging weight control may actually exacerbate problems of anorexia or bulimia. Fund-raising pleas, persistently tugging at people's heart strings, may create a numbed indifference to the plights of others, no matter how terrible or pathetic those plights might be. Campaigns promoting birth control might encourage sexual profligacy, with resulting increases in venereal diseases or divorces and/or changed attitudes toward women and family. Campaigns about drug use, whether against street drugs or drunk driving, can backfire by role modeling the undesirable behavior and communicating the commonness of the "crime," implying its minor nature.

Campaigns also serve to set agendas, direct people's attention and order people's priorities. Health programs aimed at making individuals more responsible for their diets may also divert attention away from government and industry policies putting pollutants, toxic waste and carcinogens in to the ecology and food chain. Political campaigns may focus attention on an issue such as foreign policy, justifying defense spending because of external threats while ignoring internal problems for which the candidates may be more responsible. On the other hand, political campaigns can have the effect of better educating the concerned public and increasing voter competency, but, as O'Keefe (this volume) noted, political campaigns do not seek this goal; they only seek getting elected.

The seeds planted by campaigns may bear strange fruit. Hence a complete analysis of the import and attendant ethical responsibilities of professional campaigns goes beyond the obvious considerations of what is being said (the product), and how it is being said (the process). Such an analysis also needs to consider the effects (the by-products) of that communication in the hearts and minds of the audience. It needs to reflect upon the long-term effects of campaigns, both individually and collectively. This issue of the by-products or unintended consequences of campaigns, however, is rarely researched and discussed, especially by professional persuaders and their associated technocrats, including applied academics.

CAMPAIGNS AND CULTURAL CHANGE

The professional persuasion of advertising has been termed "The Distorted Mirror" (Pollay, 1986a). While persuasion draws upon, plays to, and consequently reflects a culture, it reflects only certain behaviors, attitudes and values. It models, celebrates and reinforces only certain lifestyles and philosophies. It displays those values most readily linked to the available products, most easily dramatized, and most reliably responded to. It is a highly selective reinforcer of only some behaviors, values and ideologies.

Over time, cultural change is to be expected in the direction advocated and modeled by this kind of professional persuasion. When cultural change does indeed occur, persuasion is distorting of the culture, with effects far more substantial and enduring than the accomplishments (or lack thereof) of individual campaigns. An organized set of arguments why professionalized persuasion campaigns are felt to have cultural impact is shown in Table 7.1, and the impacts themselves are described in Table 7.2.

The nature of probable specific cultural consequences has been given considerable thought in diverse allied disciplines such as psy-

Table 7.1. Professional Persuasion and Cultural Effects

Multiple Campaigns Are:	*So Effects Are Judged to Be:*
PERVASIVE —from multiple sources, media —relentless over time —penetrating everyday life	ENVIRONMENTAL —impossible to avoid —hard to detect with detachment —affecting all (despite widespread myths of personal immunity)
CREATED TO INDUCE CHANGE —in competition with tradition —vs. influence of family, school, church, government	CHANGING BEHAVIOR, AND ALSO —thoughts and attitudes —feelings and values
ADAPTED TO A CULTURE —if easily visualized in ads —if reliably responded to by citizens	REINFORCING OF ONLY SOME VALUES —if easily linked to change desired
REPETITIVE OF COMMON THEMES —despite pluralism of sources —echoes and harmonies	INFLUENTIAL IN THE AGGREGATE —even if individual efforts fail
PROFESSIONALLY DEVELOPED —profiting from experience —researched psychologically —polished execution —tested for effectiveness	POTENTIALLY PROFOUND IN INFLUENCE —setting agenda and criteria —articulating values —moral, spiritual, and political —not just personal/practical

NOTE: For more detail and discussion, see Pollay 1986a or 1986b.

Table 7.2. Possible Specific Cultural Consequences of Change Campaigns

When Campaigns Are:	*They Also Foster:*
INTENSE ADVOCACY —insisting, exhorting —half-truths, incomplete information	SUBMISSION AND SEDUCTION —compulsive consumption, indulgence disregarding consequences —cynicism, distrust, dishonesty
EASILY UNDERSTOOD, USING —social stereotypes —strong symbols	SIMPLISTIC SYMBOLS —racism, sexism, etc. —religious and political iconoclasm
PROMOTING GOODS AND SERVICES —as satisfying all needs —as all that is important —as good for everyone	MATERIALISM —psychological belief in consumption as the source of all satisfactions —political priorities favoring private over public goods —spiritual displacement of religion
IDEALIZING "THE GOOD LIFE"	DISSATISFACTION —loss of self-esteem, self-respect —frustrations, powerlessness —criminality, revolution
APPEALING SPECIFICALLY TO: —mass markets —sexuality —fears —status —youth —newness —individuals	PROBLEMS OF: —conformity —pornography —chronic anxieties —envy, social competitiveness —disrespect of family elders —disrespect of tradition —sacrificing community, charity, co-operation, compassion

NOTE: For more detail and discussion, see Pollay 1986a or 1986b.

chology, sociology, anthropology, history, political science, linguistics, education and communication, reflecting various theories, perspectives, experience and data. Over the past few decades, a rich literature, surprisingly internally consistent, has emerged (see Pollay, 1986a,b). Summarizing greatly, the major social concerns regarding advertising include that it penetrates people's consciousness and thereby has a profound impact which tends to be underestimated; it induces people to keep working in order to consume, thereby instilling materialistic values and contributing to environmental pollution through increased production and consumption of goods; it is intrusive and irrational; it reinforces stereotypes for the sexes, race, age, occupations and family relations; and it promotes cynicism, mistrust and disrespect, anxiety and loss of self-esteem. (See also MacBride, 1980, for an inventory of similar effects).

The logic and validity of the argument of this complex of thought has been vigorously discussed and debated. The most concise, thorough and critical examinations are those by Holbrook (1987) and Pollay (1987). Their exchange clarifies the issues, though they do not reach identical conclusions except for the need to do more research. Further research is clearly called for, not just with respect to advertising, but for all professional persuasion, including that euphemistically called "information campaigns." Because many such campaigns are as ubiquitous and penetrating as advertising campaigns, their various impacts may be similarly underestimated. Whether the other impacts attributed to advertising described above emanate from information campaigns as well merits its own research.

NEW DIRECTIONS FOR RESEARCH

The assertions outlined in Tables 7.1 and 7.2 directly suggest some research thrusts. For example, the use of fear and the use of status appeals could be studied for their (sleeper effect) contributions to social anxieties and envy respectively. One could study campaigns for source credibility and longer-term changes in the credibility of various social institutions and the faith people have in them. Commercial advertising, government campaigns, political parties' efforts, non-profit and charitable organizations may have differential effects worth study, if they are perceived as differentially trustworthy, well-informed or self-serving. The aggregate persuasive pressure present at any time in a culture could be profiled to identify the common tactics and themes in use. Cultural change could be measured and compared against the profile of persuasive pressure. Measurement of the cultural character of communications is more tractable than it first appears because *values* lie at the heart of most of the concerns and at the heart of all persuasion.

The persuasion literature has given only modest attention to values, compared to other concerns, despite the fact that values are held to be the dimensions of the deep structure of personality, influencing all perceptions and judgments, attitude and preference formation, cognition and behavior. Values are the criteria of judgment applied to mundane decisions and profound political and religious issues. They guide presentation of self and the judgment of both self and others. They determine what beliefs are worth preserving, passing on to offspring and even dying for.

The term *values* is often used very loosely, as if some people had values but others did not. If the term is used more precisely, however, every individual can be described by the values operating in his or her life, just as everyone has a pattern of motivations. It is the pattern or profile of value priorities that is crucial. Almost everyone endorses common values like honoring parents, being patriotic, seeking health, being economical, and so on. When competing value considerations come into conflict, as they do in all but the most trivial situations, it is the various values' relative importance that guides behavior. This is easily seen in politicians who sound alike in their speeches but differ dramatically in their actions; however, the same holds true for average citizens in everyday actions. Value priorities also resolve the apparent contradictions involved in any culture's simultaneous valuing of both youth and maturity, or both humility and pride, or the natural and the technical, or science and religion, or the traditional and the modern. Individuals and cultures are both characterized by their operating value hierarchies and the rules governing the contexts within which specific values are most operative.

Values are also at the core of all persuasive messages. Typical campaigns model, endorse, glamorize and inevitably reinforce values. Values are manifest in persuasive appeals in every way possible, in both art and copy. It is the creative task to imbue the product (idea/service) with a sense of value so that it becomes a "good." It is a value that is displayed in any "reason why" offered as a rationale for preference or action.

There are multiple value alternatives available to the creators of ads, and their selection may be guided by either research or cultural insight, or both. Ad makers are surprisingly unrestricted by the nature of the product in choosing the values they might employ in ads. It is the ultimate rationale that manifests the value presumed by the copywriter. It is this rhetorical frontier, where the goodness of the product (service/idea) goes without further saying, that identifies the principal values the ad employs and depends upon for its impact.

The number of alternative value dimensions that might be employed and that therefore ought to be measured is large. White (1951) lists over 50 in an analysis of World War II propaganda, and Rokeach (1973) uses 36 in his self report method assessing an individual's values and developing norms for contemporary society. Pollay (1983) modifies these inventories of values to better capture those frequently used in persuasive campaigns, and develops definitions and procedures for content analysis. The application of this method to advertising, with data describing the value profile of print advertising from 1900 to 1980, is shown in Pollay (1984).

SUMMARY AND CONCLUSION

Information campaigns have become prolific in recent years. As the scope of the articles in this book so amply illustrates, communication to effect social change is now a common practice by multiple parties: governments, charities, health organizations, political parties, interest groups, religions and, of course, advertisers of commercial goods and services. The practice of persuasion has also become increasingly professionalized, with increasingly sophisticated theoretical understandings and empirically testable applied technologies. Planners of information campaigns have learned, and continue to learn, more and more about what works, when, on whom and why.

There is clearly a substantial social responsibility that accompanies the possession of the power to persuade. Information campaigners have been quicker to assign such responsibilities to advertisers than they have been to assume them for their own work. Planners of information campaigns have the obvious responsibilities to sell worthy ideas (products/services) and to do so with honesty. But, beyond that, they also have a responsibility to consider how their campaigns, individually and collectively, contribute to cultural change and associated social transformations and problems. The ecological pollution of manufacturing smokestack industries may have a parallel in a cultural and sociological pollution of persuasion industries. Like early ecological pollution, the alleged negative impacts of persuasion may at first be inadvertent and unintended. As more is learned, however, the new knowledge changes moral and political responsibilities and views. What is tolerated or excusable in naiveté can become reprehensible with awareness. There is a need to study the cultural effects of the large and still growing persuasion industry, of which information campaigns are a major part.

REFERENCES

Holbrook, M. B. (1987). Mirror, mirror, on the wall, what's unfair in the reflections on advertising? *Journal of Marketing*, 51, 95–103.

Lovelock, C. H., & Weinberg, C. B. (1984). *Marketing for public and nonprofit managers*. New York: John Wiley.

MacBride, S. (1980). *Many voices, one world: Communication and society, today and tomorrow*. New York: Unipub (UNESCO).

McGuire, W. J. (1984). Public communication as a strategy for inducing health-promoting behavioral change. *Preventive Medicine, 13*(3), 299–319.

Pollay, R. W. (1983). Measuring the cultural values manifest in advertising. *Current Issues and Research in Advertising, 1*, 71–92.

Pollay, R. W. (1984). The identification and distribution of values manifest in print advertising, 1900–1980. In R. E. Pitts & A. G. Woodside (Eds.), *Personal values and consumer behavior* (pp. 111–135). Lexington, MA: Lexington.

Pollay, R. W. (1986a). The distorted mirror: Reflections on the unintended consequences of advertising. *Journal of Marketing, 50*, 18–36.

Pollay, R. W. (1986b). The quality of life in "the padded sell": Common criticisms of advertising's cultural character and international public policies. *Current Issues and Research in Advertising, 9*(2), 173–250.

Pollay, R. W. (1987). On the value of reflections on the values in "the distorted mirror." *Journal of Marketing, 51*, 104–109.

Rokeach, M. (1973). *The nature of human values*. New York: Free Press.

Rothschild, M. L. (1979). Marketing communications in nonbusiness situations or why it's so hard to sell brotherhood like soap. *Journal of Marketing, 43*, 11–20.

White, R. K. (1951). *Value analysis: Nature and use of the method*. Ann Arbor, MI: Society for the Psychological Study of Social Issues.

PART II

THE CAMPAIGN PROCESS

PUBLICS, AUDIENCES AND MARKET SEGMENTS: SEGMENTATION PRINCIPLES FOR CAMPAIGNS

James E. Grunig

NOT LONG AGO, mass-communication literature was loaded with theories of the magical effects of the media: hypodermic needles, magic bullets, and magic keys. These theories suggested that information campaigns could have all sorts of strong effects desired by clients willing to pay the bill: fewer forest fires, fewer heart attacks, greater product sales, more wearing of seat belts, greater adherence to speed limits, reduced use of drugs and alcohol, more victories in political elections or referenda, more donations of funds and many others.

Beginning in the 1940s, theories of "communication as a magical solution" died rapidly in the academic world with the publication of such articles as Hyman and Sheatsley's (1974) "Some Reasons Why Information Campaigns Fail" and Bauer's (1964) "The Obstinate Audience." These theories of limited communication effects had their demise, in turn, when articles such as Mendelsohn's (1973) study of the national driver test, "Some Reasons Why Information Campaigns Can Succeed," were published.

The new studies showed that information campaigns can succeed but only when specific conditions are met, which had been ignored in previous campaigns. Perhaps the most important of these conditions was the requirement that campaigns be directed to carefully selected segments of the mass audience. Mendelsohn (1973, pp. 50–51) put it this way:

An impressive fund of data gathered over the past thirty years indicates that the publics who are most apt to respond to mass-mediated information messages have a prior interest in the subject areas presented. As a consequence, information directed to this segment of a potential audience requires totally different communications strategies and tactics from information that is to be disseminated to an audience that is initially indifferent. At the very least, communicators who intend to use the mass media to produce information gain or attitude and behavior modification must realize that their targets do not represent a monolithic mass, although the media they may decide to utilize have the potential of reaching huge population aggregates.

Recognition of the importance of segmentation in theories of the effect of information campaigns has reflected a similar realization by theorists who have developed broader theories of the effects of the mass media. Lowery and DeFleur (1983) pointed out that the notion of *mass* media reflects the concept of mass society that "emerged from a century and a half of theoretical analyses by a number of pioneer social scientists" (p. 4). A mass society results "when industrialization, urbanization, and modernization increasingly modify the social order" (p. 10). Mass audiences, therefore, are large, heterogeneous, disconnected, and anonymous to the communicator (Wright, 1986).

Both Lowery and DeFleur (1983) and Wright (1986) added that theorists no longer view the audiences of the media as a mass in the classical sense. Indeed, McQuail (1983) suggested that media audiences are more "massive" in size than a mass. Within massive general audiences, McQuail added, "are numerous small, selective, or local audiences" for which the possibilities for "interaction with or response to media 'senders' " are greater than suggested by the classic definition of a mass audience.

Segmentation of audiences, therefore, is crucial to the success of an information campaign—and to understanding the effects of the mass media. However, theories of segmentation in the field of mass communication are few in number and generally poorly developed. This chapter, therefore, will supplement theories of media audiences with theories of segmentation developed in public relations and marketing. It then will develop a theoretical schema for identifying, evaluating, and choosing an appropriate means of segmenting the audiences of communication campaigns. The author begins that process by defining segmentation and by identifying criteria for choosing an appropriate method of segmentation.

THE CONCEPT OF SEGMENTATION

The idea of segmenting a population into relevant categories or groups can be found in such fields as mass communication, public opinion, political science, sociology, and anthropology. Marketing theorists, however, have developed the idea of segmentation mostly as a normative concept. A normative theorist takes descriptive theories of the behavior of population segments and makes them useful to the decision maker in marketing or communication by specifying how differences in the behavior of segments can be used to increase the effectiveness of marketing or communication programs (Massy & Weitz, 1977).

Smith (1956) introduced segmentation to marketing in a seminal article over 30 years ago. In that article, he contrasted market segmentation with product differentiation. Product differentiation, he said, attempts to bend demand to the will of supply. It uses advertising and promotion to distinguish a product from competing products and, as a result, to increase demand and reduce competition for that product. Market segmentation, in contrast, works from the demand side of the market: the consumer. Segmentation bends supply to demand by identifying lucrative segments of the market and developing products specifically to fit those segments.

Segmentation became "one of the most influential and fashionable concepts in marketing," a concept that has "permeated the thinking of managers and researchers . . . more than any marketing concept since the turn of the century" (Lunn, 1986, p. 387).

Levitt (1986, p. 217) said that "the idea of segments has become a powerful organizing principle in the affairs of modern business" that dominates commercial life. "If you're not thinking segments, you're not thinking," he added (p. 128).

To think segments means you have to think about what drives customers, customer groups, and the choices that are or might be available to them. To think segments means to think beyond what's obviously out there to see. If everybody sees segments as obviously consisting of certain demographics, industries, user groups, buying practices, certain influencing groups, and the like, then the thinking that gives real power is thinking that transcends the ordinary. (pp. 128–129)

The basic idea of segmentation is simple: Divide a population, market, or audience into groups whose members are more like each other than members of other segments. Michman (1983, p. 127), for example, defined market segmentation as "the process of taking the mass market for consumer or industrial goods and breaking it up into small, more homogeneous submarkets based on relevant distinguishing characteristics." To this definition, Bonoma and Shapiro (1983, p. 1) added the idea that segmentation can be viewed "either as a process of aggregating individual customers, prospects, and buying situations into groups, or as a process of disaggregating a total market into pieces."

Kotler and Andreasen (1987) contrasted "target marketing" (in which an organization develops products for segments of a market) with "mass marketing" (in which an organization develops one market offer and attempts to get every possible person to use it) and Smith's (1956) "product-differentiated marketing" (in which products are designed "not so much for different groups but to offer alternatives to everyone in the market").

Other definitions of segmentation are similar. Cravens (1982, p. 167) described segmentation as a "niche" market strategy rather than a "mass" strategy. Lovelock and Weinberg (1984, pp. 109–111) called segmentation "segregation" as opposed to "aggregation." Both Cunningham and Cunningham (1981) and Luck and Ferrell (1985) have contrasted market segmentation with "undifferentiated marketing."

Marketing textbooks (e.g., Kotler & Andreasen, 1987; Lunn, 1986, Cunningham & Cunningham, 1981; Taylor, 1986; Luck & Ferrell, 1985; Cravens, 1982; Assael, 1984; Lovelock & Weinberg, 1984) and articles in public relations trade journals (e.g., Winkleman, 1987) contain lists of segmentation concepts. These concepts include demographics, psychographics, values and lifestyles, geodemographic clusters of postal zip codes, geographic regions, consumer behaviors, elasticities of consumer responses to products, product benefits, amount of consumption, and purchase/use situations.

This chapter will examine several of these segmentation concepts from marketing as well as others from public relations, mass communication, sociology, and political science. First, however, it is important to develop normative criteria that will help planners of a public communication campaign choose an appropriate and effective strategy for segmenting potential audiences.

Marketing theorists (e.g., Kotler & Andreasen, 1987; Taylor, 1986; Lovelock & Weinberg, 1984) have provided criteria for choosing an appropriate strategy for segmentation. In general, segments must be definable, mutually exclusive, measurable, accessible, pertinent to an organization's mission, reachable with communications in an affordable way, and large enough to be substantial and to service economically.

Kotler and Andreasen (1987, p. 124) pointed out, however, that "differential responsiveness" is "perhaps the most crucial criterion" for choosing segments. Two or more market segments may meet all of the other criteria, they explained, but still respond exactly alike to a product offer or communication strategy. Unless two segments respond differently to a public communication campaign, for example, there is no need to isolate them and treat them as separate segments.

Massy and Weitz (1977) traced normative theories of segmentation to price theory in economics. They said that price theory suggests that for all market segments serviced there should be an equal ratio of profits generated to the cost of reaching that segment. There will always be a "high-assay" segment, they added, a segment with the highest incremental response to a marketing effort. Resources should be directed to that segment until the ratio of profits to cost equals that of other segments or a budget constraint occurs.

Grunig and Hunt (1984) developed a similar process of decision making for public relations programs using simplified linear programming techniques. In their schema, organizations should appropriate resources to communication programs for publics that affect an organization most and are most likely to respond to those programs. Programs can be developed for publics of increasingly lower importance until resources budgeted for communication are exhausted.

Making such decisions, however, requires knowledge of the "differential responses" of population segments. Although the differential response desired in marketing usually will seem clear to the decision maker—purchase of a product or contribution to profit—the nature of that response will not usually be so clear for decision makers planning public communication programs.

DIFFERENTIAL RESPONSES TO PUBLIC COMMUNICATION

When marketing theorists use the term *differential response,* their unspoken assumption is that the desired response is behavioral: a purchase, adoption, use or similar desired behavior. As Flay and Cook (1981) pointed out, however, communication campaigns— including marketing communication campaigns—cannot always be evaluated by monitoring behavioral responses. Behaviors usually are less sensitive to campaigns than are variables that occur earlier in the behavioral chain that begins with seeking of or exposure to a message and continues through cognition, attitude, and behavior (see chapter by Devine and Hirt in this volume).

Advertising researchers, Flay and Cook added, recognize that advertising may not contribute directly to sales, but that it may contribute indirectly by affecting a variable that occurs earlier in the chain. Thus, advertising can be evaluated by measuring differential responses in communication or cognition rather than differential responses in behavior.

For public communication campaigns, the differential response sought may be communication behavior alone. In that situation, planners choose a segment of the population with which they will be able to communicate about the topic of the campaign. For other campaigns, planners may set an additional objective of achieving an effect from communicating with a segment of the population. Not always, however, will that effect be on behavior. Campaigns also may strive for effects on cognitions (e.g., accuracy and understanding) and on attitudes—sometimes as an intermediary effect on the path to individual or collective behavioral change, but sometimes as ends in themselves. In addition, campaign planners may attempt to affect collective behavior by creating and mobilizing activist, issue groups.[1]

Some communication campaigns may strive for all of these responses; others may strive for only one. An ideal theory of segmentation, therefore, would isolate segments of the population that differ in all of these responses. Some theories, however, may produce segments that differ in only one. Nonetheless, one can argue that a theory to be used for segmentation in communication campaigns *must* be capable of predicting when members of a segment will communicate for it to be called a communication theory. Without communication behavior, any effect on cognition, attitude, and behavior must have been produced by some variable other than communication.

A NESTED APPROACH TO SEGMENTATION

The literature in marketing, public relations, and mass communication seems to offer a seemingly inexhaustible and disorganized list of concepts for segmenting populations. As Kotler and Andreasen (1987) and Massy and Weitz (1977) pointed out, the perfect segmentation concept would make it possible for a communication planner to study each member of a market or public and to develop a personalized marketing or communication strategy for that person. Such a strategy is impractical, however.

Theorists in both communication and marketing know well that the behavior of segments can be understood better when what Frank, Massy and Wind (1972) and Kotler and Andreasen (1987) called *inferred* variables are used, rather than *objective* variables. Inferred variables are measured by questioning members of a population directly. These variables include perceptions, cognitions, or attitudes. Objective variables can be measured from secondary sources. They include demographics, geographic location, or media use.

Although inferred variables are more effective in segmentation, managers of marketing and public relations campaigns more often use objective measures because they are more available and less expensive to gather (Massy & Weitz, 1977). Kotler and Andreasen (1987, p. 125) described the problem well:

> . . . field research to determine responsiveness and information source behavior is costly and time-consuming and not every organization has the funds and the patience to make the necessary investment. Second, the sheer *number* of segmentation decisions a manager must make precludes such care and attention except in rare, very important situations.
>
> As a result, managers typically use *surrogates* for what they *ideally* would like to measure. Segmentation is often based on demographics, for example, because managers assume that such characteristics will be related to likely responses and reachability.

For communication campaigns, segmentation theories based on inferred variables predict desired communication behaviors and effects more accurately than those based on objective variables. As a result, the use of inferred variables reduces the costs of media and interpersonal communication needed to reach targeted segments. As Massy and Weitz (1977, pp. 135–136) pointed out, however, the "fundamental managerial question is at what point the marginal reduction in profit [differential response in communication behavior and effects] equals the administrative and research costs" of the more effective segmentation concepts.

Bonoma and Shapiro (1983) developed a "nested approach" to classifying segmentation concepts that is extremely useful in organizing communication theories. Although their nested framework was developed for industrial rather than consumer markets, the basic idea can be adapted readily to communication campaigns.

By *nested,* Bonoma and Shapiro (1983, p. 8) meant that "subtle, hard-to-assess" or "inferred" variables are located within general, more-easily observed "objective" variables. A variable in an inner nest can pinpoint a public or a market segment precisely. A variable in an outer nest can locate the segments in the inner nests also, although it will not be able to discriminate among several segments that could be identified by variables in the inner nest.

Figure 8.1, therefore, depicts concepts developed by scholars and practitioners in marketing and public relations, organized into nests of more-general but less-powerful concepts. The innermost nest contains variables that predict individual communication behaviors and effects—the perfect concepts for segmentation if it were feasible to organize campaigns for individuals. The second nest defines publics—individuals who communicate and behave in similar ways. For most campaigns, publics represent the optimal segment, optimal because that segment maximizes the differential responses desired by campaign planners at a reasonable cost. These first two nests are related, however, because one must understand the behaviors of individuals to understand the behaviors of publics.

Subsequent nests consist of communities; psychographics, lifestyles, subcultures, and social relationships; geodemographics; demographics and social categories; and mass audiences. The groupings in the outer nests are less powerful in isolating communication behaviors and effects than are those in the two inner nests. The outer nests may contain the publics that are the segment targeted by a communication campaign, but they also contain publics that are not targeted. To use an analogy, the inner nests catch only the fish desired. The

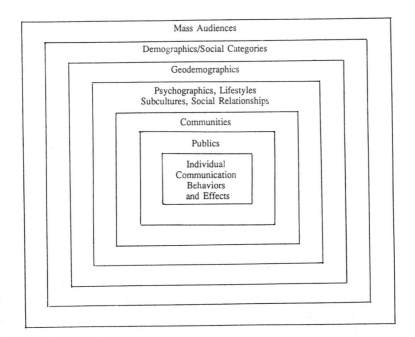

Figure 8.1 Nested Segmentation Concepts

outer nests may catch the same fish, but they also catch other, undesired fish. The farther out the nest, the larger will be the number of undesired fish that will be caught.

The variables in the outer nests can serve as surrogates for the inner nests when budget constraints prohibit identification of segments in inner nests. Bonoma and Shapiro (1983, p. 8) suggested that decision makers should begin with variables in the outer nest and work inward, until they reach the point where the additional costs of segmentation no longer justify the expected differential responses. If the variables in the inner nest are so much more effective in communication planning, it would seem more logical for decision makers to begin with the inner nests and work outward only when resources are not available for the research and time needed to work with the inner nests.

The variables in the outer nests can serve another useful function, however, when they are used in combination with the variables in the inner nests. Segments identified by the variables in the inner nests are more difficult to locate than are those identified by the variables in the outer nests. For example, it is easy to identify people who belong to demographic groups, such as age or sex, but difficult to identify members of publics. Thus, campaign planners can measure the variables in the outer nests as well as those in the inner nests to help locate the inner groups.

The rest of the chapter, then, describes the variables in each of the nests.

INDIVIDUAL COMMUNICATION BEHAVIORS AND EFFECTS

Development of a theory that will help communication planners divide a population into segments of people who will communicate similarly about the topic of a campaign must begin with concepts that explain why individuals communicate. Early theories of mass communication made no attempt to isolate such concepts. Instead, they assumed that communication begins with a message. When the message reached an individual, theorists assumed, that person would communicate by passively receiving the message.

It took Lazarsfeld, Berelson, and Gaudet's (1948) study of people's use of the mass media during a political campaign and Katz and Lazarsfeld's (1955) study of the role of the primary group in explaining use of the media to show that people can control their communication behavior. Shortly after, Festinger's (1957) theory of cognitive dissonance predicted that communication behavior would be motivated by attitudes—that people would seek information to reinforce attitudes. Although dissonance theory was tested extensively, research did not confirm that reinforcement of attitudes was a primary motivation for communication behavior (see Freedman & Sears, 1965).

The most extensive body of theory in mass communication on the variables that cause communication behavior has come under the category of "uses and gratifications." Although research in that tradition is more than 40 years old, recent interest was triggered by the volume edited by Blumler and Katz (1974) 15 years ago. In those 15 years, substantial theoretical advances have been made, as exemplified in a review by Palmgreen (1984) and the volume edited by Rosengren, Wenner and Palmgreen (1985).

The most controversial component of the uses-and-gratifications approach has been its core assumption that communication behavior is active—selective, intentional, instrumental or utilitarian, involved in processing messages, and impervious to outside influence—especially the media (Biocca, 1988; Levy & Windahl, 1984; Katz, Blumler & Gurevitch, 1974; McQuail, 1985; Palmgreen, 1984). Critics (e.g., Carey & Kreiling, 1974; Biocca, 1988) have argued that communication behavior—particularly use of the media—is more passive, consummatory and under the control of the media rather than the audience, and Grunig (1979a) has proposed an obvious solution to the controversy—that communication behavior either can be active or passive.

The crucial theoretical problem, however, is to find concepts that predict the circumstances under which communication behavior is active or passive. Nevertheless, researchers have paid little attention to the "social and psychological origins" of the "needs" that supposedly motivate communication (Palmgreen, 1984, p. 21). Levy and Windahl (1984, p. 58) even called these "background variables . . . 'complications' that await further study." Yet, "background variables" are the key to understanding communication behavior and its effects. As already noted, reinforcement of attitudes has not been a successful concept for explaining that behavior. What else does the literature suggest?

NEEDS, PROBLEMS, SITUATIONS, ISSUES

Uses-and-gratifications researchers use the concept of "need" to explain why people initiate specific kinds of communication behavior (e.g., Katz, Blumler & Gurevitch, 1974; McQuail, 1985; Levy & Windahl, 1984; Palmgreen, 1984; McGuire, 1974, 1981). "Needs" also appear in other areas of psychological and communication research—for example, Petty and Cacioppo's (1986) "need for cognition" and McCombs' (1981) "need for orientation." Similarly, "needs" and "wants" show up as the motivating concept in most marketing theories of consumer behavior (e.g., Lovelock & Weinberg, 1984; Assael, 1984).

Needs usually are defined as "inner motivational states that are aroused by external stimuli or internal cues" (Assael, 1984, p. 167). If a need is an unmeasurable inner state, it can be argued, theories that use needs to predict behavior are essentially tautological in that a need is seldom more than another name for the behavior to be explained. Theories based on needs are also deterministic in that the "needs" program people to behave in ways that they cannot control. A preferable theory of behavior would be a teleological theory that views human beings as capable of controlling their own behavior, even though they may not always do so in some situations—situations whose characteristics can be identified.

The key concepts in a teleological theory of communication behavior are "problems" and "situations." "Problem recognition" is the initiating variable in most theories of consumer behavior (e.g., Engel, Blackwell & Kollat, 1978; Lovelock & Weinberg, 1984; Assal, 1984). Most of these theorists, however, define *problem recognition* as the recognition that a person "has a set of needs to be fulfilled"—as Lovelock and Weinberg (1984, p. 68) put it. They added, however, that problem recognition results from internal or external stimuli, which suggests that the concept of need is unnecessary as an intermediary variable in explaining problem recognition.

The classic definition of a problem comes from Dewey (1910, 1938, 1939). Dewey defined problem recognition as the perception that something is lacking in a situation; he theorized that people *inquire* (seek information) and *think* when they recognize an indeterminate or problematic situation.

The concept of problem recognition has been used extensively as part of a theory of publics, in which it is one of three variables that lead to communication behavior (e.g., Grunig, 1978, 1983a, 1987; Grunig & Hunt, 1984; Grunig & Childers, 1988). Problems, as opposed to needs, can be identified and measured; they are not vague, hypothetical constructs. They may arise from the situation, environment, or social system. Or they may arise internally from curiosity or lack of understanding (Grunig & Childers, 1988).

If we use the concept of "problem" in place of "needs," it is not necessary to develop a long list of the "basic human needs." Maslow's (1970) hierarchy of needs, for example, can be translated into a hierarchy of problems—problems that change as situations change and people mature. Since new problems occur daily, it would be fruitless to try to develop a complete taxonomy of problems. But recognizing that problem recognition motivates communication behavior, researchers can ask people what problems they recognize to determine what they will communicate about and whether they will respond to a communication campaign about particular topics.

The concept of problem recognition is tied to a second concept, the *situation*. Dewey argued that problems arise in life situations or, as Dervin (1981, p. 80) called them, "specific moments in time-space when information is used." Since people communicate about *problematic situations*, analysis of how they perceive different types of life situations shows when and about what people will communicate (see also Dervin, Jacobson & Nilan, 1982).

Marketing researchers have used situations as a means of segmenting publics (e.g., Assael, 1984; Bonoma & Shapiro, 1983; Lunn, 1986; Srivastava, Alpert & Shocker, 1984; Dickson, 1982; Lehmann, Moore & Elrod, 1982). Some of the situational variables they have used include physical and social surroundings, time, the specific task for which a product is used, personal state-of-mind at purchase, social or financial pressure, uncertainty, or a situation served inadequately by existing products. Communication researchers such as Dervin and myself have defined *situations* as a somewhat more general type of recurring situation: for example, dealing with a heart problem, AIDS or environmental pollution.

A final concept similar to problems and situations is that of *issue*. An *issue* can be defined as a political or social problem—a problem whose resolution creates conflict in political or social systems (Cobb & Elder, 1972). AIDS, for example, is a problem for an affected individual; it becomes an issue when the disease becomes an epidemic or when governmental programs are developed to fight it and there is conflict over how to deal with the epidemic or over what programs are necessary.

As Becker (1982) pointed out, "issue importance" is the focal variable for the agenda-setting approach to mass media effects. Issues were key concepts in Graber's (1984) theory of how people process news and Lang and Lang's (1983) theory of "agenda building." Issues are the major concept of concern to public relations practitioners engaged in "issues management" (Heath & Nelson, 1986; Buchholz, 1982). As will be seen in discussing the second nest of segmentation concepts, the problems recognized by members of publics can be labeled "issues."

CONSTRAINTS

In addition to problematic situations/issues, a second variable that explains communication behavior is *constraint recognition* (Grunig, 1971, 1983a).

Although constraint recognition appears in fewer theories of communication or marketing than problem recognition, constraints appear as a concept in linear programming in economics and management science, a statistical process that can be used—among other things—to maximize profits within the constraints of resources available to a decision maker. In psychology, Brehm and Cohen (1962) found that individual volition (the absence of constraints) was a necessary condition for cognitive dissonance. Constraint recognition also can be seen as "personal efficacy" in Bandura's (1977) social learning theory, a theory that has been used to explain the results of several studies of communication campaigns (e.g., Maccoby & Solomon, 1981; Anderson, 1987).

In general, constraint recognition discourages communication behavior: People do not communicate about problems or issues about which they believe they can do little or about behaviors they do not believe they have the personal efficacy to execute.

INVOLVEMENT

Of the individual concepts reviewed thus far, involvement has been used most extensively in marketing and communication research: Researchers have used the concept for 40 years (Salmon, 1986). Although definitions of *involvement* vary widely, Lovelock and Weinberg (1984, p.73) provide the "common-sense interpretation" that involvement is the "degree of importance or concern" that a product or behavior generates in different individuals.

Because involvement varies with individuals as well as with products and behaviors, it can be used as a concept for segmentation (Assael, 1984; Kassarjian, 1981; Slama & Tashchian, 1985). Measures of involvement can be used to separate populations into active and passive segments, which are characterized by complex as opposed to passive purchase and communication behaviors (Assael, 1984; Lovelock & Weinberg, 1984, Ray, 1973).

The ability to distinguish active and passive segments makes the concept of involvement especially useful to communication researchers because it offers the promise of resolving the controversy generated by the uses-and-gratifications tradition, that is the question of whether media audiences are active or passive. Audiences can be either, depending on their level of involvement (Grunig, 1979a).

Involvement cannot be used indiscriminately to segment audiences, however, because several writers (Salmon, 1986; Chaffee & Roser, 1986; Grunig & Childers, 1988) found that definitions and measures of the concept differ widely in the literature—including definitions of *involvement* as a personality trait, as a state of ego involvement, as a characteristic of a situational stimulus that varies among individuals, and as a characteristic of a product or issue that is the same for most people. (See also Krugman, 1965; Sherif, Sherif & Nebergall, 1965; Preston, 1970; Ray, 1973; Rothschild & Ray, 1974; Petty & Cacioppo, 1986.)

Although most marketing and communication researchers have used the concept of involvement separately from problem recognition and constraint recognition, research shows that the three variables together explain communication behavior better than any one alone (e.g., Grunig, 1983a; Grunig & Childers, 1988). In particular, the three variables identify publics, which occupy the second nest of segmentation—the nest most useful for planners of communication campaigns.

In addition, the three concepts not only predict communication behavior but also predict that active communication behavior more often results in effects of communication—cognitions, attitudes, individual and collective behaviors—than does passive communication behavior (Grunig, 1982a, 1983a, 1987; Stamm & Grunig, 1977; Grunig & Stamm, 1979; Grunig & Ipes, 1983). Since these differential responses include most objectives for a communication campaign, the three concepts—when used to aggregate publics—provide an especially effective segmentation theory.

PUBLICS

Although the variables identified in the first nest could allow planners to target individuals for communication campaigns, such microsegmentation is seldom possible—even when interpersonal communication is a primary vehicle for the campaign. Publics, in the second nest, therefore, represent the first level of aggregation necessary for a campaign. It is a useful level of aggregation, however, because it allows researchers to place individuals into groups that differ in the extent to which they actively communicate, construct cognitions and attitudes, and engage in individual or collective behaviors—the primary differential responses sought from a campaign.

Dewey (1927) and Blumer (1946) were among the first to develop a theory of publics. They observed that publics arise around problems or issues that have consequences on them. Issues, therefore, define publics more than publics define issues (Grunig & Hunt, 1984; Price, 1987). Cobb and Elder (1972, p. 102) added that "a rather important implication that follows . . . is that there is not a single, undifferentiated public; a public is always specific to a particular situation or issue."

Dewey also recognized the crucial role that publics play in American democracy: After recognizing that problems affect them, publics organize into issue groups to pressure organizations that cause problems or that are supposed to help resolve problems. Publics, therefore, begin as disconnected systems of individuals experiencing common problems; but they can evolve into organized and powerful activist groups engaging in collective bahavior.

These classic theories of publics fit logically with the concepts of individual communication behavior and effects identified in the previous section: Publics consist of people with similar levels of problem recognition, constraint recognition, and involvement for the same issues or problems. Several studies conducted to develop public relations theory (Grunig, 1975, 1977, 1978, 1979b, 1982a, 1982b, 1983a, 1983b; Grunig, Nelson, Richburg, & White, 1988) have developed a methodology to identify publics arising from situational issues.

A typical study has taken related issues about which an organization or other sponsor of a campaign wants to communicate, such as air pollution, extinction of whales, and strip mining for an environmental campaign (Grunig, 1983a). Canonical correlation then has been used to correlate the independent variables (problem recognition, involvement, constraint recognition) with the dependent variables (active and passive communication behavior) for all of the situations. The canonical variates then have provided profiles of the active and passive publics arising from the set of situations studied.

This research has identified four kinds of publics consistently enough to assume they have theoretical regularity:

All-issue publics. Publics active on all of the issues.

Apathetic publics. Publics inattentive to all of the issues.

Single-issue publics. Publics active on one or a small subset of the issues that concerns only a small part of the population. Such issues have included the slaughter of whales or the controversy over the sale of infant formula in Third-World countries.

Hot-issue publics. Publics active only on a single issue that involves nearly everyone in the population and that has received extensive media coverage (such as the gasoline shortage, drunken driving or toxic waste disposal).

Cobb and Elder (1972) defined theoretically four types of publics that resemble these four types identified empirically—thus giving them both a theoretical and an empirical basis.

Corresponding to the all-issue public is a *specific public-identification group* (people who "have a persistent sympathy with the generic interests" of a public) (pp. 105–106).

Corresponding to the single-issue public is a *specific public-attention group* (people disinterested in most issues but . . . informed about and interested in certain specific issues) (p. 106).

A *mass public-attentive public* (a "generally informed and interested stratum of the population . . . that comes disproportionately from more educated and higher income groups") (p. 107) does not correspond perfectly with any of the author's four publics, although it could contain members of either an all-issue or hot-issue public.

Corresponding to the apathetic public is a *mass public-general public* ("that part of the population that is less active, less interested, and less informed") (pp. 107–108).

Also closely related to these theories of publics is the concept of *stakeholders* that is currently popular among public relations theorists and practitioners. Freeman (1984, p. vi) defined a stakeholder as "any group or individual who can affect, or is affected, by the achievement of a corporation's purpose." That definition essentially states that stakeholders are people upon whom an organization has a consequence, to use Dewey's terms. Stakeholders, however, are people who are potential publics of an organization or campaign; the three variables of the author's theory provide the means of identifying more specific publics from among those stakeholders (see Grunig and Hunt, 1984).

MARKETS VERSUS PUBLICS

Before leaving this second nest, it is necessary to distinguish between a market and a public and to enumerate the differential responses possible for each. Marketing theorists most often refer to segments as markets, whereas public relations theorists call these segments publics.

A "market" is a segment chosen by an organization to help meet its mission. Bonoma and Shapiro (1983, p. 2) stated, for example:

> If segmentation is done well, marketers can make intelligent choices about the fit between their company and products and the needs of each segment. Those segments that fit the company's capabilities are chosen for penetration. Those segments that do not suit the company's capabilities are left for others to serve.

Levitt (1986, p. 5) put it even more simply: "The purpose of a business is to create and keep a customer." Organizations, in other words, create and seek out markets.

Publics, in contrast, organize around issues and seek out organizations that create those issues—to seek information or help, to seek redress of grievances, to pressure the organizations, or to seek regulation of the organizations. As publics move from being latent to active, organizations have little choice other than to communicate with them (Grunig & Hunt, 1984), whereas organizations can choose to ignore markets if they wish.

Public relations practitioners, therefore, communicate with publics that threaten the organization's autonomy or provide opportunities to enhance that autonomy. Marketing practitioners, in contrast, create and seek out markets that can use or consume their products or services. Consumers provide an example of the difference. They constitute a market segment for marketing communicators, but they become a public of concern to public relations practitioners when a faulty product becomes an issue that turns a market into a public. For example, users or potential users of IUDs were a market until the product had serious consequences on health. Then, many of the users organized into a public that brought litigation and sought government regulation of the product.

The target segments for public communication campaigns may be either publics or markets. Publics, however, are usually more active than are markets—a difference that McQuail (1983) recognized when he applied the concepts of public and market to media audiences. He described a public as "an active, interactive and largely autonomous social group which is served by particular media, but does not depend on the media for its existence" (p. 152). He described a market as an "aggregate of potential consumers with a known social-economic profile at which a medium or message is directed" (p. 154). The concept of market, he added

> specifies the link between media and their audiences as a consumer-producer relationship, hence "calculative" from the point of view of the consumer and manipulative from the point of view of the sender. In any case it is not a moral or social relationship as in the case of a public . . . it gives little emphasis to the internal social relationships of the audience: they are a set of individual and equal consumers, sharing certain given demographic or cultural features. (pp. 153–154)

The distinction between a market and a public suggests that the two inner nests of Figure 1 describe publics, whereas the outer nests describe markets. Thus, public relations practitioners more often use inner nests for segmentation, and marketing practitioners use the outer nests. The exception occurs when marketing people use theories of consumer behavior (e.g., Engel, Blackwell & Kollat, 1978; Assael, 1984) for segmentation—theories that make it possible to target active and passive "markets."

ADOPTER CATEGORIES

One additional concept popular in communication and marketing research can be placed into the nested model—the diffusion of innovations. Diffusion researchers (Rogers, 1983; Lionberger & Gwin, 1982) have segmented populations of users of an innovation by the amount of time that has passed before adoption of the innovation—essentially segmentation by behavior. Segments have included five "adopter types:" innovators, early adopters, early majority, late majority and laggards (Rogers, 1983).

The diffusion model has been used for segmentation in marketing (e.g., Robertson, 1971; Assael, 1984). Myers (1986) showed that the adopter categories can be explained by the author's theory of publics, in that segments move from active to passive communication behavior (because of lower problem recognition or involvement or higher constraint recognition) as they move from innovators to laggards.

Rogers (1983), however, pointed out that information about innovations may lead to problem recognition as well as problem recognition's leading to the seeking of information. Grunig and Childers (1988) found the same: Campaigns can reach passive audiences via information processing, which can, in turn, increase active information seeking and the effects it produces.

The most important contribution that diffusion theory makes to the nested model, however, is its identification of characteristics of adopter categories that fall into outer nests, especially social relationships (Rogers, 1983). Marketing researchers call these characteristics from outer nests "descriptors of segments" (Frank, Massy & Wind, 1972; Massy and Weitz, 1977). The author turns, then, to the outer nests.

COMMUNITIES

The community nest may overlap both the public nest within it and the lifestyles nest above it, in that members of publics may be found in several communities, and several lifestyles may be found in the same community. However, it is useful to place communities at this level because communities vary according to the number and diversity of publics in them.

Two prominent studies of health campaigns, the Stanford and Minnesota heart health campaigns, have been at the community level, although differences in the communities themselves have not been variables in the studies (e.g., Mittelmark et al., 1986; Nash & Farquar, 1980). Tichenor, Donohue and Olien (1980) have provided the most useful concept for segmenting communities: the extent to which communities vary in pluralism.[2]

Pluralistic communities consist of more than one public, and these publics become more diverse as the community increases in pluralism. Thus, communication campaigns aimed at the community level should differ, depending on the pluralism of the community. Few communication campaigns have segmented communities in this way, although communication planners should do so. Advice on how to do so can be found in Grunig and Hunt (1984, chapter 13), who discussed how community relations programs should be tailored for different communities, and in Lindenmann (1980), who has used community case studies to plan public relations programs. The concept of community is treated in greater detail in the chapter by Finnegan, Bracht and Viswanath in this volume.

PSYCHOGRAPHICS, LIFESTYLES, SUBCULTURES, SOCIAL RELATIONSHIPS

The four concepts grouped into this nest are similar in that they represent population segments grouped by psychological or social characteristics, or both. These concepts are broader than publics, as the segments they produce may house several publics. The concepts should be locators of publics because people with similar activities, values, and lifestyles usually are involved in similar situations and experience similar problems and constraints.

Although the segments produced by these variables may be used alone by communication planners, the author believes they will be most valuable when used in conjunction with measures that isolate publics. Because segmentation data are available readily from commercial firms, however, planners may find it easier to use these concepts than to do original research to identify their own publics.

SOCIAL RELATIONSHIPS

Social relationships are important in explaining how people use media and how the media affect them—as Lazarsfeld, Berelson and Gaudet (1948) and Katz and Lazarsfeld (1955) found early in the history of communication research. In marketing, Assael (1984) paid the most attention to social relationships when he devoted separate chapters in his book on consumer behavior to the influence of several social groups or roles on consumer behavior: social classes, reference groups, families, opinion leaders, and the diffusion process.

To be useful in segmentation, the concept of social relationships must be converted into measurable variables. The concepts that follow—psychographics, lifestyles, and culture—provide the variables and the measures needed to convert the idea of social relationships into measured segments.

PSYCHOGRAPHICS AND LIFESTYLES

The concepts that are developed best for segmentation purposes are called either psychographics or lifestyles. Wells and Tigert (1971) introduced what they called AIO items—for activities, interests and opinions—to research in marketing and advertising. These items, they said, "focus on . . . activities, interests, prejudices, and opinions" to "draw recognizably human portraits of consumers" (p. 28). They added

> if it is granted that a communicator can usually do a better job when he can visualize his audience than when he cannot, it seems obvious that this level of descriptive detail is a significant improvement over the rather sparse and sterile demographic profiles that have been traditional in marketing research. (p. 30)

The system of lifestyle segmentation used most by marketing and public relations practitioners is VALS (for values and lifestyles)—a system developed by SRI International (1985). SRI International markets VALS at a cost to corporate and other users. Currently, 150 users pay from $20,000 to $150,000 per year to use VALS (Rice, 1988, p. 49). Although the VALS instrument is not in the public domain, a number of writers have developed similar systems that could be used by communication planners (e.g., Hanan, 1980; Blackwell & Talarzyk, 1983; Assael, 1984). Jeffres (1986) also has used lifestyles to explain use of the mass media.

The VALS typology was developed from combinations of Maslow's psychological hierarchy of needs and Riesman's sociological concepts of people who are inner- and outer-directed (Rice, 1988). The previous discussion of the relationship of needs to problems shows why the VALS categories can provide social locators of publics. The VALS typology contains nine lifestyles, whose names povide some indication of the nature of the segments: sustainers, survivors, belongers, emulators, achievers, the I-Am-Me's, experientials, socially conscious, and integrateds.

Although psychographic and lifestyle segmentation is used widely, the concepts have not been rigorously tested or validated (Lastovicka, 1982). The technique has also been criticized frequently, essentially because the profiles do not come close enough to the concepts of individual communication and consumer behavior in the innermost nest of Figure 8.1 (Lesser & Hughes, 1986). An advertising executive (Rice, 1988, p. 50), for example, criticized VALS for not being situational:

People don't always think and behave consistently in every context. Some individuals may vote as Belongers but think like Achievers when they walk into the automobile showroom.

Or as John Paluszek, president of Ketchum Public Affairs, put it in describing a campaign for the Beef Industry Council (Winkleman, 1987, p. 23):

> The health issue is intrinsic to beef. . . . Whom do we really want to talk to about beef? We want to go to the people active on the issues.

SUBCULTURES

Subcultures, the last concept in this nest, are narrower than national cultures (Assael, 1984). Like broader cultures, subcultures consist of people with similar values, customs, norms, beliefs and behaviors. Cultural groups are much like psychographic and lifestyle groups, and some researchers working in public relations use anthropological techniques to study cultures and lifestyles (Miller, 1986).

GEODEMOGRAPHICS

The next nest contains a segmentation technique that consists partly of lifestyles and partly of geographic demographics—a technique now widely used in marketing and public relations. Several commercial firms, such as Claritas, Donnelly, and National Decision System, take data from the U. S. Census or from the Nielsen, Arbitron, or Gallup firms and use cluster analysis to group postal zip codes into similar categories (Winkleman, 1987, p. 22). The best-known system, Claritas' PRIZM (Claritas, 1985), produces geodemographic clusters with names like Furs and Station Wagons, Pools and Patios, Young Influentials, and Norma Rae-ville (Winkleman, 1987).

Geodemographic segmentation, like lifestyle segmentation, suffers because it falls in an outer nest and does not predict communication behavior and the existence of publics directly. Planners of communication programs can purchase geodemographic data easily, however, and these data can provide a reasonable substitute for original research to identify publics.

DEMOGRAPHICS/SOCIAL CATEGORIES

Communication researchers and planners long have used demographic cross-tabulations to avoid unfocused dissemination of information to a mass audience, in part because demographics help to explain use of different media. Demographics also serve as useful locators of publics and other segments in inner nests, although the segments identified by demographics usually do not overlap publics closely (see Grunig, 1983a). When time or money does not permit other research, demographics may be the only segmentation tool available to the communication planner.

MASS AUDIENCES

A major premise of this chapter has been that communication campaigns will seldom be effective if they are directed to a mass audience. Mass audiences do have segments embedded in them that communicate actively, and messages directed at an unsegmented population may reach the active segments. Although there will be fewer research costs if a campaign is directed at a mass, the costs of the campaign itself will be much greater. As Cobb and Elder (1972) pointed out, however, mass/general publics are made up primarily of what the author has called apathetic publics—the most passive and unresponsive publics.

At times, communication planners may have no alternative to appealing to a mass audience. The Grunig and Childers (1988) research shows that passive audiences can become more active seekers of information after being passively exposed to messages, although the effect is a weak one. Marketing theorists such as Assael (1984), Lovelock and Weinberg (1984), and Ray (1973) have developed strategies for low-involvement consumer segments. In addition, Biocca (1988) provided evidence from cognitive psychology that messages processed passively can—through preconscious process—produce cognitive effects, a point also made by McQuail (1985).

As a result, communication planners should not write off massive audiences. At times, they may deliberately choose to target them in an effort to produce active segments of that audience.

CONCLUSION

This chapter began with the generalization suggested by previous research on communication that campaigns will be most effective if they are designed for carefully selected segments of the population. The chapter has developed criteria for constructing and choosing a theory of segmentation. It then has developed a nested theory of segmentation concepts that should help communication planners to do the segmentation that will make their campaigns more effective.

NOTES

1. See Grunig and Hunt, 1984, and Ray, 1973, for elaboration of a taxonomy of responses to campaigns.
2. See also Aiken and Mott, 1970, for related studies.

REFERENCES

Aiken, M., & Mott, P. E. (Eds.). (1970). *The structure of community power*. New York: Random House.

Anderson, R. B. (1987, May 1–3). *Reassessing the odds against finding meaningful behavioral change in mass media health promotion campaigns*. Paper presented to the Conference on Communication Theory and Public Relations, Illinois State University, Normal.

Assael, H. (1984). *Consumer behavior and marketing action* (2nd. ed.). Boston: Kent.

Bandura, A. (1977). *Social learning theory*. Englewood Cliffs, NJ: Prentice-Hall.

Bauer, R. (1964). The obstinate audience: The influence process from the point-of-view of social communication. *American Psychologist, 19,* 319–328.

Becker, L. B. (1982). The mass media and citizen assessment of issue importance: A reflection on agenda-setting research. In D. C. Whitney, E. Wartella, & S. Windahl (Eds.), *Mass communication review yearbook* (Vol. 3, pp. 521–536). Newbury Park, CA: Sage.

Biocca, F. A. (1988). Opposing conceptions of the audience: The active and passive hemispheres of mass communication theory. In J. A. Anderson (Ed.), *Communication yearbook 11* (pp. 51–80). Newbury Park, CA: Sage.

Blackwell, R. D., & Talarzyk, W. W. (1983). Life-style retailing: Competitive strategies for the 1980s. *Journal of Retailing, 59(4),* 7–27.

Blumer, H. (1946). The mass, the public, and public opinion. In B. Berelson and M. Janowitz (Eds.), *Reader in public opinion and communication* (2nd ed., 1966, pp. 43–50). New York: Free Press.

Blumler, J. G., & Katz, E. (Eds.). (1974). *The uses of mass communications*. Newbury Park, CA: Sage.

Bonoma, T. V., & Shapiro, B. P. (1983). *Segmenting the industrial market*. Lexington, MA: Lexington Books.

Brehm, J. W., & Cohen, A. R. (1962). *Explorations in cognitive dissonance*. New York: John Wiley.

Buchholz, R. A. (1982). *Business environment and public policy*. Englewood Cliffs, NJ: Prentice-Hall.

Carey, J. W., & Kreiling, A. L. (1974). Popular culture and uses and gratifications: Notes toward an accommodation. In J. G. Blumler & E. Katz (Eds.), *The uses of mass communications* (pp. 225–248). Newbury Park, CA: Sage.

Chaffee, S. H., & Roser, C. (1986). Involvement and the consistency of knowledge, attitudes, and behaviors. *Communication Research*, 13, 373–399.

Claritas (1985). *PRIZM: The integrated marketing solution*. Alexandria, VA. Author.

Cobb, R. W., & Elder, C. D. (1972). *Participation in American politics: The dynamics of agenda building*. Baltimore: Johns Hopkins University Press.

Cravens, D. W. (1982). *Strategic marketing*. Homewood, IL: Irwin.

Cunningham, W. H., & Cunningham, I. C. M. (1981). *Marketing: A managerial approach*. Cincinnati: South-Western.

Dervin B. (1981). Mass communicating: Changing conceptions of the audience. In R. E. Rice & W. J. Paisley (Eds.), *Public communication campaigns* (pp. 71–87). Newbury Park, CA: Sage.

Dervin, B., Jacobson, T. L., & Nilan, M. S. (1982). Measuring aspects of information seeking: A test of a quantitative/qualitative methodology. In M. Burgoon (Ed.), *Communication yearbook 6* (pp. 419–444). Newbury Park, CA: Sage.

Dewey, J. (1910). *How we think*. New York: Heath.

Dewey, J. (1927). *The public and its problems*. Chicago: Swallow.

Dewey, J. (1938). *Logic: The theory of inquiry*. New York: Henry Holt.

Dewey, J. (1939). *Theory of valuation*. Chicago: University of Chicago Press.

Dickson, P. R. (1982). Person-situation: Segmentation's missing link. *Journal of Marketing, 46* (Fall), 56–64.

Engel, J. G., Blackwell, R. D., & Kollat, D. T. (1978). *Consumer behavior* (3rd ed.). Hinsdale, IL: Dryden.

Festinger, L. (1957). *A theory of cognitive dissonance*. Stanford, CA: Stanford University Press.

Flay, B. R., & Cook, T. D. (1981). Evaluation of mass media prevention campaigns. In R. E. Rice & W. J. Paisley (Eds.), *Public communication campaigns* (pp. 239–264). Newbury Park, CA: Sage.

Frank, R. E., Massy, W. F., & Wind, Y. (1972). *Market segmentation*. Englewood Cliffs, NJ: Prentice-Hall.

Freedman, J. L., & Sears, D. O. (1965). Selective exposure. In L. Berkowitz (Ed.) *Advances in experimental social psychology* (Vol. 2, pp. 57–97). New York: Academic Press.

Freeman, R. E. (1984). *Strategic management: A stakeholder approach*. Boston: Pitman.

Graber, D. A. (1984). *Processing the news*. New York: Longman.

Grunig, J. E. (1971). Communication and the economic decisionmaking processes of Colombian peasants. *Economic Development and Cultural Change, 19,* 580–597.

Grunig, J. E. (1975). Some consistent types of employee publics. *Public Relations Review, 1*(4), 17–36.

Grunig, J. E. (1977). Evaluating employee communication in a research operation. *Public Relations Review, 3*(4), 61–82.

Grunig, J. E. (1978). Defining publics in public relations: The case of a suburban hospital. *Journalism Quarterly, 55,* 109–118.

Grunig, J. E. (1979a). Time budgets, level of involvement and use of the mass media. *Journalism Quarterly, 56,* 248–261.

Grunig, J. E. (1979b). A new measure of public opinions on corporate social responsibility. *Academy of Management Journal, 22,* 738–764.

Grunig, J. E. (1982a). The message-attitude-behavior relationship: Communication behaviors of organizations. *Communication Research, 9,* 163–200.

Grunig, J. E. (1982b). Developing economic education programs for the press. *Public Relations Review, 8*(3), 43–62.

Grunig, J. E. (1983a). Communication behaviors and attitudes of environmental publics: Two studies. *Journalism Monographs, 81.*

Grunig, J. E. (1983b). Washington reporter publics of corporate public affairs programs. *Journalism Quarterly, 60,* 603–615.

Grunig, J. E. (1987). *When active publics become activists: Extending a situational theory of publics.* Paper presented to the International Communication Association, Montreal.

Grunig, J. E., & Childers, L. (1988). *Reconstruction of a situational theory of communication: Internal and external concepts as identifiers of publics for AIDS.* Paper presented to the Association for Education in Journalism and Mass Communication, Portland, OR.

Grunig, J. E., & Hunt, T. (1984). *Managing public relations.* New York: Holt, Rinehart and Winston.

Grunig, J. E., & Ipes, D. A. (1983). The anatomy of a campaign against drunk driving. *Public Relations Review, 9*(2), 36–53.

Grunig, J. E., & Stamm, K. R. (1979). Cognitive strategies and the resolution of environmental issues: A second study. *Journalism Quarterly, 56,* 715–726.

Grunig, J. E., Nelson, C. L., Richburg, S. J., & White, T. J. (1988). Communication by agricultural publics: Internal and external orientations. *Journalism Quarterly, 65,* 26–38.

Hanan, M. (1980). *Life-styled marketing* (rev. ed.). New York: Amacom.

Heath, R. L. & Nelson, R. A. (1986). *Issues management.* Newbury Park, CA: Sage.

Hyman, H. H., & Sheatsley, P. B. (1947). Some reasons why information campaigns fail. *Public Opinion Quarterly, 11,* 412–423.

Jeffres, L. W. (1986). *Mass media processes and effects.* Prospect Heights, IL: Waveland.

Kassarjian, H. H. (1981). Low involvement—a second look. In K. B. Monroe (Ed.), *Advances in consumer research,* (Vol. 8, pp. 31–34). Ann Arbor, MI: Association for Consumer Research.

Katz, E., Blumler, J. G., & Gurevitch, M. (1974). Utilization of mass communication by the individual. In J. G. Blumler & E. Katz (Eds.) *The uses of mass communications* (pp. 19–32). Newbury Park, CA: Sage.

Katz, E., & Lazarsfeld, P. F. (1955). *Personal influence*. Glencoe, IL: Free Press.

Kotler, P., & Andreasen, A. R. (1987). *Strategic marketing for nonprofit organizations* (3rd ed.). Englewood Cliffs, NJ: Prentice-Hall.

Krugman, H. E. (1965). The impact of television advertising: Learning without involvement. *Public Opinion Quarterly, 29,* 349–356.

Lang, G. E., & Lang, K. (1983). *The battle for public opinion*. New York: Columbia University Press.

Lastovicka, J. L. (1982). On the validation of lifestyle traits: A review and illustration. *Journal of Marketing Research, 19 (February),* 126–138.

Lazarsfeld, P. F., Berelson, B., & Gaudet, H. (1948). *The people's choice*. New York: Columbia University Press.

Lehmann, D. R., Moore, W. L., & Elrod, T. (1982). The development of distinct choice process segments over time: A stochastic modeling approach. *Journal of Marketing, 46*(Spring), 48–59.

Lesser, J. A., & Hughes, M. A. (1986). The generalizability of psychographic market segments across geographic locations. *Journal of Marketing, 50* (January), 18–27.

Levitt, T. (1986). *The marketing imagination* (exp. ed.). New York: Free Press.

Levy, M. R., & Windahl, S. (1984). Audience activity and gratification: A conceptual clarification and exploration. *Communication Research, 11,* 51–78.

Lindenmann, W. K. (1980). Use of community case studies in opinion research. *Public Relations Review, 6*(2), 40–50.

Lionberger, H. F., & Gwin, P. H. (1982). *Communication strategies: A guide for agricultural change agents*. Danville, IL: Interstate.

Lovelock, C. H., & Weinberg, C. B. (1984). *Marketing for public and nonprofit managers*. New York: John Wiley.

Lowery, S., & De Fleur, M. L. (1983). *Milestones in mass communication research*. New York: Longman.

Luck, D. J., & Ferrell, O. C. (1985). *Marketing strategy and plans* (2nd ed.). Englewood Cliffs, NJ: Prentice-Hall.

Lunn, T. (1986). Segmenting and constructing markets. In R. M. Worcester & J. Downham (Eds.), *Consumer market research handbook* (3rd ed., pp. 387–423). Amsterdam: North Holland.

Maccoby, N., & Solomon, D. S. (1981). Heart disease prevention: Community studies. In R. E. Rice & W. J. Paisley (Eds.), *Public communication campaigns* (pp. 105–126). Newbury Park, CA: Sage.

Maslow, A. H. (1970). *Motivation and personality* (2nd ed.). New York: Harper & Row.

Massy, W. F., & Weitz. B. A. (1977). A normative theory of market segmentation. In F. M. Nicosia & Y. Wind (Eds.), *Behavioral models for market analysis: Foundations for marketing action* (pp. 121–144). Hinsdale, IL: Dryden.

McCombs, M. E. (1981). The agenda-setting approach. In D. D. Nimmo & K. R. Sanders (Eds.), *Handbook of political communication* (pp. 121–140). Newbury Park, CA: Sage.

McGuire, W. J. (1974). Psychological motives and communication gratification. In J. G. Blumler & E. Katz (Eds.), *The uses of mass communications* (pp. 167–196). Newbury Park, CA: Sage.

McGuire, W. J. (1981). Theoretical foundations of campaigns. In R. E. Rice & W. J. Paisley (Eds.), *Public communication campaigns* (pp. 41–70). Newbury Park, CA: Sage

McQuail, D. (1983). *Mass communication theory*. Newbury Park, CA: Sage.

McQuail, D. (1985). With the benefit of hindsight: Reflections on uses and gratifications research. In M. Gurevitch and M. R. Levy (Eds.) *Mass communication review yearbook* (Vol. 5, pp. 125–141). Newbury Park, CA: Sage.

Mendelsohn, H. (1973). Some reasons why information campaigns can succeed. *Public Opinion Quarterly, 37,* 50–61.

Michman, R. C. (1983). *Marketing to changing consumer markets*. New York: Praeger.

Miller, D. A. (1986). *Psychographics . . . a study in diversity*. Unpublished manuscript, University of Maryland, College Park.

Mittelmark, M. B., Luepker, M. D., Jacobs, D. R., Bracht, N. F., Carlaw, R. W., Crow, R. S., Finnegan, J., Grimm, R. H., Jeffery, R. W., Kline, G. F., Mullis, R. M., Murray, D. M., Pechacek, T. F., Perry, C. L., Pirie, P. L., & Blackburn, H. (1986). Community-wide prevention of cardiovascular disease: Education strategies of the Minnesota Heart Health Program. *Preventive Medicine, 15,* 661–672.

Myers, R. E., Jr. (1986). Communication behaviors of Maryland farmers: an analysis of adopters and nonadopters of innovations to reduce agricultural pollution of the Chesapeake Bay. (Masters thesis, University of Maryland, College Park, 1985). *Journalism Abstracts, 24,* 75.

Nash, J. D., & Farquhar, J. W. (1980) Applications of behavioral medicine to disease prevention in a total community setting: A review of the three community study. In J. M. Ferguson & C. B. Taylor (Eds.), *The comprehensive handbook of behavioral medicine* (pp. 313–335). New York: Spectrum.

Palmgreen, P. (1984). Uses and gratifications: A theoretical perspective. In R. N. Bostrom (Ed.), *Communication yearbook 8* (pp. 20–55). Newbury Park, CA: Sage.

Petty, R. E., & Cacioppo, J. T. (1986). *Communication and persuasion: Central and peripheral routes to attitude change*. New York: Springer-Verlag.

Preston, I. L. (1970). A reinterpretation of the meaning of involvement in Krugman's models of advertising communication. *Journalism Quarterly, 47,* 287–295.

Price, V. (1988). Effects of communicating group conflicts of opinion: An experimental investigation. (Doctoral dissertation, Stanford University, 1987). *Dissertation Abstracts International, 7,* 1572A.

Ray, M. L. (1973). Marketing communication and the hierarchy of effects. In P. Clarke (Ed.), *New models for mass communication research* (pp. 147–176). Beverly Hills, CA: Sage.

Rice, B. (1988, March). The selling of lifestyles. *Psychology Today, 22,* 46–50.

Robertson, T. S. (1971). *Innovative behavior and communication*. New York: Holt, Rinehart & Winston.

Rogers, E. M. (1983). *Diffusion of innovations* (3rd ed.). New York: Free Press.

Rosengren, K. E., Wenner, L. A., & Palmgreen, P. (Eds.). (1985). *Media gratifications research: Current perspectives*. Newbury Park, CA: Sage.

Rothschild, M. L., & Ray, M. L. (1974). Involvement and political advertising effect: An exploratory experiment. *Communication Research, 1,* 264–285.

Salmon, C. T. (1986). Perspectives on involvement in consumer and communication research. In B. Dervin & M. J. Voigt, *Progress in communication sciences* (Vol. 7, pp. 243–269). Norwood, N.J.: Ablex.

Sherif, C. W., Sherif, M., & Nebergall, R. E. (1965). *Attitude and attitude change: The social judgment-involvement approach*. Westport, CT: Greenwood Press.

Slama, M. E., & Tashchian, A. (1985). Selected socioeconomic and demographic characteristics associated with purchasing involvement. *Journal of Marketing, 49* (Winter), 72–82.

Smith, W. R. (1956). Product differentiation and market segmentation as alternative marketing strategies. In C. G. Walters & D. P. Robin (Eds.), *Classics in marketing* (pp. 433–439). Santa Monica, CA: Goodyear.

SRI International (1985). *VALS—values and lifestyles of Americans*. Menlo Park, CA: Author

Srivastava, R. K., Alpert, M. I., & Shocker, A. D. (1984). A customer-oriented approach for determining market structures. *Journal of Marketing, 48*(Spring), 32–45.

Stamm, K. R., & Grunig, J. E. (1977). Communication situations and cognitive strategies for the resolution of environmental issues. *Journalism Quarterly, 54,* 713–720.

Taylor, J. W. (1986). *Competitive marketing strategies*. Radnor, PA: Chilton.

Tichenor, P. J., Donohue, G. A., & Olien, C. N. (1980). *Community conflict and the press*. Newbury Park, CA: Sage.

Wells, W. D., & Tigert, D. J. (1971). Activities, interests, and opinions. *Journal of Advertising Research, 11*(August), 27–35.

Winkleman, M. (1987). Their aim is true. *Public Relations Journal, 43* (August), 18–19, 22–23, 39.

Wright, C. R. (1986). *Mass communication: A sociological perspective* (3rd ed.). New York: Random House.

Chapter 9

MESSAGE STRATEGIES FOR INFORMATION CAMPAIGNS: A SOCIAL-PSYCHOLOGICAL ANALYSIS

Patricia G. Devine and Edward R. Hirt

EVERY DAY, WE ARE BOMBARDED with persuasive communications from a number of sources. Advertisers attempt to convince us that their products are the very best available on the market. Political campaign planners try to get our votes by convincing us that their candidate is the best person for the job. Social reform advocates point out shortcomings in existing public policy and attempt to rally support for proposed policy changes. In this chapter we will discuss several social psychological theories and identify their implications for understanding, creating and evaluating information campaigns. Following a comparison of the information campaign and attitude-behavior literatures, we offer two general approaches to influencing audience behavior: message-based and behavioral-based models of persuasion. We then discuss research findings on the link between attitudes and behavior, and finally offer recommendations for considerations in the design of message strategies.

However, before getting into the theoretical issues, we feel it is essential to consider issues concerning the definition of information campaigns and measures of campaign effectiveness. Typically, information about a product or a political candidate is presented as part of a systematic, organized information campaign. The term *information campaign* has been variably defined in the literature (Rogers & Storey, 1987). In order to develop a working definition of information campaigns for this chapter, we abstracted the common elements from the many existing definitions. Thus, for purposes of this chapter, information campaigns are defined as organized attempts to influence another's beliefs about, attitudes toward, and/or behaviors with respect to some object (e.g., product, issue, person, etc.) through the use of mass media or other communication channels. This definition suggests that campaign effectiveness could be assessed against a variety of criteria.

In general, there appear to be three outcomes that are identified as goals of information campaigns: to *inform,* to *persuade,* and to *mobilize* the public (Rogers & Storey, 1987). However, examination of the campaign literature suggests that what constitutes a successful information campaign is ambiguous at best. Campaign goals are typically not well specified, and measures of effectiveness differ from campaign to campaign (see the chapter by Salmon in this volume). Without clear goal specification, it is impossible to ascertain what would be appropriate and valid measures of campaign effectiveness.

Historically, discussions of the effectiveness of information campaigns have focused on questions of "outcome" rather than "process." we would like to argue, however, that there are limitations to the outcome-oriented approach to information campaigns.[1] For example, day-after recall findings are not directly related to the purchasing behavior of consumers. Recall can be high for disliked products (e.g., products with which the consumer has had an unfavorable experience and which he or she therefore avoids), but the effect on persuasion is a boomerang. In this instance, high recall is functional so that the disliked product can be avoided. In addition, low recall for an advertisement does not necessarily imply that the consumer will not purchase the product (see Greenwald, 1968, for a discussion of related research). Likewise, consumers may have positive attitudes toward expensive cars but have no intention whatsoever of purchasing one, due to financial restrictions. Other factors besides attitudes toward the product can affect purchases without changing purchase intentions or attitudes toward the product. For example, availability of the product or the availability of alternatives may influence one's purchase. If a store is out of the laundry detergent that one typically purchases, a consumer is likely to choose the next best detergent. This does not imply that the consumer did not intend to buy the regular brand or that the regular brand is no longer liked.[2]

Taking an outcome approach irrespective of process limits campaigners' opportunities to learn from the campaign. That is, campaigners can ascertain *whether* a campaign was effective by examining outcomes, but they cannot tell from this strategy *why* one campaign was successful and another was a failure. New campaigns are often modeled after previous campaigns that were identified as successful; unsuccessful campaign strategies are typically avoided. To the extent that new campaigns are modeled after campaigns whose success was serendipitous, campaigners cannot be sure that the new campaign will produce desired outcomes.

In this chapter, we argue that even if the central issue for campaigners is to obtain a specific outcome—whether it be knowledge, attitudes, or behavior—the key to successful campaigns is an understanding of the processes that lead to that outcome. In fact, the central theme unifying this chapter is that an understanding of persuasion as a process allows campaign planners to expeditiously design message strategies to achieve desired goals. In the absence of this understanding, campaigners may use inappropriate or inefficient strategies, or strategies needlessly targeted at a secondary rather than a primary goal of most campaigns—namely, human behavior.

PARALLELS IN THE INFORMATION CAMPAIGN AND ATTITUDE-BEHAVIOR LITERATURES

There are parallels in the types of questions asked in the history of research on information campaigns and the history of research on the relation between attitudes and behavior (Rogers & Storey, 1987). For example, Zanna and Fazio (1982) suggested that the history of attitude-behavior research can be divided into three generations, characterized by the type of questions that guided the research in each generation. The questions guiding the three generations of research have been referred to as the "Is," "When," and "How" questions. "Is" questions essentially ask whether there is a relation between attitudes and behavior. The parallel in the first era of campaign research was to ask whether information campaigns "are" effective. The pessimism in early attitude-behavior research (Wicker, 1969) also has parallels in the campaign research; whereas attitudes were shown not to be reliably related to behavior, campaigns in this era were shown not to be consistently successful. Neither attitude nor campaign researchers were willing to dispose of their concepts, and the second generation of research was directed to discovering the conditions under which and the types of people for whom attitudes could be expected to guide behavior, in the attitude domain, and the conditions under which and the types of people for whom campaigns could be expected to be successful, in the campaign domain. Addressing the "When" questions has been productive in both domains. Many variables have been identified that moderate the attitude-behavior relation (see Fazio, 1986, for a review) and the effectiveness of information campaigns (see Rogers & Storey, 1987, for a review). It has not necessarily been made clear, however, why or how these variables have their effects.

The third-generation "How" questions in the attitude-behavior domain are designed to address this issue. "How" questions focus on the *process* by which attitudes guide behavior (see Fazio, 1986). The emphasis on process may reveal why many of the factors identified during the "When" generation of research produce their effects. We would like to argue that a similar emphasis on process in the information campaign research, in addition to the current emphasis on outcome, would be similarly productive. In the area of persuasion, the work of Greenwald (1968; see also Petty, Ostrom, & Brock, 1981) on the role of cognitive responses in persuasion and the work of Petty and Cacioppo (1981, 1986a, 1986b) on the Elaboration Likelihood Model can generally be considered in the domain of "How" questions. Although the research done to test these models usually takes advantage of single communication settings in contrast to the typical multiple communication settings of information campaigns, the process implications of these models can easily be generalized to campaign settings. These process models and their relevance for information campaigns are more fully elaborated in the section dealing with theories of persuasion.

THEORIES OF PERSUASION: MESSAGE-BASED AND BEHAVIORAL-BASED MODELS

Most theories of persuasion operate under the assumption that producing attitude change is the key to producing behavior change (McGuire, 1981; Petty & Cacioppo, 1981). This assumption argues for a directional influence from attitudes to behavior (A $--\rightarrow$ B). Some persuasion strategies try to affect attitudes directly through message factors, whereas other strategies attempt to influence attitudes indirectly through behavior. The primary difference between message-based and behavioral-based persuasion concerns the source of that initial information that provides the basis for the attitude (i.e., either a message from a communicator or the recipient's own experience).

Whether the goal is attitude formation or attitude change, the focus of such strategies is on producing positive attitudes toward the topic of the persuasive communication. It is assumed that if positive attitudes can be elicited, for example, then behavior consistent with those attitudes will follow. The issue of how attitudes guide behavior has been of secondary interest to those who study persuasion from the message-based perspective, and they have not typically been specific concerning this part of the process. Recent work in social psychology on the attitude-behavior relation (e.g., Fazio, 1986; Fazio, Chen, McDonel, & Sherman, 1982; Fazio, Powell, & Herr, 1983) suggests that attitudes do not necessarily guide behavior and require very specific conditions to do so.

MESSAGE-BASED PERSUASION

Taking a message-based persuasion (A $--\rightarrow$ B) approach, the important question concerns how attitudes can be affected directly. In message-based persuasion, the persuasive communication itself provides the information about the attitude object. That is, communications are constructed to convey information about the attitude object (e.g., sets of arguments in favor of the object) with the expectation that the communication will be compelling enough to lead to positive attitudes about the object and that the positive attitudes, in turn, will lead to positive behavior toward the object. For example, political campaigners develop communications to convey information regarding the candidate's stands on important domestic and foreign policy issues with the goal of creating a positive view of the candidate (e.g., as a leader and trustworthy person who is worthy of votes), with the expectation that this positive view will lead voters to actually vote for the candidate.

The best examples of message-based persuasion are McGuire's (1981) information-processing model, Greenwald's (1968) cognitive response theory, and Petty and Cacioppo's (1986a, 1986b)

Elaboration-Likelihood Model. An important assumption of these models is that any effect on behavior will be mediated by communication recipients' attitudes toward the topic of the communication.

Information-Processing Model

McGuire's model suggests that responses to a persuasive communication occur in the following series of stages: exposure, attention, comprehension, yielding, retention of the message. Behavior, according to this model, occurs at some point after these five stages and requires that the message and one's attitude be recalled from memory. The empirical efforts derived from this theoretical model have focused on determining aspects of the message (e.g., one- vs. two-sided communications, complexity of message, message repetition, arousal of fear, etc.), the source (e.g., credibility, attractiveness, similarity to communication recipients), the audience (e.g., self-esteem, intelligence) and the medium (or channel) of communication (e.g., print, radio, television, face-to-face communications, etc.) that influence the likelihood that communication recipients will form positive attitudes toward the communication. To review the effects associated with all the variables listed is beyond the scope of this chapter, and we refer readers to Petty and Cacioppo (1981) for a review. What is important for the present purposes is that the stages are assumed to occur in a fixed sequence, and, to the extent that one of the stages fails (e.g., the audience does not attend to or understand the message), the process stops.

An interesting aspect of the model is that yielding, which is a key stage in the model, either occurs or it does not. However, it is not clear in the model *why* yielding occurs. Researchers know that certain factors make yielding more likely (e.g., highly credible sources—at least in some circumstances), but the processes underlying yielding are left unspecified. We argue that the information processing model is an outcome-based model and suffers from the limitations of outcome-based models discussed previously.

Consider, for example, that some of the obtained findings in the persuasion literature are inexplicable from the perspective of outcome-based models of persuasion. The sometimes observed boomerang effects (i.e., attitude change in the opposite direction than expected) are difficult to explain from outcome-based models, and the persuasive communications that generated the boomerang outcome can be categorized simply as ineffective in eliciting persuasion. Outcome-based models do not specify the processes involved in responding to a persuasive communication that would render boomerang effects explainable. In contrast, the cognitive-response and elaboration likelihood models are message-based models that focus on process rather than outcome.

Cognitive-Response Theory

Greenwald (1968) provides an analysis of the persuasion process that suggests that the cognitive responses (positive or negative thoughts relevant to the communication) that communication recipients generate in response to the persuasive communication are the key to determining the outcome of the persuasion attempt. According to the cognitive-response approach to persuasion, persuasion is a function of the number of positive compared to the number of negative thoughts elicited by the communication. When there are a greater number of positive thoughts (proarguments) than negative thoughts (counterarguments), persuasion occurs. But when recipients generate more negative thoughts than positive thoughts, boomerang occurs.

A study by Sternthal, Dholakia, and Leavitt (1978) provides another compelling example of the need to focus on process issues. These authors demonstrated that sources low in credibility can be more persuasive than sources high in credibility, an effect unexpected from the outcome-based information-processing model. This counterintuitive finding cannot be explained without appealing to the processes involved in responding to the persuasive communication and the precommunication attitudes of the subjects in the study.

Subjects in Sternthal et al.'s study were supportive of the position advocated in the communication. The authors suggested that when the topic is important to the audience and the communicator is low in credibility, audience members cannot trust the communicator to represent their views adequately. As the audience listens to the communication, they try to bolster or strengthen the arguments presented to them by the low-credibility source. Thus, in addition to the arguments given to them by the low credibility source, the audience has an additional set of self-generated, communication-supportive thoughts that contribute to the audience's reaction to the communication. Because high-credibility sources are expected to represent the audience's views well, audience members do not engage in this bolstering process. In Sternthal et al.'s study, the number of proarguments generated in response to the communication from the low-credibility communicator exceeded the number of proarguments generated in response to the high-credibility communicator. In a sense, the subjects responding to the low-credibility communicator persuaded themselves. It was only by focusing on the types of cognitive responses generated in the process of responding to the persuasive communication that the researchers were able to render a puzzling, previously inexplicable finding not only understandable but expected. The greatest advantage of the cognitive-response approach to persuasion is that it provides an analysis of the process by which people elaborate upon persuasive messages.

Elaboration-Likelihood Model

Petty and Cacioppo (1981, 1986a) have also offered a process model concerning how communication recipients respond to persuasive messages. In general, their Elaboration-Likelihood Model suggests that there are two primary routes to persuasion: central and peripheral. Which route to persuasion dominates in the persuasion setting depends on the probability that communication recipients carefully scrutinize and elaborate upon message arguments. Elaboration likelihood is high when the communication issue has personal relevance for recipients, recipients have high need for cognition, and recipients have ample time to consider the message. The high elaboration likelihood component, or central route processing, of Petty and Cacioppo's model essentially subsumes the cognitive-response approach to persuasion. If message arguments are of high quality (e.g., cogent, sensible), recipients are expected to generate favorable thoughts related to the communication. Low quality (weak, specious) arguments elicit primarily counterarguments. Attitude change (whether it be persuasion or boomerang) depends upon the communication recipients' cognitive responses (pro vs. counterarguments, etc.) to the message. When both personal relevance and message quality are high, persuasion is expected. When personal relevance is high but message quality is low, persuasion is not expected, and boomerang would certainly be possible (Petty & Cacioppo, 1979; Petty, Cacioppo, & Goldman, 1981).

When elaboration likelihood is low (e.g., conditions of low personal relevance, low need for cognition, time pressure), the peripheral route to persuasion dominates. Communication recipients do not think carefully about message arguments and are more responsive to positive or negative cues associated with the message (e.g., source credibility or attractiveness) or the use of simple decision rules that obviate the need for careful scrutiny of the content of message arguments (e.g., the more arguments, the better). For elaboration likelihood to be high, communication recipients must have both the motivation and the ability to process the communication. To the extent that either motivation or ability is absent (e.g., low personal relevance or distraction, respectively), communication recipients will not elaborate on the communication and the peripheral route to persuasion dominates.

In contrast to the information processing model, the Elaboration Likelihood Model of persuasion focuses on how a persuasive communication has its effect on attitudes and not simply whether or not the communication exerts an influence on attitudes. The Elaboration Likelihood Model suggests that attitude changes that occur through the central route are likely to persist longer than attitude changes that occur through the peripheral route (Cialdini et al., 1975). In addition, Petty and Cacioppo (1986b) argue that attitudes formed through the central route (under conditions of high personal relevance or vested interest) are more predictive of behavior than attitudes formed through the peripheral route (Sivacek & Crano, 1982).

It is with this type of process focus that we begin to get a clearer sense of why and when the previously examined variables such as source credibility, message repetition, etc., influence recipients' attitudes. Moreover, the process orientation suggests how such variables are likely to interact with each other to determine the ultimate impact on attitudes. The Elaboration-Likelihood Model is particularly appealing in the sense that it attempts to specify the processes by which a persuasive communication has its impact on attitudes. More than any other model of persuasion posed to date, the Elaboration-Likelihood Model provides insights on how and why persuasive communications are (or are not) effective in producing attitude change. It accounts for persuasion effects under conditions in which audience members carefully scrutinize persuasive messages (i.e., high elaboration likelihood) and when they do not (i.e., low elaboration likelihood).

In line with other models of message-based persuasion, the

Elaboration-Likelihood Model suggests that changes in behavior result from changes in attitudes. One shortcoming of the message-based models is that they have, by and large, failed to test the assumed link between changes in attitudes and changes in behavior. In fairness to these models of persuasion, we recognize that these models were developed to explain the persuasion process, conceptualized as attitude change. If, however, these models are to be useful to information campaigners (and we think they can be useful), greater emphasis needs to be placed on strengthening the attitude-behavior link. Strategies for strengthening the attitude-behavior link are discussed later in the chapter.

BEHAVIORAL-BASED PERSUASION

In behavioral-based persuasion, the process requires that campaigners must first get the target of the campaign to perform some behavior before attitude formation or change occurs. The subsequently formed attitude could be based on positive experiences with the object or could serve as justification for the initial behavior. As such, behavior must precede attitude ($B_1 \dashrightarrow A$). The behavior serves as an important source of information upon which an attitude (favorable or unfavorable) can be formed (or modified). Then, as in message-based persuasion, the assumption is that once an attitude is formed, it will guide behavior in attitude-consistent directions ($B_1 \dashrightarrow A \dashrightarrow B_2$). However, in order to fully utilize and understand the process of behavioral-based persuasion, campaigners must focus on two major issues: (1) How can one initiate behavior (e.g., induce trial)?, and (2) How does that behavior then get translated into the formation (or change) of an attitude? This section examines how various social psychological theories might help campaigners to address these critical questions.

Social-Learning Theory

Social psychology has many theories that suggest methods by which information campaigns can induce trial behavior. Social-learning theory (Bandura, 1969, 1977; Peter & Olson, 1987), for instance, argues that we often imitate the behavior of models. Thus, in information campaigns, an effective approach for initiating behavior would be to show someone performing the targeted behavior (e.g., buying some product). To the extent that the viewer of this model sees that the model had a positive experience with the product (i.e., was positively reinforced for purchasing and using it), the viewer will be likely to imitate that behavior on a future occasion. Likewise, if a model has negative experiences with an "inferior brand" of a product, viewers may avoid the bargain brand in favor of the superior, nonbargain brand through processes of negative reinforcement (e.g., avoid having trash strewn all over one's driveway by avoiding bargain brand trash bags, avoid embarrassing dandruff by using a shampoo that controls dandruff, and so on).

However, campaigners would be wise to consider the importance of such factors as their choice of a model or models (e.g., a celebrity, a person-on-the-street, an authority figure, a child) to maximize the degree to which the audience will identify with the model(s). It is certainly not the case that we will identify with or compare ourselves to any model. Social comparison theory (Festinger, 1954) suggests that we are likely to compare ourselves with similar others. Brock (1965) demonstrated the effectiveness of making sources similar to recipients in a purchase situation. When the clerk in a paint store indicated to consumers that he was similar to them in important ways, he was able to convince the consumers to purchase one brand of paint over another. This is not to deny the effectiveness of high-credibility sources (who likely have more expertise on a topic) or highly attractive communicators (who may have more positive features than we do), but there are some instances (or some products) that may benefit from making sources similar to recipients. Under ambiguous situations (e.g., deciding what kinds of clothes, music, political beliefs are in fashion), we tend to look toward similar others for information or "social proof" (Cialdini, 1988). For example, charity telethons repeatedly point out to us the large number of people (just like ourselves) who have already contributed to the cause, indicating that it must be the "right" thing to do.

Heuristic Effects

This previous example leads us to consider other techniques by which campaigners can induce compliance with behavioral requests. As will be seen, many of these techniques take advantage of simple or heuristic rules that people employ in making decisions. By and large, these rules are reasonable guides for judgment; however, under certain circumstances, they can be inappropriately applied, leading to serious errors in judgment (see also Nisbett & Ross, 1980). People tend to automatically apply these heuristic rules in situations without consideration of the possible consequences, allowing campaigners to use the techniques to their full advantage (Cialdini, 1988). For instance, people tend to follow the prescriptions of authority figures. In general, authority figures (e.g., our parents, law enforcement officials, doctors, and so on) give us good advice; however, the blind obedience to authority figures is unwarranted and can have negative consequences (e.g., Milgram, 1974; Cohen & Davis, 1981). Communicators with the trappings of authority (e.g., Robert Young and other TV doctors) are often utilized in advertisements in order to get people to comply with recommended behaviors. Similarly, people tend to find it difficult to refuse requests made to them by individuals that they like. As a result, an effective technique in inducing compliance is to use friends and neighbors rather than total strangers to deliver the request. Campaigners can effectively use this rule to elicit compliance in communication recipients by making it appear that people like us (and therefore people we tend to like, Byrne, 1969) also use product X, plan to vote for candidate Y, or favor social reform policy Z.

Probably the most directly relevant of these heuristic rules for eliciting compliance is the reciprocity rule. Very simply, this rule suggests that when someone does you a favor, you are obliged to return the favor. This rule underlies many successful sales tactics. The "free sample," according to this idea, may not be "free" after all if it obligates the customer to feel the need to return the favor by purchasing the product.

Self-Perception Theory

Each of the heuristic rules we have summarized are most likely to be effective in eliciting one-time behaviors rather than repeated behaviors (i.e., behaviors over time, such as wearing seat belts or exercising). However, the most important question regarding behavioral-based persuasion concerns how these "one-time" behaviors are translated into positive attitudes ($B_1 \dashrightarrow A$) which can lead to subsequent attitude-consistent behaviors ($A \dashrightarrow B_2$). Several social psychological theories have addressed the issue of how behavior affects attitudes. For example, self-perception theory (Bem, 1972) suggests that individuals infer their attitudes by observing their own behavior. To the extent that our behavior does not appear to be under environmental constraints (and thus is freely chosen), we infer that our behavior must reflect our own underlying attitudes or dispositions. Many compliance techniques are designed to encourage people to engage in self-perception processes in response to the induced behaviors.

The foot-in-the-door technique (Freedman & Fraser, 1966; De-Jong, 1979) exemplifies these processes well. The foot-in-the-door phenomenon suggests that after complying with a small initial request (e.g., donating $1.00 to a cause), people are more likely to comply with a subsequent larger request (e.g., donating $10.00 to the cause) than if the initial small request had not been made. Explanations for this phenomenon have focused on changes that occur in peoples' self-perceptions as a function of having complied with the initial request. Those who make the initial donation may come to see themselves as socially conscious individuals who support worthy causes. As a result of these self-perception processes, people may infer attitudes consistent with their behavior and become *committed* to subsequent behaviors consistent with their newly formed attitudes.

A specific example of such processes in the domain of information campaigns is found in a study of energy conservation by Pallak, Cook, and Sullivan (1980). These researchers initially induced homeowners to reduce their energy consumption by the promise of public recognition in the form of having their names listed in local newspapers as public-spirited, fuel-conserving citizens. Their ultimate fuel consumption was compared with a group of homeowners who were informed of the benefits of conserving energy and were asked to make such efforts but were not promised any public recognition. Within just one month, the group promised public recognition for conserving energy had drastically cut their fuel consumption, whereas the comparison group had not. The promise of public recognition had its intended effects. Pallak et al. then removed the original reason for the residents' conservation efforts—they were told that their names would *not* be published in the newspaper. Taking away this original reason, however, did not undermine conservation efforts. In fact, their conservation efforts for the remaining part of the winter actually increased! Pallak et al. argued that, once made, the commitment to energy-conservation generated its own support. These homeowners began to acquire energy conservation habits, felt good about their public-spirited efforts, liked the idea of reducing American dependence on foreign fuel, liked the money that they saved on fuel bills, and, perhaps most importantly, came to view themselves as conservation-minded people. They were now committed to the new behavior and attitudes that followed from it. These commitments set up the possibility for the behavior to persist over time and thus to become a repeated behavior (Ronis, Yates, & Dirscht, 1989).

Dissonance Theory

An alternative theory that specifies how behaviors affect attitudes focuses specifically on situations in which one's behavior is discrepant or inconsistent with existing attitudes. Festinger (1957) argued that when behavior contradicts one's attitudes, the person experiences an uncomfortable psychological tension state called cognitive dissonance. One method of alleviating the negative-arousal state of dissonance is to change one's attitude to bring it in line with the undeniable counterattitudinal behavior. For campaigners to take advantage of dissonance-related attitude change, they would need to induce compliance with a request under conditions in which there is insufficient external justification for behavior. It would appear that opportunities for campaigners to employ dissonance techniques are few and far between.

Both self-perception and cognititve dissonance models make process assumptions concerning the manner in which behavior is translated into attitudes (the $B_1 \dashrightarrow A$ link). These models differ in that self-perception theory argues that the inference process is informationally based (e.g., observation of one's own behavior provides the information that serves as a basis for inferences), whereas dissonance theory argues for a motivationally based process (e.g., the discrepancy between behavior and attitudes arouses dissonance, a negative drive state that must be reduced). Although both models make process assumptions, validation of these processes has relied primarily on outcome measures (e.g., attitude change) rather than on specific measures of the underlying mechanisms presumed to lead to attitude change. We would suggest that research efforts focused on delineating the mechanisms that strengthen the $B_1 \dashrightarrow A$

link (i.e., development of some commitment to the new attitude) would be productive.

Operant Conditioning

Operant conditioning also has been applied to the attitude formation process. In operant conditioning, the goal is to elicit some behavior and then to manipulate the consequences that follow the behavior. It has been repeatedly demonstrated that these consequences have implications for the likelihood of repeating the behavior and for the formation of attitudes with regard to the object of the behavior. Consider, for example, a situation in which a behavior is elicited (e.g., a statement in favor of candidate X) and is followed by some positive or negative consequence (e.g., praise or ridicule by one's peers for the behavior). Many studies have supported the notion that we come to hold attitudes that yield rewards and reject attitudes that lead to punishments (Bostrom, Vlandis, & Rosenbaum, 1961; Insko, 1965; Insko & Cialdini, 1969; Scott, 1957). Thus, the consequences following one's behavior can lead to the formation of an attitude that, once in place, could be used to guide subsequent behavior with respect to the attitude object. If campaigners can control the reinforcement contigencies for behavior concerning the topic or issue of their campaign (e.g., have follow-up calls that reinforce campaign-consistent behaviors, provide support services or incentives for those attempting to extinguish undesirable behaviors), they could possibly exert a powerful influence on the formation of topic- or issue-related attitudes.[3]

Summary

In this section, we have identified two persuasion strategies: message-based and behavioral-based.[4] These persuasion strategies may be differentially appropriate to certain types of situations, issues and/or desired outcomes. For instance, under conditions in which people are sufficiently motivated to carefully attend to and evaluate the communication (i.e., conditions of high personal relevance), message-based persuasion may be the most appropriate strategy. If message arguments are strong (i.e., cogent, well-reasoned), persuasion is likely to occur (Petty & Cacioppo, 1979; 1986a,b; Petty et al., 1981). However, under conditions of low personal relevance, behavioral-based persuasion may be most effective. For example, in advertising situations in which consumers need to make decisions among essentially equivalent products (e.g., choosing among brands of laundry detergent or toothpaste), inducing the consumer to try the product may provide the most compelling information about the product. Given a favorable experience with the product, the consumer may then be willing to purchase the product again, potentially leading to the development of commitment or brand loyalty. Message-based strategies would be hard-pressed to develop convincing arguments that would sufficiently differentiate among the products.

This is not to say that message-based persuasion strategies only work under situations of high personal relevance or that behavioral-based persuasion strategies only work under situations of low personal relevance. The research of Petty and Cacioppo has demonstrated that peripheral characteristics of a message (e.g., source characteristics, number of arguments) have large effects on persuasion under situations of low personal relevance, indicating that a message-based strategy can still be effective under these conditions. Moreover, in situations of high personal relevance, one important way that people gain information about the object is to gain experience with the object. For example, when buying a new car, the consumer may not only read *Consumer Reports* (i.e., messages about the cars) but may also test drive the various cars. Test driving can be considered a form of behavioral-based information and may play an important role in the formation and/or change of the consumer's attitudes toward the cars and in the purchasing decision.

ESTABLISHING THE ATTITUDE TO BEHAVIOR LINK

We suggested early in this chapter that the ultimate goal of information campaigns is to affect behavior. We also suggested that there is an implicit assumption that if one can successfully change communication recipients' attitudes toward the target of the communication, behavior consistent with that attitude will follow (e.g., an attitude-to-behavior link). Although this idea has intuitive appeal, it has been difficult to establish empirically (Ajzen & Fishbein, 1977; Calder & Ross, 1973; DeFleur & Westie, 1958; Wicker, 1969). Thus, regardless of whether attitudes are a function of message-based or behavioral-based persuasion strategies, a key issue concerns how attitudes are translated into attitude-consistent behavior. Much of the theoretical work in the area of persuasion and information campaigns has focused on how to influence attitudes. Much less attention in persuasion has focused on the connection between attitudes and behavior. Moreover, persuasion research is relevant to the ultimate goal of behavior change only to the extent to which changes in attitude can be linked to changes in behavior.

We have indicated the directional effect of attitudes on behavior with a dashed line, suggesting that there is a possible but not a necessary one-to-one correspondence between attitudes and behavior (A $--\rightarrow$ B). If information campaigns are going to be effective in terms of producing campaign-consistent behaviors, much more attention will need to be focused on strengthening the connection between attitudes and behavior in the context of the campaign. Abelson (1972) argues that our culture does not encourage people to translate their attitudes into action. If this is true, then campaigners need to be sensitive to this issue and provide campaign recipients with guidelines on how to translate attitudes into campaign-consistent behaviors.

SPECIFYING BEHAVIORAL OPTIONS

The clarity of the behavioral implications that should follow from information campaigns seems to vary across the type of campaign. For example, in most advertising campaigns, the behavioral implication of having a positive attitude toward the product is fairly clear—buy the product. In other domains, however, there is considerably more ambiguity concerning the appropriate behavioral implications of holding favorable or unfavorable attitudes toward the target of the information campaign.

Consider the domain of political campaigns. The most important behavior to elicit from communication recipients is a vote for the candidate. One common difficulty in political settings is actually getting people out to vote. A common notion is that one vote won't make a difference, and those who accept this notion—although eligible to vote—often stay away from the polls. Rarely is the message—"go out and vote"—included in political advertisements. Political advertisements are designed primarily to provide information that will create positive attitudes toward the candidate (or negative attitudes about rival candidates). By and large, the behavioral implications are left unspecified and to be inferred by the recipients. Political information campaigns could be revised to outline a *set* of behaviors that could follow from having a positive attitude toward the candidate (e.g., placing bumper stickers on one's car or signs on one's lawn, attending political rallies, handing out fliers, making donations to the campaign, etc.). Increasing the behavioral options available may increase the likelihood that communication recipients will find at least one option appealing. To the extent that they commit themselves to even one of the suggested alternatives, it may have the effect of increasing their commitment to the cause, which, in turn may serve to get them out to vote (the primary goal) on election day.

Health-promotion and social-reform campaigns encounter the same types of ambiguities on the behavioral side of the campaigns. For example, one can come to believe that the type of social reform called for by an information campaign is a good idea but not really have a good sense of what the positive attitude would imply behaviorally. The communication recipient may wonder where he or she fits into the process. Should a letter be written to a member of Congress, or should a donation be contributed to the cause? Likewise, one may come to believe that diet and exercise are sensible but be unclear on what to do or how to start a diet or exercise program. Should the person seek a doctor's advice, go to Weight Watchers, try one of the "wonder diets" advertised on television or in magazines, etc.? There are many behavioral possibilities, but which behavior should follow from a positive (or negative) attitude may be unclear. Information campaigns that suggest or prescribe appropriate behavioral plans or strategies may turn out to be the most effective. Such strategies may help to change the now dashed line between attitude and behavior into a solid line such that the connection between attitude and the appropriate behavior is more direct.

The technique of providing behavioral instruction has been used productively in examining the role of fear appeals in the persuasive process (see Leventhal, 1970, for a review). For example, it has been demonstrated that recipients are more persuaded by fear-arousing communications when a direct behavioral plan for dealing with the expected negative outcomes are provided (e.g., how to deal with bad oral hygiene or how to stop smoking) and when communication recipients are provided with assurances that the recommendations will help to eliminate the negative consequences. A key to the success of these communications is that the recipients are provided with a specific plan of action. Research on fear-arousing communications that did not include such behavioral suggestions (Janis & Feshbach, 1953) indicated that arousing fear alone was not successful in producing communication-consistent behaviors. It would seem productive, then, for campaigners to provide instruction on how the attitudes can be translated into campaign-consistent behavior.

THE MEASUREMENT-SPECIFICITY ISSUE AND CAMPAIGN EFFECTIVENESS

Another advantage to identifying a range of behaviors that could follow from one's attitude toward a campaign issue concerns evaluating the effectiveness of campaigns. Given that a range of appropriate behaviors exists for many campaign issues, better measures of effectiveness would follow from attempts to examine consistency of the entire range of appropriate behaviors with the general attitude, rather than examining the consistency of the general attitude with only a single behavior. This is especially true in domains in which *the appropriate* behavior is not clearly specified (or there are many possible attitude-consistent behaviors). This problem parallels the measurement specificity issue outlined by Ajzen and Fishbein (Ajzen & Fishbein, 1977, 1980; Fishbein & Ajzen, 1974; Weigel & Newman, 1976) in the attitude-behavior domain. Attempts to predict specific behaviors from global attitude measures generally suggest that there is little correspondence between attitudes and behavior. Global attitudes, however, are predictive of a wider range of behaviors relevant to the attitudinal domain. To the extent that appropriate behaviors are not specified in the context of the information campaign, measuring a single behavior to assess *effectiveness* may actually reflect an underestimation of the campaign's effectiveness.

In our social reform example, if campaigners only measured campaign recipients' donations and not whether they wrote letters to Congress or participated in a rally, they might not have a good measure of the effectiveness of the campaign. In the case of each behavior, various factors may interfere with the relationship between attitudes and behavior (e.g., a person may have another appointment on the day of the rally or may be particularly short on cash when the request for donations is presented, etc.), but the particular combination of factors that could interfere with the attitude-behavior relation is likely to differ from one behavior to another. Measuring the range of behaviors relevant to the attitude object would tend to eliminate the influence of unique factors associated with any given action. Our general suggestion, then, is to broaden the operationalization of effectiveness to provide a more fair and informative test of the success or failure of an information campaign.

It should be noted that campaigners should not only broaden the behaviors that they measure but that they should also measure behaviors over time. Just as a variety of factors can influence any single behavior, many factors can influence behavior at any one measurement time. For example, if one were to measure product buying at only one point in time, it is likely that factors other than one's attitude toward the product would influence purchasing behavior. For example, if the store happens to be temporarily out of stock of a given product, the consumer may purchase an alternate brand. In addition, sales promotions often offer very good deals to entice consumers to try an alternative product. A consumer may decide to take advantage of a good deal without changing his or her attitude toward the original brand. In summary, measuring a variety of behaviors and taking behavioral measures over time may lead to a clearer, more productive assessment of effectiveness.

STRENGTHENING THE ATTITUDE − − → BEHAVIOR CONNECTION

In addition to suggesting specific behavioral plans regarding how to translate attitudes into behavior, campaigners could look to the social psychological literature for some suggestions on how to strengthen the attitude-behavior link. Several factors have been identified that improve the correlation between attitudes and behavior. For example, attitudes formed on the basis of direct behavioral experience with attitude objects are more predictive of behavior than attitudes formed on the basis of indirect, nonbehavioral experience (Regan & Fazio, 1977; Fazio et al., 1982). This type of finding suggests that to the extent that advertisers can provide the opportunity for direct behavioral experience (i.e., induce trial) with a new product (e.g., free samples, cents-off coupons), attitudes toward the product will be more predictive of behavior than attitudes formed on the basis of message-based advertising strategies that involve indirect experience alone (e.g., television or magazine ads). A series of other factors (e.g., vested interest, stability of the attitude, etc.) have been identified as moderators of the attitude-behavior connection (see Fazio, 1986, for a review). To the extent that campaigners can take advantage of such factors, the likelihood of a campaign's success can be increased (provided that the experience with the attitude object was positive).

Recently, Fazio (1986, 1989) has proposed a process model of how attitudes guide behavior. In general, the model assumes that before an attitude can influence behavior, it must be activated from memory (i.e., accessible). Attitude accessibility varies as a function of the strength of the association between the attitude object and one's evaluative reaction to the object. The stronger the object-evaluation association, the greater the accessibility of the attitude. Fazio (Fazio et al., 1982; Powell & Fazio, 1984) has demonstrated in a series of studies that manipulations that serve to increase the accessibility of the attitude (e.g., repeated expression of the attitude, direct experience with the attitude object) increase the attitude-behavior relation. Relatively inaccessible atttitudes are much less likely to guide subsequent behavior with respect to the attitude object. Fazio (1986) has suggested that many of the variables that have been shown to increase the correlation between attitudes and behavior do so through their effects on attitude accessibility. For example, attitudes formed on the basis of direct experience are relatively more accessible in memory than attitudes formed on the basis of indirect experience. It seems likely that knowledge of *how* attitudes exert their influence on behavior would be extremely useful to designers of campaigns to influence behavior. Although Fazio's model suggests that attitudes will not always guide behavior (e.g., situational norms or other attitudes may influence behavior in the immediate setting), it also specifies conditions that are necessary (e.g., attitude accessibility) before attitudes *can* guide behavior.

Another strategy that might be useful in strengthening the connection between atttitudes and behavior that could be used in information campaigns takes advantage of strategies that increase individuals' commitment to the advocated behavior or set of behaviors. Sherman's (1980) research on the self-erasing nature of errors of prediction suggests that it might be productive to induce communication recipients to make self-predictions concerning their future behavior with respect to the campaign issue. This technique would be particularly useful when campaigns advocate socially desirable behaviors, such as in political campaigns (e.g., voting) or health promotion campaigns (e.g., brushing one's teeth, wearing safety belts, or not driving drunk). Sherman found that people tend to predict in such instances that they will do the socially desirable behavior. These self-predictions differ from the actual behavior of a separate but comparable group of subjects who do not make predictions but are only presented with the behavioral opportunity. Sherman argued that the predictions are errors in prediction but that these errors in prediction are self-erasing. Having made the prediction, subjects tend to follow through with prediction-consistent behaviors. The self-prediction apparently increases subjects' commitment to the behavioral request.

Similarly, Gregory Cialdini, and Carpenter (1982) and Anderson (1983) have demonstrated that instructions to imagine scenarios in which the subject is performing the target behavior (e.g., enjoying cable television or donating blood) increase subjects' behavioral intentions to actually perform the behavior. Behavioral intentions also have a direct influence on behavior (see also Ajzen & Fishbein, 1980). In the Gregory et al. study, for example, subjects who imagined themselves enjoying the benefits of cable television were also more likely to make the commitment to subscribe to cable TV than a comparable group of subjects who were merely informed about the benefits of cable TV. These imagination strategies, like the self-predictions in Sherman's research, increased subjects' commitment to the behavior enacted in the imagined scenario.

These self-prediction and imagination techniques, coupled with specific instructions on how to translate attitudes into attitude-consistent behaviors, would likely be very effective in producing successful campaigns. For example, an information campaign designed to decrease the incidence of drunk driving might do well to provide a set of behavioral instructions on how to avoid driving drunk (e.g., make arrangements for tranportation in advance of going out, set up a rule that if one consumes two or more drinks he or she will call a cab for transportation home, choose a designated driver) and follow the communication with a question to the communication recipients asking what they will do the next time they plan to go out and drink alcohol. This type of communication is most likely to be effective when recipients have the motivation and the ability to process the message arguments (e.g., elaboration likelihood is high), because recipients would need time to think about the socially desirable implications of their behavior, and they would need time to make the type of predictions requested.

CONCLUSIONS

The major goal of this chapter has been to relate social psychological theory on attitude and behavior change to the information campaign literature. Social psychology has provided a number of suggestions to improve the measurement of campaign effectiveness. For example, measures of effectiveness should be specific to the goal identified. If the goal identified is global, then campaigners would be wise to measure a broad range of campaign-relevant behaviors if they are to fully measure campaign effectiveness. Otherwise, they may conclude that a campaign has not been effective when, in reality, they simply failed to measure the right behavior(s). In addition, the social psychological literature would encourage campaigners to measure such behaviors (or attitudes or information) over time when the goal is to produce long-term changes. The decision of when to assess effectiveness appears to be somewhat arbitrary, and campaigners may "miss" the changes produced (e.g., if they try to measure effectiveness too early).

In considering the implications of the social psychological literature for information campaigns, we drew a distinction between what we have labeled message-based persuasion and behavioral persuasion. In both types of persuasion, the goal is to influence attitudes, and it is assumed that attitudes will then guide behavior with respect to the attitude object. We would like to briefly explore now some of the conditions under which message-based and behavioral-based persuasion strategies are more or less applicable to the information campaign setting. In information campaigns, the goal is to reach a wide audience. Message-based persuasion, which is dependent on providing audience members with a message and arguments to support the message, would be most effective under conditions in which (1) mass media are available and affordable, (2) there is little opportunity for interpersonal contact among campaigners and the target audience, (3) the campaign conveys a compelling and understandable message, (4) the audience has at least some general familiarity with the topic (e.g., issue, product, social policy) of the campaign and (5) the goal is to produce repeated behaviors.

Behavioral-based persuasion strategies, on the other hand, seem to be better suited to situations in which (1) mass media presentation of messages is limited; (2) there are opportunities for interpersonal contact that may allow campaigners to take advantage of some of the heuristic (e.g., reciprocity) processes summarized previously; (3) there is little difference among response alternatives (e.g., laundry detergents); (4) the audience is unfamiliar with the attributes of the topic of the campaign (e.g., issue, product, social policy); (5) the goal is to produce one-time and/or repeated behaviors. Consider, for example, the situation in which there is little meaningful difference among the response alternatives. Under such circumstances, it may be difficult to develop strong, persuasive messages; actual experience with the product may be more likely to influence one's attitude toward the product (i.e., induce trial to provide behavioral experience with the new product). As another example, if audience members are presented with a message designed to provide information on all the special features of a product (e.g., a new camera) and the audience members are not familiar with product features, the message may not make sense. A better strategy would be to allow the audience to try the camera, see the wonderful pictures it produces, and form their attitudes on the basis of behavioral experience with the product.

It seems quite clear that when resources are available, a blend of message-based and behavioral-based persuasion would be the ideal strategy. Big companies promoting new products, such as toothpaste, deodorant, laundry detergent, etc., often initiate a mass media campaign (e.g., television, radio, magazine ads) while simultaneously distributing free samples to induce trial with the product. The major point, however, is that neither strategy is necessarily better than the other: Each has its own strengths. Information campaigners should develop campaign strategies to best take advantage of these strengths, given their particular circumstances (i.e., type of product, resources available, targeted audience, goal, etc.).

The ultimate goal in most information campaigns is to produce campaign-consistent behaviors, and, as such, behavior change is crucial for the success of campaigns. Most of the social psychological literature that we reviewed focused on attitude change or attitude formation (see the sections on message-based and behavioral-based persuasion). Social psychology's theories of persuasion (see the section on message-based persuasion) have focused almost exclusively on attitude change strategies. What is of particular interest, given this emphasis, is that the link between attitudes and behavior is uncertain, a relationship which we have characterized as a dashed line $(A \dashrightarrow B)$. That is, the first generation of research on the attitude-behavior relation focused on asking whether attitudes predicted behavior. The answer to this question was a resounding "sometimes" (Zanna & Fazio, 1982). With the tenuous connection between attitudes and behavior, it is necessary to carefully evaluate the contribution of this literature to behavior change. That is, changes in attitudes are not sufficient if behavior change is the desired outcome.

Perhaps the area in which social psychology can make its strongest contribution to the campaign literature is in its most recent efforts to develop ways to strengthen the attitude-behavior link. These are strategies that we argued could help to change the now dashed line between attitudes and behavior $(A \dashrightarrow B)$ into a solid line $(A \rightarrow B)$. The theoretical and empirical work focusing on second generation "When" and third generation "How" questions are most relevant here. For example, social psychologists have identified several factors that increase attitude-behavior consistency (e.g., direct experience, vested interest, confidence, low self-monitoring). In addition, Fazio and his colleagues have developed a model that specifies the processes by which attitudes guide behavior (e.g., accessibility of attitudes). We have suggested that a variety of other techniques (e.g., self-prediction, imagination, and role playing) could contribute to improving the attitude-behavior relation. These recent advances in the attitude-behavior connection, used in conjunction with message-based and behavioral-based persuasion, could productively be applied to the campaign literature and could help to increase the likelihood of successful campaigns.

In summary, we believe that there is much to be gained from both the social psychological and information campaign literatures by examining what each has to offer to the other. The parallels in the history of research on the attitude-behavior relation in the social psychological literature (see also Zanna & Fazio, 1982) and the campaign-behavior relation in the information campaign literature (Rogers & Storey, 1987) are quite striking. To achieve the goals of this volume, we have focused primarily on the contribution of social psychology to the campaign literature. But it seems clear that social psychology's theories of persuasion could be enhanced by examining some of the information campaign domains in which the theories might find ready applications. We would like to encourage systematic interchange of theoretical and empirical efforts in these very much related fields.

NOTES

1. The dominant theoretical framework in the communication and marketing literatures, hierarchy-of-effects models (Ray, 1973; Preston & Thorson, 1984), reflects the emphasis on outcomes with little or no emphasis on process. Hierarchy-of-effects models argue that attitudes consist of three interrelated components: affect, cognition, and behavior (see Breckler, 1984, for a review). The basic assumption of hierarchy-of-effects models is that changes in the affect, behavior, and cognition components occur in different possible sequences or orders of these three components. Although hierarchy-of-effects models have been influential in the information campaign literature, they provide little insight into the process by which the changes occur (see Devine & Hirt, 1988, for a complete discussion). At best, these models are descriptive and not really models of the persuasion process.

2. Note that this would be undesirable from the marketer's perspective, because it sets up the possibility for the consumer to gain behaviorally based information about the positive qualities of a competitor.

3. Classical conditioning has also been shown to play a role in attitude formation processes. For example, Staats and Staats (1957) demonstrated that by repeatedly pairing attitude objects (i.e., conditioned stimuli) with positive or negative events (i.e., unconditioned stimuli), the attitude objects would come to elicit the same favorable or unfavorable response as the positive or negative event (i.e., a conditioned response). Thus, an attitude would be formed toward the object (i.e., slogan). Classical conditioning is not really an example of behavioral-based or message-based persuasion (or attitude formation), but it can play an important role in the attitude formation process. Campaigners could increase the likelihood that individuals would form positive attitudes toward their product, topic, or issue to the extent that they could ensure that the message is associated with positive events that should elicit favorable reactions reflexively.

4. In our discussion of message-based and behavioral-based persuasion, our emphasis has been on behavior change that is mediated through attitude change. The reader may have noted, however, that changes in behavior can be produced with no necessary implications for attitude change. In some circumstances (e.g., one-time behaviors), attitude change may be less important because single changes in behavior are sufficient to reach the desired outcome. In other instances, compliance with a request or law may be involved, and, as such, attitude change may be less important for producing the behavior.

Consider, for example, the distinction between informational and normative social influence (Sherif, 1936). Whereas informational social influence's effectiveness derives from a desire to be correct, normative social influence's effectiveness follows from a desire to be liked or accepted by others. In situations of normative social influence, a referent person or group sets the standard for appropriate behavior, and the individual complies or conforms to the standard so that the individual will be rewarded (or not punished) by the referent group (see also Kelman's, 1961, discussion of compliance). Behavior that follows from normative social influence holds no necessary implications for attitudes or subsequent behavior. The behavior is likely to be repeated only to the extent that the powerful influence agent (i.e., those who control rewards and punishments) is present.

It should be noted that many of the models concerned with the relation between attitudes and behavior recognize the importance of normative social influence as a powerful determinant of behavior. For example, Fishbein and Ajzen (1974) argue that behavioral intentions (which are the immediate precursors to behavior) are a function of both people's attitudes and their subjective norms. Subjective norms consist of people's beliefs about what important referent others would like them to do and their motivation to comply with these norms. If one is going to be able to predict behavior, both components must be taken into consideration. Fazio (1986) has also built this normative component into his model of attitude accessibility.

REFERENCES

Abelson, R. P. (1972). Are attitudes necessary? In B. T. King & E. McGinnies (Eds.), *Attitudes, conflict, and social change* (pp. 19–32). New York: Academic Press.

Ajzen, I., & Fishbein, M. (1977). Attitude-behavior relations: A theoretical analysis and review of empirical research. *Psychological Bulletin, 84*, 888–918

Ajzen, I., & Fishbein, M. (1980). *Understanding attitudes and predicting social behavior*. Englewood Cliffs, NJ: Prentice-Hall.

Anderson, C. (1983). Imagination and expectation: The effects of imagining behavioral scripts on behavioral intentions. *Journal of Personality and Social Psychology, 45*, 293–305.

Bandura, A. (1969). *Principles of behavior modification*. New York: Holt, Rinehart and Winston.

Bandura, A. (1977). *Social learning theory*. Englewood Cliffs, NJ: Prentice-Hall.

Bem, D. J. (1972). Self-perception. In L. Berkowitz (Ed.), *Advances in experimental social psychology* (Vol. 6, pp. 1–62). New York: Academic Press.

Bostrom, R. N., Vlandis, J. W., & Rosenbaum, M. E. (1961). Grades as reinforcing contingencies and attitude change. *Journal of Educational Psychology, 52*, 112–115.

Breckler, S. J. (1984). Empirical validation of affect, behavior, and cognition as distinct components of attitude. *Journal of Personality and Social Psychology, 47*, 1191–1205.

Brock, T. C. (1965). Communicator-recipient similarity and decision change. *Journal of Personality and Social Psychology, 1*, 650–654.

Byrne, D. (1969). Attitudes and attraction. In L. Berkowitz (Ed.), *Advances in experimental social psychology* (Vol. 4, pp. 36–89). New York: Academic Press.

Calder, B. J., & Ross, M. (1973). *Attitudes and behavior*. Morristown, NJ: General Learning Press.

Cialdini, R. B. (1988). *Influence: Science and practice*. Glenview, IL: Scott Foresman.

Cialdini, R. B., Vincent, J. E., Lewis, S. K., Catalan, J., Wheeler, D., & Darby, B. L. (1975). Reciprocal concessions procedure for inducing compliance: The door-in-the-face technique. *Journal of Personality and Social Psychology, 31*, 206–215.

Cohen, M., & Davis, M. (1981). *Medication errors: Causes and prevention.* Philadelphia: G. F. Stickley.

DeFleur, M. L., & Westie, F. R. (1958). Verbal attitudes and overt acts: An experiment on the salience of attitudes. *American Sociological Review, 23*, 667–673.

DeJong, W. (1979). An examination of self-perception mediation of the foot-in-the-door effect. *Journal of Personality and Social Psychology, 37*, 2221–2239.

Devine, P. G., & Hirt, E. R. (1988). *Hierarchy-of-effects models: A critical review.* Unpublished manuscript, University of Wisconsin-Madison.

Fazio, R. H. (1986). How do attitudes guide behavior? In R. M. Sorrentino & E. T. Higgins (Eds.), *Handbook of motivation and cognition: Foundations of social behavior* (pp. 204–243). New York: Guilford.

Fazio, R. H. (1989). On the power and functionality of attitudes: The role of attitude accesibility. In A. R. Pratkanis, S. J. Breckler & A. G. Greenwald (Eds.), *Attitude structure and function* (pp. 153–179). Hillsdale, NJ: Lawrence Erlbaum.

Fazio, R. H., Chen, J., McDonel, E. C., & Sherman, S. J. (1982). Attitude accessibility, attitude-behavior consistency, and the strength of the object-evaluation association. *Journal of Experimental Social Psychology, 18*, 339–357.

Fazio, R. H., Powell, M. C., & Herr, P. M. (1983). Toward a process model of the attitude-behavior relation: Accessing one's attitude upon mere observation of the attitude object. *Journal of Personality and Social Psychology, 44*, 723–735.

Fazio, R. H., & Zanna, M. P. (1981). Direct experience and attitude-behavior consistency. In L. Berkowitz (Ed.), *Advances in experimental social psychology* (Vol. 14, pp. 161–202). New York: Academic Press.

Festinger, L. (1954). A theory of social comparison processes. *Human Relations, 7*, 117–140.

Festinger, L. (1957). *A theory of cognitive dissonance.* Stanford, CA: Stanford University Press.

Fishbein, M., & Ajzen, I. (1974). Attitudes toward objects as predictors of single and multiple behavioral criteria. *Psychological Review, 81*, 59–74.

Freedman, J. L., & Fraser, S. C. (1966). Compliance without pressure: The foot-in-the-door technique. *Journal of Personality and Social Psychology, 4*, 195–203.

Greenwald, A. G. (1968). Cognitive learning, cognitive response to persuasion and attitude change. In A. G. Greenwald, T. C. Brock, & T. M. Ostrom (Eds.), *Psychological foundations of attitudes* (pp. 361–388). New York: Academic Press.

Gregory, W. L., Cialdini, R. B., & Carpenter, K. (1982). Self-relevant scenarios as mediators of likelihood estimates and compliance: Does imagining make it so? *Journal of Personality and Social Psychology, 43*, 89–99.

Insko, C. A. (1965). Verbal reinforcement of attitude. *Journal of Personality and Social Psychology, 2*, 621–623.

Insko, C. A., & Cialdini, R. B. (1969). A test of three interpretations of attitudinal verbal reinforcement. *Journal of Personality and Social Psychology, 12*, 333–341.

Janis, I. L., & Feshbach, S. (1953). Effects of fear-arousing communications. *Journal of Abnormal and Social Psychology, 48*,78–92.

Kelman, H. C. (1961). Processes of opinion change. *Public Opinion Quarterly, 25*, 57–78.

Leventhal, H. (1970). Findings and theory in the study of fear communications. In L. Berkowitz (Ed.), *Advances in experimental social psychology* (Vol. 5, pp. 120–186). New York: Academic Press.

McGuire, W. J. (1981). Theoretical foundations of campaigns. In R. E. Rice & W. J. Paisley (Eds.), *Public communication campaigns* (pp. 41–70). Beverly Hills, CA: Sage.

Milgram, S. (1974). *Obedience to authority*. New York: Harper & Row.

Nisbett, R., & Ross, L. (1980). *Human inference: Strategies and shortcomings of social judgment*. Englewood Cliffs, N.J.: Prentice-Hall.

Paisley, W. J. (1981). Public communication campaigns: The American experience. In R. E. Rice & W. J. Paisley (Eds.), *Public communication campaigns* (pp. 15–40). Beverly Hills, CA: Sage.

Pallak, M. S., Cook, D. A., & Sullivan, J. J. (1980). Commitment and energy conservation. *Applied Social Psychology Annual, 1*, 235–253.

Peter, J. P., & Olson, J. C. (1987). *Consumer behavior*. Homeword, IL: Irwin.

Petty, R. E., & Cacioppo, J. T. (1979). Issue-involvement can increase or decrease persuasion by enhancing message-relevant cognitive responses. *Journal of Personality and Social Psychology, 37*, 1915–1926.

Petty, R. E., & Cacioppo, J. T. (1981). *Attitudes and persuasion: Classic and contemporary approaches*. Dubuque, IA: William C. Brown.

Petty, R. E., & Cacioppo, J. T. (1986a). *Communication in persuasion: Central and peripheral routes to attitude change*. New York: Springer/Verlag.

Petty, R. E., & Cacioppo, J. T. (1986b). The Elaboration Likelihood model of persuasion. In L. Berkowitz (Ed.), *Advances in experimental social psychology* (Vol.19, pp. 123–205). New York: Academic Press.

Petty, R. E., Cacioppo, J. T., & Goldman, R. (1981). Personal involvement as a determinant of argument-based persuasion. *Journal of Personality and Social Psychology, 41*, 847–855.

Petty, R. E., Ostrom, T. M., & Brock, T. C. (1981). *Cognitive responses in persuasion*. Hillsdale, NJ: Erlbaum.

Powell, M. C., & Fazio, R. H. (1984). Attitude accessibility as a function of repeated attitudinal expression. *Personality and Social Psychology Bulletin, 10*, 139–148.

Preston, I. L., & Thorson, E. (1984). The expanded association model: Keeping the hierarchy concept alive. *Journal of Advertising Research, 24*, 59–65.

Ray, M. L. (1973). Marketing communication and the hierarchy-of-effects. In P. Clarke (Ed.), *New models for communication research* (pp. 147–176). Beverly Hills: Sage.

Regan, D. T., & Fazio, R. H. (1977). On the consistency between attitudes and behavior: Look to the method of attitude formation. *Journal of Experimental Social Psychology, 13*, 28–45.

Rogers, E. M., & Storey, J. D. (1987). Communication campaigns. In C. R. Berger & S. H. Chaffee (Eds.), *Handbook of communication science*. Newbury Park, CA: Sage.

Ronis, D. L., Yates, J. F., & Dirscht, J. P. (1989). Attitudes, decisions, and habits as determinants of repeated behavior. In A. R. Pratkanis, S. J. Breckler, & A. G. Greenwald (Eds.), *Attitude structure and function* (pp. 213–239). Hillsdale, NJ: Erlbaum.

Scott, W. A. (1957). Attitude change through reward of verbal behavior. *Journal of Abnormal and Social Psychology, 55*, 72–75.

Sherif, M. (1936). *The psychology of group norms.* New York: Harper & Row.

Sherman, S. J. (1980). On the self-erasing nature of errors of prediction. *Journal of Personality and Social Psychology, 39,* 211–221.

Sivacek, J., & Crano, W. D. (1982). Vested interest as a moderator of attitude-behavior consistency. *Journal of Personality and Social Psychology, 43,* 210–221.

Staats, A. W., & Staats, C. K. (1957). Attitudes established by classical conditioning. *Journal of Abnormal and Social Psychology, 57,* 37–40.

Sternthal, B., Dholakia, R., & Leavitt, C. (1978). The persuasive impact of source credibility: A test of cognitive response. *Journal of Consumer Research, 4,* 252–260.

Weigel, R. H., & Newman, L. S. (1976). Increasing the attitude-behavior correspondence by broadening the scope of the behavioral measure. *Journal of Personality and Social Psychology, 33,* 793–802.

Wicker, A. W. (1969). Attitudes versus actions: The relationship of verbal and overt behavioral responses to attitude objects. *Journal of Social Issues, 25,* 41–78.

Zanna, M. P. & Fazio, R. H. (1982). The attitude-behavior relation: Moving toward a third generation of research. In M. P. Zanna, E. T. Higgins, & C. P. Herman (Eds.), *Consistency in social behavior: The Ontario Symposium* (Vol. 2, pp. 283–301). Hillsdale, NJ: Lawrence Erlbaum.

Chapter 10

STRATEGIES AND TACTICS IN POLITICAL CAMPAIGNS

Garrett J. O'Keefe

POLITICAL CAMPAIGNS: STRATEGIES AND TACTICS

THIS CHAPTER EXAMINES the structure and processes of contemporary political campaigns, and analyzes the strategies and tactics used in them. A recurring theme is that such campaigns are a breed apart: They have numerous characteristics that clearly differentiate them from other types of campaigns discussed in this volume. Political campaigns are also highly dynamic with respect to changes in political and social structure, and they may, in fact, work to partially effect such changes.

The past few decades have seen several alterations in political campaigns themselves and in citizen response to these campaigns. The alterations have been extensively documented elsewhere (see also Nie, Verba, & Petrocik, 1976; O'Keefe and Atwood, 1981; Kinder and Sears, 1985; Salmore and Salmore, 1985); the author's concern here is limited to the workings of contemporary campaigns. For a number of reasons, political campaigns now have greater potential for impact upon the electorate than they had previously. The decline of party organizations and concurrent changes in party nomination procedures, changes in campaign finance laws, the advent of television and other media technologies, and numerous demographic and social changes within the country have all contributed to the development of a new role for political campaigns in social change processes.

Political campaigns are primarily designed to benefit their planners: typically candidates for office or special interest groups. However, these campaigns often benefit their audiences as well in terms of increased voter knowledge, participation, etc. (Rogers and Storey, 1987). The campaigns target organized groups as well as individual citizens, since fund-raising and the generation of support from activist organizations are critical to their success. Below, I will consider how political campaigns attempt to accomplish their tasks by examining their functions, stages of conduct, organization, financial aspects, marketing strategies and communication tactics.

POLITICAL CAMPAIGNS IN CONTEXT

As a working definition of *political campaigns* for the purposes of this chapter, the author adopts a previous one by Chaffee (1981) that they "consist of an organized set of communication operations to achieve a political goal. The goal(s) might be attaining elected office, raising campaign funds, building acceptance of an idea, enacting a statute, gaining public subsidy for a special societal group or commercial entity, and so on" (p. 182). Political campaigns thus entail programs in which appropriate target groups are reached by a range of communication channels toward the basic end of mobilizing support for one's cause or candidate.

Chaffee also emphasizes a duality of contexts, in that political campaigns often attempt to simultaneously benefit the society as a whole while being propagated by special interest groups in direct conflict with one another. Thus these campaigns are similar to public-interest-oriented information campaigns, in that some notion of "public good" is an ultimate aim (see Chapter 1 by Salmon in this volume). However, there is no direct effort at bettering the lot of the audience by providing appropriate information or advice or by advocating improved health habits, safer behaviors, and the like. Political education or increased citizen competency in politics may be an indirect result of many campaigns, but that is by no means an explicit goal. Rather, most political campaigns resemble the most hotly competitive of commercial campaigns, in that they vie, often with extensive resources, for "the purchase"—the choosing by citizens of one candidate, issue or policy over others. However, while commercial campaigns may only occasionally be pitted directly against each other at he same time, in the most common type of political contest—electoral ones—the shared time frame is dictated.

Candidate contests are by far the most frequent form of political campaign, and they will be the focus of most attention here, since they have been the most researched as well. Inherent in these candidate contests is another unique factor: In no other type of campaign is the fundamental "object" of promotion a person. Arguments that contemporary campaigns overly package candidates, much like products, notwithstanding, in no other promotional situation do strategists have to attempt to "sell" the complexities of another human personality to an audience. And, in no other campaign situation are target audiences required to take into account not only ideas, issues, and policies, but also such human traits as honesty, professional expertise, and managerial style. Moreover, the emphasis in campaigns on the personality of the candidate, as opposed to parties or issues, appears to be steadily increasing (Goldenberg and Traugott, 1984; Salmore and Salmore, 1985). Such person-centered campaigns can also be expected to generate far more emotive response from audiences than any form of product appeal, and the implicit import of politics in everyday life adds to this salience even more. Even in elections over state ballot issues, voters' emotional responses can run far higher than they do in nonpolitical campaign settings (Zisk, 1987).

Most of what has been researched and written about political campaigns has centered upon presidential ones. However, as Salmore and Salmore (1985) rightly contend, lower-level campaigns are apt to have greater impact on citizens because of generally lower public consciousness of the candidates of these campaigns outside the campaign context. This allows senatorial and congressional office seekers, as well as those at state and local levels, to typically have more freedom to manipulate information about themselves to the public through campaigns. Thus, the strategies chosen in less-visible contests have more potential bearing on winning or losing. This is also true for various kinds of ballot issue campaigns at the state and local levels (Zisk, 1987).

STAGES AND SCHEDULES

A rather precise sequence of regularly scheduled and often mandated campaign steps leads to any election day. An overlooked aspect of this campaign routine is that the vast majority of voters and other participants in any race have been through similar ones before. Even first-timers have had ample opportunity to observe from the sidelines. Citizens have a fairly good understanding of the rules and rituals, and they can have quite clear expectations of what is to come. Voters also often have well-identified expectations, based upon their past experiences, of how they will go about making their voting choices and the extent to which they will actively participate in the campaign. They are likely to anticipate which information sources they will use and rely on most (O'Keefe and Mendelsohn, 1979). Most voters are thus more likely to have well-structured cognitive sets toward election campaigns than they have toward other campaign types. Campaign planners would do well to be more attentive to the kinds of voter expectations involved and the cognitions underlying those.

Trent and Friedenberg (1983) identify four rather discrete campaign stages, each with its own panoply of functions and strategies. In the pre-primary or "surfacing" stage, candidates and potential candidates simultaneously test the waters and vie for recognition. Critical early fund-raising begins, as does the development of partisan support from a variety of special interest groups in the private and not-for-profit sectors. The electorate receives early indications of candidates' fitness for office in terms of trust, expertise and presence. Other instrumental functions of this stage include the development of voter expectations about candidates' administrative and personal style and the general campaign themes to be employed. The development of an overriding and clearly-spelled-out campaign theme appears critical at this point if further support is to be generated (Hershey, 1974, 1984; Beaudry & Schaeffer, 1986). A "sifting and winnowing" among candidates occurs, in which media may play a major role. The news media may be highly influential at this stage as candidates seek their support, and interaction between press and contenders may help shape the issues and images that voters eventually confront (Weaver, 1987). The press may also overly constrict the range of political possibilities in this early phase (Paletz and Entman, 1981).

The second, or primary, stage of election campaigns involves selection of candidates by the respective parties. The previous functions now become more sharply focused, and feedback from voters to candidates pertains more to issue stances, organization and staffing, and other more technical specifics. Voters are able to observe candidates on more of a firsthand basis, and stronger perceptions of images and issue positions are formed. Also, more citizens become involved in the process through political action, parasocial interaction, and greater exposure to candidates through the media. In the presidential campaign process, success in the early primaries insures even greater press coverage and subsequent voter recognition, and something of a "frontloading" process can take place, in which early victors find it easier to raise money and volunteer support (Ranney, 1983).

Following the primaries comes a nominating convention stage, which has become more symbolic or ritualistic in recent years. Trent and Friedenberg emphasize that the conventions remain important, however, in that the media coverage accorded them provides voters with a sense of party unity as the winners are formally "anointed" and legitimized. Thus, while the national party conventions may, with much justification, seem like "spectacles" designed for television (Ranney, 1983), they remain relevant in the campaign processes. Also, "brokered" conventions, in which preordained candidates do not exist, often occur at statewide and local levels. National campaigns' attention to television coverage may well become more tempered, given decreased network coverage and viewership of them in 1988.

The final "general election" stage of the race becomes more intense and direct, and it is more media-dominated. Focus shifts more to parties than to candidates, and emphasis is placed on getting votes rather than on mobilizing support (Chaffee, 1981). A wider range of voters gains campaign-relevant information as a consequence of their own higher interest and of increased news coverage and advertising. In major campaigns, even the least attentive citizens are apt to pick up at least some knowledge of the contestants and issues. The additional information may also lead to cognitive restructuring among some voters. The campaign itself, including its more ritualistic elements, also provides a sense of legitimacy in the system. A critical final step is getting out the vote, which can require the most extensive field strategy in the entire campaign with staffs, volunteers and interest groups combing the precincts, encouraging and assisting citizens to get to the polls (Salmore and Salmore, 1985).

COMPLEXITY OF CAMPAIGN ORGANIZATION

Political campaigns also stand out in terms of their organizational complexity. In no other type of campaign must planners be concerned with such a diverse array of day-to-day activities as (1) fund-raising; (2) recruitment and coordination of sometimes vast numbers of volunteers; (3) personal contact with target-audience members through door-to-door and telephone canvassing, speeches, small group meetings, etc.; (4) scheduling of a multitude of types of appearances by the candidate and surrogates; (5) production and distribution of pamphlets, direct mail pieces, etc.; (6) ongoing press releases and other forms of cooperation with media for "free" time; (7) the production and dissemination of paid media materials; and (8) constant evaluation of audience feedback through polling and other research techniques. These are in addition to the development of campaign themes, subgroup targeting and reactions to competing candidates and other external forces, all of which typically undergo at least some change over a campaign's course. Within each general activity is a host of other more specific ones which require comprehensive coordination and timing (see also Belker, 1982; Schwartzman, 1984; Denton & Woodward, 1985; Beaudry & Schaeffer, 1986).

Moreover, as Hershey (1974) notes, political campaign organizations are rarely the kinds of unified or controlled task groups found in industry or in the public sector, and campaigning is not guided by a set of principles widely accepted by all participants. The candidate's own personality and managerial style, party attachments or lack thereof, issue cleavages, and perceptions of the electorate are some of the factors that can lead to high variability across campaign organizations.

Given the above, it is understandable that an increased diversification of roles has occurred among campaign staffs (Kayden, 1978), leading to the use of specialized consultants in larger campaigns. Campaign consultants typically offer expertise in such specific areas as polling, media production and distribution, and direct-mail appeals, and, in some cases, they play major roles in campaign planning and strategy (Hershey, 1984). Consultants often work with several clients during any one election period, but they usually limit themselves to one political party or ideological faction. Sabato (1981, 1983) credits these consultants with being instrumental in the development of advanced campaign techniques and technologies, particularly among political action committees and other special interest groups. Sabato also finds that the more prominent among these campaign consultants can be quite influential in selecting of nominees, fund-raising and impacting public opinion. The addition of a "star" consultant to a campaign staff can signal greater legitimacy and prospects for victory.

Perhaps the greatest asset to the internal management of modern campaigns has been the computer (Meadow, 1985). Even modest office microcomputers allow several advantages, not the least of which may be careful tracking of fund-raising and expenditures to comply with finance regulations. Keeping tabs on contributors is another asset, as is more accurate projecting of future budget needs. Computers also are the virtual backbone of direct-mail production and distribution, allowing careful targeting of specialized messages to their appropriate audiences. Meadow also notes that computers can more efficiently coordinate volunteer efforts than campaign staffs can, and that they allow optimal scheduling of a candidate's time. In a larger context, accurate and timely polling would be virtually impossible without computers, as would targeting of precincts and other districts by demographics and past voting patterns.

THE CAMPAIGN PROCESS

Given the uniqueness of political campaigns in terms of time considerations and organization, it comes as no great surprise that the processes by which they occur contain several distinctive features. Paramount among these are (1) the ways in which these campaigns are financed and budgeted, (2) the methods of strategic planning involved and (3) the methods of communication used.

FUND-RAISING AND SPENDING

Political campaigns are set apart from others by the way in which the money to finance them is gathered, spent and regulated. Political campaigns rely almost completely on voluntary contributions. (An exception are the federal funds used in presidential campaigns to match certain of the voluntary contributions; there are also similar provisions for some state campaigns.) Funding demands necessitate that contestants have a well-organized set of conduits to tap the array of potential funding sources available to them. The increased reliance on paid media over the years, as well as the cost of polling, consultants, and the like, has greatly increased the cost of electoral campaigns. Moreover, federal-level campaigns face a host of rather complex fund-raising restrictions. How the money is spent needs to be carefully accounted for and reported. Statewide and local campaign fund-raising and spending often need to meet certain requirements as well.

The most significant changes in fund-raising and spending have followed from the federal regulations enacted in the early 1970s. In brief summary, they allow each candidate's campaign organization to accept not more than $1,000 from any one individual for each election, including primaries. (Candidates themselves, however, may spend as much of their own money as they choose.) A candidate cannot accept more than $5,000 per election from organized groups, or political action committees (PACs). Political parties may directly contribute only limited amounts of money to a campaign, but they have far more leeway in providing both in-kind services and coordinated external support. In-kind services may include such items as polling and advertising production. Coordinated support may take the form of promotional materials produced on behalf of the party but supportive of individual candidates as well. Importantly, political action committees may spend as much as they choose on behalf of a candidate, as long as the efforts are in no way coordinated with the candidate or the campaign committee. Thus the National Conservative Political Action Committee has been able to spend millions of dollars in support of various Republican candidates, as long as these "shadow campaigns" are carried out independently of the candidates' own efforts.

These regulations were intended to reduce the impact of inordinately large contributions to campaigns by special interests (Alexander, 1984). What the regulations have accomplished is a far-reaching restructuring of the campaign fund-raising process that puts primary emphasis on getting smaller amounts of money out of more people. One major outgrowth has been the increased reliance on direct mail solicitation of campaign funds, a technique aided and abetted by advances in computer mailing technologies.

Moreover, PACs have become a key source of support and they have multiplied accordingly in number and influence. PACs are typically created by corporations, unions, and various kinds of public advocacy groups, and the money they raise is volunteered by individuals. By 1984, over 4,000 PACs were in place, and they contributed nearly one-third of all contributions to congressional candidates

(Salmore & Salmore, 1985). Candidates have clearly come to rely on PACs as a major, and often critical, supplier of campaign funds. While a goal of the financing laws is increased representativeness of contributions and enhanced citizen participation, Conway (1983) contends that the proliferation of PACs may weaken the role of individual citizens by allowing special interest groups to have greater impact. Incumbents, particularly those chairing the more powerful committees, tend to receive disproportionate amounts of PAC money, and Conway voices concern over the often intense lobbying efforts that follow such contributions. He also notes that PACs may contribute to a "nationalization" of politics, in which contributions received from groups outside of a candidate's own constituency can lessen accountability. Sabato (1984) suggests a decrease in the power of PACs through less limitation on individual campaign contributions and more flexibility in party spending on campaigns. PACs have also been tied to increased effectiveness of interest groups in contemporary campaigns, and to the concept of "single-issue" voting, focusing on such issues as abortion (Loomis and Cigler, 1983). There is some evidence that PAC contributions have directly influenced congressional voting patterns (Ginsberg and Green, 1986).

From the point of view of campaign strategy, however, the impact of PACs has heightened the need for contestants to seek them out and hear their own particular issue concerns, in order to remain financially competitive. The question of candidates' seeking out support from PACs or other groups may often depend upon the kinds of constraints that may place on other forms of fund-raising and politicking (Mauser, 1983).

STRATEGIC PLANNING FOR CAMPAIGNS

More formal strategies for political campaigns have recently evolved, utilizing contemporary marketing principles and techniques borrowed from product campaigns aimed at consumers. The main advantage of these more formal strategies may be that they attempt to bridge the gap between the traditional and highly pragmatic "seat-of-the-pants" strategies, based upon past experience and anecdotal evidence on what has worked before, and the more theoretical assessments of voter behavior, derived from the political science and communication research literature. More formal marketers use rather sophisticated empirical models of voter behavior to pragmatically devise campaign strategies.

The analogy of candidates to consumer products is, of course, nothing new, particularly with respect to advertising techniques (see McGinniss, 1969). However, the application of sophisticated marketing models to direct the entire campaign process is new. As Kotler (1982) has noted, candidates can be viewed as going through roughly the same series of steps in their campaign as a product does, in that they first establish a personality or "brand image"; get organizational approval (party sanction and fund-raising); are "test marketed" in the primaries; campaign formally (advertising and distribution); gain an adequate "market share" for election; and, if "repeat sales" are strong, they stay in office. While the models may place more explicit emphasis on reaching individuals as members of voting blocs, it is important to remember that the behind-the-scenes gathering of support and funds from more formal partisan groups entails much the same kind of analysis. These organizations must be researched extensively to determine the extent of compatibility between their positions and policies and the candidate's own and to decide upon the kinds of group support that will allow winning coalitions to be built among them.

Marketing Models

Two of the most explicitly delineated, and empirically tested such models are those of Mauser (1983) and Newman and Sheth (1987). Both deserve attention in some detail.

Mauser begins with the premise that election campaigns pose problems highly similar to those faced in marketing a new product: (1) Parties and candidates need to seek a differential advantage over their competition in order to get a significant share of the vote or "market"; (2) The same psychological and sociological processes are found in voters and consumers: They are both attempting to decide among alternatives that will help further their personal goals, and they are using whatever information is available to them; and (3) The interpersonal and mediated channels of information and persuasion used in consumer and political campaigns are identical.

For Mauser, the campaign process must include an initial analysis of not only the candidate's goals and organization, but also such external factors as the competitors, the electorate, and the general political climate as well. Voter surveys are seen as crucial at this point, with the end result being the choosing of a campaign strategy that will put the candidate in a favorable light and yield a competitive advantage that will differentiate the candidate from others. Analysis of the situation and strategy formulation then continue in an iterative fashion as the actual mechanics of campaigning begin.

More specifically, Mauser relies upon a spatial model of the strategic positioning of candidates that is derived from procedures used to analyze markets for facilitating the introduction of new products. His techniques include repeated surveys at various stages of the campaign to determine what types of candidates and issue positions yield maximum advantage over others. The iterative procedure used is as mathematically complex as it is expensive, requiring sequential samples of voters. Mauser is quick to point out that marketing strategies obviously cannot guarantee success and that the key to winning rests largely in the intuition of the candidate or manager in asking the right questions and correctly interpreting the results to design an effective campaign.

An interesting counterpoint to Mauser's model involves recent research on how candidates position themselves depending upon the competitiveness of the race. At least in congressional campaigns, there appears to be a tendency for opposing candidates to take more moderate or intermediate positions in more competitive races (Goldenberg and Traugott, 1984). This conservative strategy aims at building winning coalitions for each candidate, rather than going out on a limb trying to generate support from more splintered groups.

Newman and Sheth (1987) formulate a more general marketing approach to electoral campaigns but one still closely tied to identifying the values of voters and parlaying analyses of those values into effective strategies. Taking more of a market-segmentation approach, Newman and Sheth argue that the candidate needs to identify and appeal to distinct target markets. In order to do that effectively, without attracting some markets while alienating others, an analysis is needed of those values common to all target markets, so that a platform and image can be developed accommodating as many of those values as possible.

Newman and Sheth postulate that voter choice is driven by one or more of five distinct values: (1) political issues, or the personal beliefs of a voter about the candidate's stand on issues important to the voter; (2) social imagery, or the candidate's image to the voter in terms of demographic, socioeconomic, cultural-ethnic, and political-ideological attributes; (3) the candidate's personality in terms of the emotional feelings aroused, including hope, anger, patriotism, pessimism, etc.; (4) the situational contingencies present, e.g., transitive events impacting on a campaign, such as war, economic distress, scandal, and so on; and (5) epistemic value, referring to such drives as curiosity about a new candidate, boredom with an incumbent, desire for novelty, satiation with campaign exposure, and so forth.

Newman and Sheth recommend examining these groupings of values in voters through focus groups and related techniques, and then identifying the most salient ones through discriminant analysis. Target markets for the candidate—as well as for other contestants—based upon these values are identified both prior to the campaign and at various later stages of it. A "candidate position" is then formed, with the aim of posturing the candidate to attract the greatest number of voters while still differentiating the candidate from others. Specific types of strategies are then implemented, depending upon situational constraints. These may include reinforcing voters' existing beliefs regarding candidates, offering rationalizations when inconsistent beliefs are found, providing inducements for citizens to vote according to their key beliefs, and, perhaps as a last resort to be used when all else fails, confronting voters with negative information about the opposition.

An obvious benefit of Newman and Sheth's model is that it provides a rather encompassing framework from which a mix of specific strategies can be aimed at particular markets. At a minimum, it yields a body of rather cohesive data upon which campaign-management plans can be based. Moreover, the authors' greater emphasis on focus-group techniques minimizes research costs; however, ongoing concerns over the generalizability of such methods continue. The model also emphasizes distinctions between more informationally-based campaigns and more persuasive or emotive ones. The former may be chosen by candidates for societal benefits, but such campaigns may only be more effective if voter values center more upon advocacy of specific issues and policies. More emotional persuasive campaign tactics may be more effective when voters perceive the candidate as a strong, effective and honest leader, regardless of any policy differences they may have with the candidate.

Considerations for Incumbents Versus Challengers

Campaign marketing strategies also need to account for situations in which existing products compete against newly introduced ones. In the political arena, the issue becomes that of incumbent versus challenger, and the complexities are far more compelling. The differing strategies in each case merit individual attention.

Incumbency offers numerous benefits to the candidate (Alford and Hibbing, 1981), but, as Salmore and Salmore (1985) note, it can have its disadvantages as well. The most notable advantages include recognition by voters and the evidence of a track record. Obviously, both quickly become liabilities if the office holder has a tarnished personal reputation or is seen as having a poor record. Also, the higher the visibility of the office, the greater the potential asset of incumbency. The uniqueness of the presidency offers incumbents extensive symbolic trappings, as well as a sense of ultimate legitimacy, competence and excitement (Trent and Friedenberg, 1983). On the other hand, incumbent district attorneys, state representatives and the like may have substantially less recognition and may be particularly vulnerable to higher-visibility challengers. Incumbent ties with partisan interest groups are likely to be more solidified, with greater congruence between candidate needs and support-group expectations. Fund-raising is apt to be easier for incumbents, particularly in the earliest stages of campaign planning. This accelerates opportunities for preliminary polling and related information-gathering and helps get an organized apparatus in place well before the "public" campaign begins (Salmore & Salmore, 1985). These assets translate into what Trent and Friedenberg (1983) denote as an incumbent campaigning "style." It basically involves taking advantage of the powers and assets of the office to promote an image of experience, trust and effectiveness. Incumbents in congressional races have been found more likely to use polling to determine what voters perceive their strengths to be, and what attributes to emphasize with which group (Weaver-Lariscy, Tinkham, & Nordstrom, 1987).

Challengers, on the other hand, have a quite different set of concerns. Their main disadvantage, as Salmore and Salmore note, is that they are not incumbents. In most cases, they lack recognition, a pertinent record, money and appropriate campaign experience. At higher office levels, however, they may well have at least moderately appealing track records in lesser public positions. Seeking support from specific interest groups is likely to be more haphazard and based far more on promises than experience. Early success at fund-raising is even more critical for challengers than it is for other candidates, since they must counter with paid media time or publicity the greater press coverage accorded incumbents. Early development of support staffs and volunteers are also more important to challengers, since incumbents usually have well-oiled organizations already in place. A working rapport must be quickly developed with the news media, which tend to scrutinize newcomers quite heavily. Media judgment as to the viability of relatively unknown candidates can potentially make or break them. Other things equal, challengers for higher public offices have the more formidable task, if for no other reason than that incumbents have more resources at their disposal. Thus, polling among challengers focuses more on name recognition, finding opponents' weak spots, and fund-raising; polling overall may be more critical for challengers than it is for incumbents (Weaver-Lariscy et al., 1987). The challenger "style" depicted by Trent and Friedenberg is "a series of communication strategies designed to persuade voters that change is needed and that the challenger is the best person to bring about the change."

METHODS OF COMMUNICATION

While the mention of political communication may immediately conjure up ubiquitous, flag-draped television commercials, another factor setting political campaigns apart from other types of campaigns is the immense diversity of communication channels they use in implementing strategy. Arterton (1984) views political organization as inherently a communications process, noting that U. S. political parties were initially structured to facilitate communication along rather permanent geographic lines with vertical, interpersonal links. These party organizations remained largely as constants, regardless of changes in candidates and constituents. Contemporary, more candidate-based organizations, however, are relatively temporary and must overcome greater geographic mobility and other barriers to established interpersonal channels; thus, the greater emphasis in contemporary political campaigns on the telephone, direct mail, mass media, and polling for feedback.

Interpersonal Communication

Often overlooked, and certainly underresearched, are the inter-personal and "quasi-interpersonal" channels essential to the conduct of election campaigns. If a poll were taken of candidates and their staffs asking them the communication technology they could least do without, chances are the telephone would win hands-down over tele-vision. Certainly, in the formative stages of a campaign, when fund-raising and other garnering of support takes place, effective interper-sonal networks must be formed and exhaustively worked (Trent and Friedenberg, 1983). As the contest develops, candidates must speak to the "right" organizations at the "right" times, hold innumerable coffee talks in voters' homes, stage rallies and generally be accessi-ble in person and over the telephone to a wide range of parties-at-interest. Campaign staff and volunteers play major interpersonal roles in telephone solicitation, neighborhood canvassing, and gener-ally representing the candidate to the community. The development and effectiveness of these interpersonal activities across all levels of voter contact deserve much further study. Such interpersonal strate-gies are often "the campaign" in local government races, but they can obviously make or break contests at the highest levels of office as well. Moreover, while everyday conversations and discussions among voters are out of the candidate's control, they can have ma-jor effects on eventual vote choices (O'Keefe, 1982; Trent and Friedenberg, 1983).

Mediated Communication: Controlled and Uncontrolled

Turning to mass media and appropriate "mixes" of communication channels, Goldenberg and Traugott (1984) identified factors related to the effectiveness of various forms of information used in congres-sional campaigns. Campaigners can basically exhibit high control over the production of advertisements, billboards and yard signs, for example, but these vehicles offer little control over their distribution in the sense of effectively reaching appropriate target audiences. More effective from the point of view of both production and dissemi-nation, in Goldenberg and Traugott's view, are newsletters and other forms of direct mail, as well as telephone canvassing. Conversely, candidates have low control over both the production and dissemination of news items, endorsements, and opinion columns. However, they can more carefully target the dissemination of government pamphlets and other materials giving favorable mention to their candidates by using them as direct mail pieces. The efficiency of various media also often depends upon the level of office being sought (Rust, Haley, & Bajaj, 1984).

Controlled media. The design, production and dissemination of media advertising are the instances in which political campaigns perhaps most resemble other types of campaigns, and common, textbook approaches to production and time-buying are typically followed in political campaigns. Messages are developed in an effort to imaginatively and attractively present the key campaign themes. Polling helps identify key audience groups, and time and space are purchased on television and radio, in newspapers and magazines to reach those audiences. Pretesting of commercials, usually among focus groups, is regarded as a must. Media professionals are hired to produce the messages, and additional consultants may be brought in as well.

Two elements do, however, make the generation of successful political advertisements more problematical. One is the previously mentioned need to promote a personality along with a theme, a challenge not found in product or public information campaigns. The other is the occasional necessity of producing advertisements in quick response to an unexpected turn in the campaign, such as a damaging charge by an opponent. This kind of event, particularly near election day, can mightily test the capabilities of a candidate's media staff.

Television's predominant role in election advertising rests on its ability to project both image and issue-related information, albeit in a highly capsulized form (Diamond and Bates, 1984). Selective audience segments may be reached to some extent by choosing particular programs for spot placement, but television is also valued for being able to reach less-politically interested citizens, who are heavier viewers (Patterson & McClure, 1976). Generally, radio is useful for targeting audiences according to station format, and it is also less expensive, allowing greater reach by repetition as well as updating of spots. Newspapers and other print media allow fuller presentation of issue-related information (see also Schwartzman, 1984).

The creative element in advertising design is, of course, a critical—and difficult to measure—feature. Interestingly, in a study of consultants and the thematic and emotive appeals of their television commercials in the late 1970s, Sabato found wide variation—and even hot dispute—among the types of appeals that were favored for political campaigns. Joslyn (1986a) examined the content themes of some 500 televised political commercials aired between 1960 and 1984, in the context of the campaign functions described earlier. He found that campaigners focused quite heavily on "benevolent leader" appeals in their advertising approaches. Personality-based appeals appeared in over half the spots, followed closely by the retrospective policy satisfaction "time for a change" theme. Forty percent included ritualistic elements, and only 15% contained prospective policy choice appeals. Joslyn finds this disturbing, arguing that the prospective-policy approach is the most consistent with prevailing notions of democratic theory.

Salmore and Salmore (1985) found that in early stages of statewide and congressional races, paid media messages were far more apt to include positive statements about the candidate's background, personality and accomplishments. Incumbent messages were tied more to public records, while challengers tended to use more personal and biographical information. Issue-related positive messages may follow later in the campaign. While the 1986 campaigns gave the appearance of more negative television advertising being used, particularly closer to election day, there is little evidence as to the impact of this negative advertising. The danger, of course, is that voters can be turned off quickly by strong personal attacks on an opponent. Salmore and Salmore contend that the most effective negative communications attempt to distance the opponent from the needs of the electorate while demonstrating the concern of the attacker for those same needs. Moreover, those authors indicate that while challengers may have more use for such negative tactics, an incumbent threatened by a viable challenger may need to take a more aggressive stance as well. Comparative ads also seem to be gaining in use. These are ads in which a candidate compares records or other qualities with a contestant's, of course, in a highly selective light. While the fairness of these messages may sometimes be questionable, they may run less risk of offending voters than outright, one-sided attacks.

Research on the impact of political advertising has mainly focused on television spots, and there are indications that voters can gain issue-related information from them (Patterson and McClure, 1976; Patterson, 1980) and that these spots can affect image perceptions of candidates as well (Cundy, 1986; Garramone, 1986). A wide range of receiver factors can work to inhibit attention, recall and attitudinal change (Kaid, 1981). However, there is little evidence of advertisements alone having direct persuasive "conversion" effects on voters (Kaid, 1981; O'Keefe & Atwood, 1981). Political advertising may serve other important functions in terms of reinforcing supporters, building staff morale, fund-raising, countering opposition attacks, and basically giving candidates their own media links to voters, bypassing the press (Devlin, 1986).

Quasi-interpersonal channels merit more attention as well, if for no other reason than their being newer and technologically based. The most prominent is direct mail, used in fund-raising as well as in seeking votes. Meadow (1985) regards direct mail as a surrogate for direct personal contact with the candidate, and, with carefully targeted, computerized mailing lists, it is an opportunity to tailor specific issue concerns to voting blocs. Interest-group mailing lists, as well as zip-code programs identifying neighborhood demographic compositions, allow candidates to aim select letters at, for example, various ethnic groups, senior citizens, young urban professionals and a range of other cohorts. In early 1988, Republican presidential hopeful Pat Robertson may have brought this format to a new level by mailing a recorded spoken appeal on tens of thousands of audio cassettes to residences in key primary states. Similarly, recognizing that most U.S. homes have video recorders, many candidates have taped appeals on video cassettes for neighborhood sharing among voters. The impact of these techniques remains open to study, as do the kinds of designs, formats, and contents that are most effective.

Uncontrolled media. Yet another distinguishing feature of political campaigns is that no other campaign format is so heavily dependent on news media, nor has any other such a curious symbiotic relationship with the press. Successful political strategists must typically devote a good majority of their time to dealing with the press in order to insure adequate and, they hope, favorable coverage. The news media, in turn, need access to campaigns and candidates both to fulfill their responsibilities to the citizenry and to satisfy an apparent craving by the U.S. public for information about the professional and personal lives of office seekers. Journalists are highly drawn to the unexpected happening and, in many cases, the negative event. Also, they are often attracted by the "horse race" or competitive aspects of election contests (Patterson, 1980). While the press carries an aura of legitimacy greater than that of political advertising, reporting is not without its faults (Blumler, 1987), and public acceptance of political journalism can vary, as was evident in the case involving presidential candidate Gary Hart in 1987. The importance of news media varies with the level of campaign. Presidential, statewide and major municipal contests generate far more interest among journalists than do lesser races.

"Free" media time poses other constraints on political campaigns. News coverage in print and electronic media, along with appearances in interview formats, debates, and the like, gives candidates less control over the message reaching the audience. Nonetheless, some degree of coverage is essential for nearly all office seekers, and the need rises sharply with the importance of the position being sought. Contestants for the least prestigious local offices rely most upon newspapers for such exposure, and use of television rises with the importance of the post. Salmore and Salmore (1985) found that statewide campaign managers tried to strike a balance between free newspaper and television coverage, if for no other reason than the possibility of over-emphasis on television resulting in charges by print journalists of "media-event" staging.

Another important variable in the free media mix is that of the quality of local news media and the extent to which media market-distribution patterns overlap with electoral boundaries. Goldenberg and Traugott (1984) found, for example, that the effectiveness of news coverage of congressional campaigns varied considerably, according to how much attention local news editors decide to pay these campaigns. Moreover, geographically smaller districts in heavily urbanized, major-media-market areas were slighted in coverage because of the large number of other districts, as well as other races, competing for the fixed amount of media space and time. In addition, there is evidence that newspaper campaign coverage, at least, rather clearly favors incumbents (Clarke and Evans, 1983).

Campaign strategies directed toward the press thus typically try to maximize the element of information control as much as possible. Arterton (1984) points to several distinct goals in campaign news strategies: (1) aiming for high initial news exposure to promote name recognition; (2) generating a favorable image or campaign theme, preferably by casting the same basic message into fresh forms to keep it newsworthy; (3) projecting a view of the candidate's prospects of winning as being favorable; (4) insulating journalists as much as possible from internal campaign operations; and (5) using coverage for intracampaign communication when needed to facilitate agreement and understanding among campaign staffs. Toward these ends, Arterton distinguishes between campaign strategies and "scenarios," the latter being public statements of plans and goals used to influence the perceptions of journalists (and the electorate) about the campaign's progress and prospects. Thus, a presidential candidate's public scenario might emphasize staying out of certain early primaries to let other contestants "winnow out" one another, while the actual strategy might be based more on saving limited financial resources for primaries in which the candidate has a better chance. Candidates thus try more for an overall "orchestration" of press coverage as opposed to outright manipulation, which is more likely to backfire. There is also emphasis on presenting "diffuse" positions on issues rather than more specific ones to the press, in keeping with the candidate's interest in coalition building as opposed to confrontation (Patterson, 1982).

The pace of technological—primarily electronic—innovation in news coverage has not slowed. Fleets of satellite-linked minivans from local television stations across the country now rush from one presidential primary or caucus state to another, all reporting back directly to their home market audiences on candidates and issues of local concern, bypassing the national television networks. Instead of so much travel, candidates are now able to go from van to van for interviews sure to be screened in locales thousands of miles away. The "big three" networks face extensive and diversified coverage from such all-news or all-politics entities as Cable News Network and C-Span. All of this also leads to far greater immediacy of campaign reporting, which, on occasion, may require quickened candidate response as well (Bieder, 1982). One can debate qualitative improvements in campaign press coverage, but quantity has clearly increased, leaving open at least the potential for more informed voters.

News media may be more successful at generating campaign interest among voters than at persuading them to vote for one candidate or another (Patterson, 1980; O'Keefe and Atwood, 1981). However, strategists need to be aware of more subtle cognitive effects on citizens, such as influencing their personal agendas as to which issues (or candidates) are more important (Weaver, 1987) or "priming" them to attend more to some aspects of political life at the expense of others (Iyendar and Kinder, 1987).

CONCLUSIONS AND FUTURE DIRECTIONS

While each campaign is carried out to serve its own ends, democratic theory holds that the public good is served through the competition among campaigns for citizen support. Furthermore, while the seeking of votes may be at the heart of electoral campaigns, the process by which that vote seeking is accomplished rests upon the solicitation of resources from other parties-at-interest. These factors, as well as numerous other ones cited above, render political campaigns a unique and highly complex public communication phenomenon. This raises important issues in terms of how these campaigns are to be studied and evaluated.

Mauser (1983), Meadow (1985), and Newman and Sheth (1987), among others, have argued for more comprehensive empirically-based models for designing, implementing and evaluating political campaigns. They note that academic research in the area has generally been more concerned with the study of theoretical models of voting and communication behavior, while the more pragmatic campaign specialists have relied more upon their own experience and anecdotal evidence. The middle ground of systematically testing and building generalizable models of what works and what does not work in political campaigns has been largely neglected.

Major roadblocks to testing and building generalizable models include, on the one hand, adequate cooperation between campaign strategists and researchers during the contest periods and, on the other, adequate resources for not only formative precampaign research (already to some extent underway), but also careful postelection evaluative measures. The latter are particularly lacking because of the central concern with "who won." Unlike the case with most other campaigns, clear winners and losers emerge from political campaigns as mandated. There is an implicit tendency to regard the winning candidate as having had the best campaign, which, of course, may be fallacious. Rigorous testing of voter perceptions, attitudes, motives and campaign-related behaviors is needed to identify more precisely which aspects of the campaign were having what kinds of impact. It would also be beneficial to borrow more from social science models of social influence and communication, as Mauser (1983), Newman and Sheth (1987), and Hershey (1984) have done in the strategy planning stages. At the least, such models provide a more cohesive framework for campaign organization and coordination. An encouraging sign is a rising interest among academicians in studying internal components of various political campaigns types (Goldenberg and Traugott, 1984; Salmore and Salmore, 1985; Zisk, 1987). This is particularly important because of the decided lack of knowledge about how campaigns interact with partisan interest groups and the press.

More system-level research on political campaigns is also warranted. An apparent trend for both political parties and interest groups to become more centralized has been referred to as a "nationalization" of politics (Benjamin, 1982; Conway, 1983; Salmore and Salmore, 1985). Computers, direct mail, and television have allowed far greater cross-country communication and cohesion among groups that may otherwise be more splintered. Single-issue or ideology adherents now have far more ability to cooperate to get their message out to the public and, in many cases, have more influence over candidates as well. The proliferation of PACs has had considerable impact here. As for parties, some observers see a resurgence for them (Everson, 1982; Salmore & Salmore, 1985; Kolar, 1986). However, they may become more relevant as facilitators, as opposed to controllers, of campaigns. In particular, the previous direct-mail, fund-raising success of the Republican Party to date has made it far more able to support candidates financially, thus potentially increasing their loyalty. In the long run, this might make for more of a balance among candidate, party and interest-group politics.

While legitimate concern may be voiced over the increasing role of political campaign consultants and their influence over voting processes, one thing they do not do, as Blumenthal (1980) notes, is control the candidate in the same way as formerly powerful party bosses did. For better or worse, the "candidate-centered" campaign gives far more independence to the contestants. This may not always result in more responsiveness to the electorate, but it likely makes politicians more knowledgeable about what public concerns actually are. Furthermore, consultants increasingly continue to advise candidates after they are elected on polling, press relations, and strategies for dealing with constituents. This situation can offer the same advantages, and possible disadvantages, as occur during campaigns.

Another underinvestigated aspect of political campaigns is the simple matter of how well the public accepts them. During the 1988 presidential primaries, Elizabeth Drew (1988) wrote that the process of choosing candidates "resembles a demolition derby more than a rational procedure. It's an elimination contest, offering us the last man—or men—standing at the end of a long, grueling and expensive series of matches, in some strange arenas . . . it should be no surprise that people are increasingly unhappy about how we choose our President." Just how unhappy is the public? How much confidence do people have in the appropriateness of current campaign processes and techniques? What facets of them would they prefer to see changed? It is clear from polling data that while campaigns may be getting underway earlier, many citizens are postponing voting decisions until later in the contest, with increased numbers failing to vote at all. What does that portend for the future conduct of campaigns and for citizen participation in elections? As Mauser (1983) indicates, those politicians inclined to cynically cater to the public will use campaign strategies toward that end; on the other hand, more competent and honest office seekers can use those same techniques to more effectively communicate with voters, likely educating them in the process.

REFERENCES

Alexander, H. E. (1984). *Financing elections: Money, elections and political reform* (3rd ed.). Washington, DC: CQ Press.

Alford, J. R., & Hibbing, J. (1981). Increased incumbency advantage in the house. *Journal of Politics, 43,* 1042–1061.

Arterton, F. C. (1984). *Media politics.* Lexington, MA: Lexington Books.

Beaudry, A., & Schaeffer, B. (1986). *Winning local and state elections: The guide to organizing your own campaign.* New York: Free Press.

Belker, L. B. (1982). *Organizing for political victory.* Chicago: Nelson-Hall.

Benjamin, G. (1982). Innovations in telecommunications and politics. In G. Benjamin (Ed.), *The communications revolution in politics* (pp. 1–12). New York: Academy of Political Science.

Bieder, J. (1982). Television reporting. In G. Benjamin (Ed.), *The communications revolution in politics* (pp. 36–48). New York: Academy of Political Science.

Blumenthal, S. (1980). *The permanent campaign: Inside the world of elite political operatives.* Boston: Beacon.

Blumler, J. G. (1987). Election communication and the democratic political system. In D. Paletz (Ed.), *Political communication research: Approaches, studies, assessments* (pp. 167–175). Norwood, NJ: Ablex.

Chaffee, S. H. (1981). Mass media in political campaigns: An expanding role. In R. E. Rice and W. J. Paisley (Eds.), *Public communication campaigns* (pp. 181–198). Beverly Hills, CA: Sage.

Clarke, P., & Evans, S. H. (1983). *Covering campaigns: Journalism in congressional elections.* Stanford, CA: Stanford University Press.

Conway, M. M. (1983). PACs, the new politics, and congressional campaigns. In A. J. Cigler and B. A. Loomis (Eds.), *Interest group politics* (pp. 126–144). Washington, DC: CQ Press.

Cundy, D. T. (1986). Political commercials and candidate image, the effect can be substantial. In L. L. Kaid, D. Nimmo, & K. R. Sanders (Eds.), *New perspectives on political advertising* (pp. 210–234). Carbondale: Southern Illinois University Press.

Denton, R. E., & Woodward, G. C.(1985). *Political communication in America*. New York: Praeger.

Devlin, L. P. (1986). An analysis of presidential television commercials. In L. L. Kaid, D. Nimmo, & K. R. Sanders (Eds.), *New perspectives on political advertising* (pp. 21–54). Carbondale: Southern Illinois University Press.

Diamond, E., & Bates, S. (1984). *The spot: The rise of political advertising on television*. Cambridge: MIT Press.

Drew, E. (1988, March 7). Letter from Washington. *The New Yorker,* pp. 99–113.

Everson, D. H. (1982). The decline of political parties. In G. Benjamin (Ed.), *The communications revolution in politics* (pp. 49–60). New York: Academy of Political Science.

Garramone, G. (1986). Candidate image formation: The role of information processing. In L. L. Kaid, D. Nimmo, & K. R. Sanders (Eds.), *New perspectives on political advertising* (pp. 235–247). Carbondale: Southern Illinois University Press.

Ginsberg, B., & Green, J. C. (1986). The best Congress money can buy. In B. Ginsberg & A. Stone (Eds.), *Do elections matter?* (pp. 75–89). Armonk, NY: M. E. Sharpe.

Goldenberg, E. N., & Traugott, M. W. (1984). *Campaigning for Congress*. Washington, DC: CQ Press.

Hershey, M. R. (1974). *The making of campaign strategy*. Lexington MA: Lexington Books.

Hershey, M. R. (1984). *Running for office: The political education of campaigners*. Chatham, NJ: Chatham House.

Iyendar, S., & Kinder, D. R. (1987). *News that matters: Television and American opinion*. Chicago: University of Chicago Press.

Joslyn, R. (1986a). Candidate appeals and the meaning of elections. In B. Ginsberg and A. Stone (Eds.), *Do elections matter?* (pp. 90–114). Armonk, NY: M. E. Sharpe.

Joslyn, R. (1986b) Political advertising and the meaning of elections. In L. L. Kaid, D. Nimmo, & K. R. Sanders (Eds.), *New perspectives on political advertising* (pp. 139–183). Carbondale: Southern Illinois University Press.

Kaid, L. L. (1981). Political advertising. In D. D. Nimmo and K. R. Sanders (Eds.), *Handbook of political communication* (pp. 249–272). Beverly Hills, CA: Sage.

Kayden, X. (1978). *Campaign organization*. Lexington, MA: D. C. Heath.

Kinder, D. R., & Sears, D. O. (1985). Public opinion and political action. In G. Lindzey and E. Aronson (Eds.), *The handbook of social psychology* (Vol. II pp. 659–742). New York: Random House.

Kolar, B. (1986). Fighting back: American political parties take to the airwaves. In L. L. Kaid, D. Nimmo, & K. R. Sanders (Eds.), *New perspectives on political advertising* (pp. 55–81). Carbondale: Southern Illinois University Press.

Kotler, P. (1982). *Marketing for nonprofit organizations*. Englewood Cliffs, NJ: Prentice-Hall.

Loomis, B. A., & Cigler, A. J. (1983). Introduction: The changing nature of interest group politics. In A. J. Cigler and B. A. Loomis (Eds.), *Interest group politics* (pp. 1–30). Washington, DC: CQ Press.

Mauser, G. A. (1983). *Political marketing: An approach to campaign strategy.* New York: Praeger.

McGinniss, J. (1969). *The selling of the president, 1968.* New York: Trident Press.

Meadow, R. G. (1985). Political campaigns, new technology, and political communication research. In K. R. Sanders, L. L. Kaid, & D. Nimmo (Eds.), *Political communication yearbook, 1984* (pp. 135–152). Carbondale: Southern Illinois University Press.

Newman, B. I., & Sheth, J. N. (1987). *A theory of politics choice behavior.* New York: Praeger.

Nie, N. H., Verba, S., & Petrocik, J. R. (1976). *The changing American voter.* Cambridge, MA: Harvard University Press.

O'Keefe, G. J. (1982). The changing context of interpersonal communication in political campaigns. In M. Burgoon (Ed.), *Communication Yearbook 5* (pp. 667–684). New Brunswick, NJ: Transaction Books.

O'Keefe, G. J., & Atwood, L. E. (1981). Communication and election campaigns. In D. D. Nimmo and K. R. Sanders (Eds.), *Handbook of political communication* (pp. 329–358). Beverly Hills, CA: Sage.

O'Keefe, G. J., & Mendelsohn, H. (1979). Media influences and their anticipation. In S. Kraus (Ed.), *The great debates: Carter vs. Ford 1976* (pp. 405–417). Bloomington: Indiana University Press.

Paletz, D. L., & Entman, R. M. (1981). *Media power politics.* New York: Free Press.

Patterson, T. E. (1980). *The mass media election: How Americans choose their president.* New York: Praeger.

Patterson, T. E. (1982). Television and election strategy. In G. Benjamin (Ed.), *The communications revolution in politics* (pp. 24–35). New York: Academy of Political Science.

Patterson, T. E., & McClure, R. D. (1976). *The unseeing eye: The myth of television power in national elections.* New York: Putnam.

Ranney, A. (1983). *Channels of power: The impact of television on American politics.* New York: Basic Books.

Rogers, E. M., & Storey, J. D. (1987). Communication campaigns. In C. R. Berger and S. H. Chaffee (Eds.), *Handbook of communication science* (pp. 817–846). Newbury Park, CA: Sage.

Rust, R., Haley, G., & Bajaj, M. (1984). Efficient and inefficient media for political campaign advertising. *Journal of Advertising, 13,* 45–49.

Sabato, L. J. (1981). *The rise of political consultants: New ways of winning elections.* New York: Basic Books.

Sabato, L. J. (1983). Political consultants and the new campaign technology. In A. J. Cigler & B. A. Loomis (Eds.), *Interest group politics* (pp. 195–224). Washington, D.C.: CQ Press.

Sabato, L. J. (1984). *PAC power: Inside the world of political action committees.* New York: W. W. Norton.

Salmore, S. A., & Salmore, B. G. (1985). *Candidates, parties, and campaigns: Electoral politics in America.* Washington, DC: CQ Press.

Schwartzman, E. (1984). *Political campaign craftsmanship: A professional's guide to campaigning for public office*. New York: Van Nostrand-Reinhold.

Trent, J. S., & Friedenberg, R. V. (1983). *Political campaign communication: Principles and practices*. New York: Praeger.

Weaver, D. (1987). Media agenda setting and elections: Assumptions and implications. In D. Paletz (Ed.), *Political communication research: Approaches, studies, assessments*. Norwood, NJ: Ablex.

Weaver-Lariscy, R. A., Tinkham, S. F., & Nordstrom, K. E. (1987). The use and impact of polling as a strategic planning tool in congressional campaigns. *Political Communication Review, 12*, 1–24.

Zisk, B. H. (1987). *Money, media and the grass roots: State ballot issues and the electoral process*. Newbury Park, CA: Sage.

Chapter 11

ESTIMATING THE MAGNITUDE OF THREATS TO VALIDITY OF INFORMATION CAMPAIGN EFFECTS

Steven H. Chaffee, Connie Roser and June Flora

THREE DECADES AGO, Campbell (1957) introduced the methodological concept of categorical threats to the validity of an empirical inference. His outline of ways to control these threats through experimental design has been elaborated in major monographs (Campbell and Stanley, 1966; Cook and Campbell, 1979) and integrated into most leading textbooks on social research methods. Widely disseminated via graduate programs throughout the social and behavioral sciences, this approach focuses attention on the inferences that researchers draw. Study design, rather than being determined a priori, flows from anticipated inferences and the need to defend them against alternative explanations.

In evaluating a communication campaign, the expected inference is ordinarily clear-cut. Campaigns are mounted to achieve prespecified goals: to build public knowledge, to modify behaviors, to elect a

AUTHORS' NOTE: The research reported here was supported in part by U.S. Public Health Service Grant HL-21906 from the National Heart, Lung, and Blood Institute, to John W. Farquhar, M.D., Principal Investigator. We are indebted to Dr. Farquhar, Stephen Fortmann, Nathan Maccoby, Donald Barrett, Edward Maibach and our other colleagues at the Stanford Center for Research in Disease Prevention for their support and help in the preparation of this study. An earlier version of this paper was presented to the annual convention of the Association for Education in Journalism and Mass Communication, at Portland, Oregon, in July, 1988.

candidate, to prevent disease, to improve agricultural practices, or to create a social climate supportive of desired values. When evidence of a campaign effect is found, that conclusion becomes the inference against which threats to its validity, or alternative explanations of the findings, are arrayed. Campbell's typology of threats is a general scheme for categorizing alternative explanations so that threats that have been anticipated can be "eliminated" from consideration because they have been controlled by experimental study design. Those which were not anticipated in the design must be dealt with singly by specific measurement and statistical control in multivariate analyses.

Campaign research methodology, then, implicitly separates threats to validity into two groups: (1) those whose influence has not been dealt with by design and which have, therefore, been measured to provide quantitative estimates of their magnitude, and (2) those which are eliminated by design so that no immediate occasion for estimating their magnitude has arisen. It is, however, a central premise of this chapter that estimation of the latter, controlled effects can also be useful to campaign designers and evaluators. It is not enough to show that threats to validity are statistically nonsignificant (Yeaton & Sechrest, 1986). Any threats are substantive competitors to the campaign's effect, and their magnitude provides a context for evaluating a campaign's *comparative effect* as well as its absolute effect.

Designing a campaign evaluation is largely a problem of resource allocation. The sample size (N), for example, is calibrated to provide enough statistical power to avoid the alternative explanation that one's results are due to chance. A control group, which can double the required N, is added to meet other threats to the validity to the inference that the campaign has been effective. The considerable expense of a large N or a control group adds nothing to the campaign itself. Indeed, in a typical fixed-budget campaign, funds that are put into these evaluation components are taken directly from the communication campaign effort itself. The same is true of added waves of measurement, of some trade-offs between cross-sectional and panel designs, and of unobtrusive measurement procedures. Since each of these design components consumes resources that might otherwise be dedicated to campaign efforts, it makes good sense to make estimates of the benefits that each might provide. Not every conceivable threat to validity is of a magnitude that warrants a major expenditure to control for it. The benefit of a control is directly proportional to the size of the threat. One might say that threats to validity compete with the campaign itself for resources at the beginning of a project and for effects at the end. This chapter is concerned with the comparison between effects of a major health communication campaign and other effects that can be estimated with this project's quasi-experimental design.

NON-EQUIVALENCES AS THREATS TO VALIDITY

No design for the study of human behavior can be free from threats to validity. In the "perfect" design, one would need to observe the same person under different conditions. This is patently impossible; no one is literally the same person twice. All research designs represent compromises that fall short of the ideal of comparing truly identical time-person combinations. Failing the possibility of literal identicality, the key methodological concept becomes *equivalence* in estimated population values (Reichardt, 1979). To the extent that two persons, or times or observations, can be considered equivalent, they can be compared with respect to a variable, such as exposure to a campaign or message. Threats to the validity of such a comparison arise from non-equivalences—of persons, times or observations. In Campbell's terminology, these non-equivalences include:

—*Selection,* or non-equivalence at one time (prior to the communication event) of the different persons being compared.

—*Maturation,* or non-equivalence of the same person at different times.

—*History,* or events that occur between times that render them non-equivalent.

—*Instrument decay,* or non-equivalence of measures at different times or for different persons at one time.

—*Mortality,* or non-equivalence of groups of persons over time due to attrition.

—*Testing,* or changes in persons over time following reactive measurement.

—*Sensitization,* or the interaction between testing and the communication whose effect is being studied.

The last of these seven, sensitization, is a threat to the external validity, or generalizability, of a study. That is, would the observed effect also occur with persons who had not been reactively measured before receiving the communication? The other six listed above are threats to internal validity; that is, the issue of whether the differences observed in these persons at these times with these measures represents an effect of the communication or of one of the threats. The essence of experimental design is to minimize these kinds of threats in advance through procedures that maximize the equivalence of the persons, times and measures in a study. In a field quasi-experiment (such as the one reported here), the design is elaborated so that threats can be evaluated and inferences modified accordingly—rather than practically eliminating the threat, as might be the case in a tightly controlled laboratory experiment.

Campbell notes other threats to validity as well, such as the statistical regression fallacy (see also Heimendinger and Laird, 1983), the interaction of selection with other elements of a study and the problem of isolating a single effect of the communication. The example presented here does not deal with those concerns, except that the regression fallacy remains a possibility if selection proves to be a significant threat. (It does; see below.) This analysis is also unable to estimate effects of instrument decay or to separate clearly the effects of maturation from those of testing. The experimental design controls simultaneously for maturation along with testing but does not yield sufficient data for distinct estimates of each. Other approaches for evaluating maturation will be suggested later. In summary, they will outline procedures for estimating the magnitude of a campaign's effect relative to the following threats: selection, mortality, history, maturation/testing, and sensitization.

THE FIELD QUASI-EXPERIMENTAL DESIGN

The context for our analysis is the Stanford Heart Disease Prevention Program, which began in several central California cities in the late 1970s and continued into the mid-1980s. This is called the Five City Project (FCP), although the field intervention took place in only two of those cities. The full design, a description of the campaign itself and its effects on reduction of the risk of cardiovascular disease are reported elsewhere (Farquhar et al., 1985; Farquhar, Fortmann, Flora et al., 1986, 1988). Only those aspects of the FCP that are relevant to the purposes of this chapter will be described.

The main criterion variable selected in this chapter is the *acquisition of knowledge* about cardiovascular disease risk and how to modify one's lifestyle to reduce it. The FCP measures include behaviors, attitudes, physiological factors associated with heart disease and actual morbidity and mortality data. But the communication campaign was built mainly around a public education approach, and it presumably operated via knowledge acquisition to achieve its ultimate goals. Knowledge about heart disease risk reduction is a rich topic and one that is particularly susceptible to several of the major threats to validity that are of concern here. By focusing on effects on knowledge, these analyses will be relevant to the widest range of other communication campaigns, most of which share this goal.

The knowledge index consists of 17 factual items that were covered in the heart disease risk reduction campaign and in every wave of survey data collection; these were summed to form an index. Approximately half of the items were true-false questions, and the remainder were multiple choice. Substantive areas covered in the questions reflect major themes of the campaign: the effects of cholesterol and foods that contain it; the contributions of high blood pressure and cholesterol to heart disease risk; the benefits of exercise and the amount of exercise needed; the effects of smoking; which foods are healthy or unhealthy; and the role of diet and smoking in serious illnesses, such as cancer and heart disease.

The measures reported in this chapter represent the mean percentage of correct answers to these 17 questions, adjusted for age, sex, and education of respondent as in other analyses of the FCP data. Reliability of this index was tested by confirmatory factor analysis (Roser, Chaffee, Flora and Farquhar, 1988). A satisfactory single-factor solution was obtained. The adjusted goodness-of-fit index (.96), the root mean square residual (.04) and the ratio of chi-square to degrees of freedom (3.07) were all within standard levels for acceptability.

In all, the FCP campaign ran for more than five years in the two "Education cities." Data reported here were collected from 1979, some months before the campaign began, through 1985. The evaluation utilized both a panel design, in which the same individuals were remeasured annually—some as many as six times—and a repeated cross-sections design, for which a new random sample was drawn annually from each community. The panel and cross-section survey periods alternated, each occupying a different six-months period of each year of the study.

The various waves of survey measurement in this elaborate design are labeled either Ci for the panel (the "C" stands for *cohort,* a term in the language of epidemiology equivalent to *panel*), or Ii for the *independent* cross-sections. For example, the first survey is labeled I1, and subsequent cross-sections are called I2, I3, etc. The panel begins with C2, which consists of all those persons from I1 who could be contacted and remeasured a year later. The original measures on the members of C2 become, retrospectively, C1. Subsequent waves of panel remeasurement are labeled C3, C4, etc; group Ns vary for these waves, as efforts were made each year to recontact everyone who was measured in any earlier panel wave. In standard experimental design fashion, there is a control group, called here the *reference cities,* where no campaign occurs. (Use of the term control group here would suggest a greater degree of control over extraneous factors than is possible in such a large-scale and extended field experiment.)

Identical time designations do not represent exactly the same times, except for Time-1. That is, I1 and C1 represent the same time period in 1979. But C2 was conducted in the six-month period prior to I2; after that, six-month data collection periods alternated so that C3 precedes I3 and so forth. Rather than treat surveys with the same time designations as comparable (e.g., I3 as a control for C3), successive cross-sectional waves of data collection were averaged so that their estimates-of-knowledge scores represent calendar years (1979 through 1985) rather than any single wave of data collection.

ESTIMATION PROCEDURES

Selection, or non-equivalence of cities in this project, is a major threat to validity in any information campaign and the one that has occasioned the most concern among evaluation methodologists (Alwin and Sullivan, 1976; Reichardt, 1979; Berry, 1983; Mark, 1983; Muthen and Joreskog, 1983; Newcomb, 1984; Achen, 1986). Data reported here were collected in just two education sites and two reference sites. Because the number in each condition (N=2) is small, and due to pragmatic constraints such as the FCP's need for somewhat overlapping media markets for the education campaign, statistical equivalence could not be achieved through random assignment. This lack of randomization in assignment to the two conditions (education vs. reference) is the primary reason this design is best called a quasi-experiment rather than a "true" experiment (Cook and Campbell, 1979).

The measurement of knowledge before the campaign began is designed to give estimates of the effects of selection. There are two tests, one nested within the other, of initial differences between the education and references cities. One is a comparison of the independent cross-sections (Iled-Ilref), and the other is a comparison of the panel data (Cled-Clref). These should yield similar results, as C1 is a large subset of I1. The difference in either comparison represents the magnitude of differences between the sites before the campaign began. In the absence of these "before" measures, preexisting differences could later be mistaken for campaign effects, or else they could neutralize real subsequent campaign effects, depending upon the direction of the difference.

History was a serious threat to validity during the period of the FCP campaign because information regarding heart disease risk reduction became a topic of considerable currency in American society. Newspapers, magazines, and television carried information on saturated fats, how to reduce stress, aerobic exercise and other topics that were also being emphasized by the FCP. Even without FCP efforts, antismoking publicity appeared on television, and some restaurants began to feature low-sodium and low-calorie menu items. A secular trend toward greater public knowledge about heart disease would in the FCP evaluation design be reflected in the reference cities. More specifically put, knowledge gains over time in the independent cross-sections for the reference sites would represent the effect of history alone, while those in the education sites would represent the combined effects of history and the FCP campaign. Thus, subtraction provides an estimate of the effect of history across each time span in the project. Using conventional notation where i indicates a given point in time and j the next point in time,

History = Ijref—Iiref

Mortality is a threat in any panel study, and some elaborate statistical approaches have been developed to cope with it (e.g., Muthen and Joreskog, 1983). Mortality refers to the possibility that those who drop out of the sample from time *i* to time *j* differ from those who remain in it. Specifically, it could be that the campaign, instead of informing people, simply has the effect of encouraging those who are already well-informed to remain in the panel. To address this possibility, the authors need to evaluate differential mortality, that is, between the education and reference cities. The independent cross-sections provide an estimate of the effect of mortality in this sense by comparing the Time-1 knowledge levels of those who stayed in the panel with the full Time-1 sample to see if this difference is greater for those who were exposed to the campaign:

Mortality = [Cled−Iled]−[Clref−Ilref]

This procedure can be repeated for later waves of the panel, as its size (N) shrinks further through C3, C4, etc.

Maturation differs from history in that it occurs over time within an individual but not necessarily in the community at large. (As individuals age, some move or die and are replaced by new members of the community.) For maturation effects, the comparison between the panel and cross-sectional data is useful. Specifically, knowledge gains in the panel might represent the effects of maturation over time of those particular individuals, whereas gains from one cross-sectional sample to the next would represent change in the community separately from change in any individual member of it. Again, subtraction is needed, to separate the combined effects of history and maturation (knowledge gain in the panel, from C_i to C_j) from the effects of history alone (knowledge increase from one cross-section of the community to the next, or I_i to I_j).

Testing, however, is a second threat to validity that might account for these same differences. Testing is only a threat when measurement is reactive, but that is surely the case here—as it is with most knowledge measures (Salmon, Mrja and Carroll, 1983). Indeed, it is difficult to think of a more obtrusive test, or one more likely to induce people to seek exactly what the campaign provides, than asking them knowledge questions that have right-and-wrong answers. With less obtrusive measures, such as some of the physiological tests administered in the FCP survey, the effects of testing might be considered minimal and the differences attributed mainly to maturation. But in this analysis of information holding, testing effects should be large relative to maturation. The FCP design provides an opportunity to draw some informed inferences about comparative effects of these threats. Testing effects are likely to be greatest in the earliest panel waves (T1 to T2), while maturation in this adult population should manifest itself in steady, gradual increments of about equal magnitude from year to year.

The combined effects of maturation and testing will be algebraically additive, which leaves open the possibility that one could be negative. If, for example, maturation causes forgetting, it would subtract from the apparent effect of testing here. Estimates of these effects are based on averaged (mean) gains from any time Ti to any later time Tj:

$$\text{Maturation} + \text{Testing} = (.5 \, [\text{Cjed}-\text{Cied}) + (\text{Cjref}-\text{Ciref})]) \\ - (.5 \, [(\text{Ijed}-\text{Iied}) + (\text{Ijref}-\text{Iiref})])$$

The foregoing exhausts the list of threats to internal validity that are estimated empirically in this chapter. These threats are to be compared to the campaign effect itself, which is estimated in straightforward fashion by subtracting changes in the reference cities from changes in the education cities. Collectively, the panel and the cross-sectional data represent more controls for threats to validity than does either data set alone, so data are combined in estimating the net effects of the campaign:

$$\text{Campaign Effect} = (.5 \, [(\text{Cjed}-\text{Cied})-(\text{Cjref}-\text{Ciref})]) \\ + (.5 \, [(\text{Ijed}-\text{Iied})-(\text{Ijref}-\text{Iiref})])$$

Sensitization has been a much-discussed threat to the external validity, or generalizability, of a before-after, mass-communication experiment, since the early work of Hovland, Lumsdaine and Sheffield (1949). When, as in this study, there is a high likelihood of reactive measurement producing a testing effect, there is a further possibility that those who have been pretested are thereby "sensitized" to the campaign's content. They may then attend to and learn it better than they would have in the absence of pretesting. Sensitization is not a threat to internal validity; it does not challenge the findings as artifacts of uncontrolled factors the way history or testing do. Rather, it threatens external validity; it raises the question whether the campaign effects found would generalize to other populations that had not been pretested.

The rather expensive textbook solution to the threat of sensitization is Solomon's (1949) Four-Group design, consisting of both before-after and after-only experimental and control groups (Cook and Campbell, 1979). (For a rare example in the communication literature, see Chaffee and McLeod, 1973.) The FCP design can be viewed as a time-lagged variant of this Four-Group design. The panel data (Ci, Cj) are before-after measures in one time period, and the cross-sections (Ij) are after-only measures prior to and following the same period. Formally, sensitization is tested as a statistical interaction between the effects of testing and of the campaign. Estimating sensitization involves the third possible combination of contrasts beyond those of campaign effects and testing/maturation effects:

$$\text{Sensitization} = (.5\,[(\text{Cjed}-\text{Cied}) + (\text{Ijref}-\text{Iiref})]) \\ - (.5\,[(\text{Cjref}-\text{Ciref}) + (\text{Ijed}-\text{Iied})])$$

To summarize these last three, seemingly complicated sets of estimates, one might view them as in a 2 x 2 design.[1] If the campaign conditions are represented in the columns (education vs. reference) and the type of survey in the rows (panel vs. cross-section), then column mean differences are campaign effects, row mean differences are testing/maturation effects and differences between the means of the two diagonals (i.e., the interaction) are sensitization effects. The various time periods of the FCP study will provide several estimates of each of these types of effect.

RESULTS AND DISCUSSION

The basic data from which estimates will be made are shown in Table 11.1. This table gives demographically adjusted estimates of the percentage of correct answers to the 17 heart-disease related knowledge questions in each year of the FCP campaign. These are shown in columns that represent the main divisions of the quasi-experimental design: education vs. reference, and panel vs. cross-section. Entries in parentheses in Table 11.1 are gain scores for the same figures for each of the six adjacent pairs of years (subtracting Tj-Ti).

Table 11.1 Percent Correct Knowledge (adjusted), by City, Survey Design and Year

	Education Cities		Reference Cities	
	(Ied) Cross-section	*(Ced)* Panel	*(Iref)* Cross-section	*(Cref)* Panel
1979	30.75%	36.98%	32.62%	40.00%
1980	34.60	44.55	34.59	45.21
(Gain 1979–80)	(+3.86)	(+7.57)	(+1.97)	(+5.21)
1981	38.45	47.09	36.57	46.81
(Gain 1980–81)	(+3.85)	(+2.54)	(+1.98)	(+1.60)
1982	37.31	49.63	35.44	48.41
(Gain 1981–82)	(−1.14)	(+2.54)	(−1.13)	(+1.60)
1983	36.16	50.31	34.31	49.39
(Gain 1982–83)	(−1.15)	(+.68)	(−1.13)	(+.98)
1984	38.19	50.98	36.33	50.37
(Gain 1983–84)	(+2.03)	(+.67)	(+2.02)	(+.98)
1985	40.23		38.35	
(Gain 1984–85)	(+2.04)		(+2.02)	

NOTE: Cell entries are estimated group percentages of correct answers to the seventeen knowledge questions, adjusted for respondent's education, age and gender. When survey waves overlap calendar years, data from successive years have been averaged in calculating these estimates. Approximate Ns for each year's entries range from 450 to 490 for panel data and from 750 to 950 for cross-sectional data.

Table 11.2 Algorithms for Calculating Threats to Validity and Campaign Effects

Selection (Cross-section)	=	$Il_{ed} - Il_{ref}$
Selection (panel)	=	$Cl_{ed} - Cl_{ref}$
History	=	$Ij_{ref} - Ii_{ref}$
Mortality	=	$[Cl_{ed} - Il_{ed}] - [Cl_{ref} - Il_{ref}]$
Maturation + Testing	=	$(.5 [Cj_{ed} - Ci_{ed}) + (Cj_{ref} - Ci_{ref})])$ $- (.5 [Ij_{ed} - Ii_{ed}) + (Ij_{ref} - Ii_{ref})])$
Sensitization	=	$(.5 [(Cj_{ed} - Ci_{ed}) + (Ij_{ref} - Ii_{ref})])$ $- (.5 [(Cj_{ref} - Ci_{ref}) + (Ij_{ed} - Ii_{ed})])$
Campaign Effect	=	$(.5 [(Cj_{ed} - Ci_{ed}) - (Cj_{ref} - Ci_{ref})])$ $+ (.5 [(Ij_{ed} - Ii_{ed}) - (Ij_{ref} - Ii_{ref})])$

Table 11.3 Effects on Knowledge of Threats to Validity,
by Campaign Period

Effect	1979–1980	1980–1981	1981–1982	1982–1983	1983–1984	Net 1979–84
*Selection (cross-section)	−1.87%					
*Selection (panel)	−3.02					
History	+1.97	+1.98	−1.13	−1.13	+2.02	+3.71
Mortality	− .58	+ .37	+ .37	+ .14	+ .14	+ .29
Testing + Maturation	+3.48	− .85	+3.21	+1.97	−1.20	+6.61
Sensitization	+ .24	− .47	+ .48	− .14	− .16	− .05
Campaign	+2.13	+1.41	+ .47	− .16	− .15	+3.68

NOTE: Cell entries represent net change in the percentage correct answers on the adjusted knowledge index, as described in the note to Table 11.1. Gains have been calculated for the period indicated in each column for the effect listed in each row, according to the algorithms in Table 11.2.
* Data are from 1979, prior to the start of the campaign.

Algorithms are summarized in Table 11.2 for calculating the various effects from the basic data of Table 11.1. The estimates of effects of various threats, and of the campaign in this comparative context, are summarized in Table 11.3.

SELECTION

The choice of communities for the education and reference conditions did not result in a perfect match. The cross-sectional data indicate a significant precampaign superiority of the reference cities in terms of the knowledge index. This was, if anything, more marked in the panel data. These initial differences created a situation in which the campaign was, in effect, playing "catch-up"; indeed, the net impact of the campaign in its first year or two was to bring up to approximate equality the knowledge levels in the two sets of cities. This initial difference favoring the reference cities also raises some possibility of a regression phenomenon, a hypothesis not tested here.

HISTORY

Over the campaign years, there was an upward secular trend in public knowledge related to heart disease, independent of that attributable to the FCP campaign. Although the history-effect estimates display some inexplicable fluctuations across the years in Table 11.3, their net overall impact seems to have been about as strong as that of the FCP campaign itself. The campaign was, in a sense, in the unenviable position of attempting to outstrip a widespread general campaign devoted to approximately the same goals. The FCP staff could only be pleased that its message was gaining such broad acceptance and media assistance, but from a technical-evaluation perspective, this positive secular trend made the specific campaign's impact more difficult to discern.

MORTALITY

Calculation of the effects of mortality was undertaken for each time period by comparing the results for those who survived in the panel to what the expected results would have been without any attrition of panel members from one wave to another. Even when calculated for the entire 1979–84 period, however, mortality appears to have produced little, if any, net impact that could have been confused for a campaign effect.

TESTING AND MATURATION

A sizable effect that could be attributed to either testing or maturation is shown in Table 11.3. It is, on the whole, greater than the net effect of the campaign itself. A large testing effect is not surprising, given the highly reactive nature of the knowledge test. Can any of this be attributed to maturation as well? Probably not much. The large initial (1979–80) effect is what the authors would expect testing alone to produce. After being asked these knowledge questions in 1979, respondents were better able to answer them a year later; thereafter, the scores fluctuate up and down, although there is some further net gain through the full 1980–84 span. Maturation, if it is having an independent effect on these adult respondents, should presumably be gradual and steady, producing estimated gains of about the same magnitude in each time period. It would be possible to explore the maturation issue further, such as in a decomposition of cohort, period and aging effects, using the successive cross-sections, an analysis not attempted here.

In comparing the rows of Table 11.3, it is obvious that the two greatest threats, history and testing/maturation, go up and down over time in mirror-image patterns. That is, in the periods 1980–81 and 1983–84 the effect of history appears to be positive and that of testing/

maturation negative; in 1981–82 and 1982–83 the reverse is found. This occurs, in large measure, because history is represented by changes in the cross-sectional means for the reference cities, which is a subtractive term in the algorithm for estimating testing/maturation effects. The negative effect of history in the 1981–83 period could be due to unexplained vagaries of instrumentation during one cross-sectional survey period in those two cities. It is worth noting at the bottom of Table 11.1 that a further year's estimate of history effects is available, and it shows an additional gain of +2.02 for 1984–85. Overall, the secular trend (history) of knowledge about heart disease appears to be a steady and significant one throughout the early 1980s.

SENSITIZATION

The interaction of testing with the campaign produces essentially a zero net effect. The only serious hint of sensitization occurs in 1981–82, accompanying the strong apparent effect of testing in that same period. It is as if the panel respondents, having been asked these knowledge questions twice, began to take note of answers to them in their surrounding communication environment. This perhaps sensitized them to the campaign, along with any other information relevant to these questions. But overall sensitization (as distinct from testing) is a minor threat, if any, even with this highly reactive form of measurement.

CAMPAIGN EFFECTS

This chapter is not the place to evaluate the campaign itself; the purpose of including campaign effects here is solely for comparison with the threats to validity. Information transmission was only an intermediate goal of the FCP, and more sophisticated statistical analyses than reported here have shown significant overall gains in knowledge, along with campaign effects on other heart-disease risk factors (Farquhar et al., 1988).

Looking at Table 11.3, though, it appears clear that the campaign's effect on this knowledge index was concentrated mainly in the early years of the educational intervention. Campaign effects were greatest in the first year and gradually tailed off until after the fifth year, when they became approximately zero.

In comparison with threats to the inference that the intervention had its intended effect, campaign effects overall were of about the same magnitude as those of history and selection, and less than the combined effects of testing and maturation. Most of the latter is attributable to testing alone. Maturation, like mortality and sensitization, was probably of lesser, perhaps negligible, magnitude.

CONCLUSIONS

The main value of this chapter lies in the questions raised more than in the specific answers found. That is, the problem of anticipating the magnitude of various threats to validity is a basic one for campaign planners and particularly for evaluators. But this particular study is only one—and quite probably an unusual one—in a potentially long series of attempts to make the same kinds of estimates from other information campaign evaluation projects. Doubtless, future investigators will develop more elegant statistical techniques for making these estimates.

Selection, history, and testing were threats of considerable magnitude in this case, while mortality, maturation, and sensitization were not. But conditions fostering history and testing effects were practically maximal here. As noted, this was an unusual historical period in which there was a nationwide campaign of sorts aimed at heart-disease risk reduction in parallel with the FCP intervention. This secular trend somewhat overshadowed the Stanford project's specific effects. As for testing, a knowledge test that is repeated verbatim in several successive panel waves is probably the most reactive measure possible in terms of affecting the same respondents' ability to answer the same questions at later times. History and testing, then, are by no means always major threats to validity; their likely magnitude should be assessed in light of what a would-be campaign evaluator knows of the historical context and measurement conditions of the particular project at hand.

Selection, on the other hand, remains a major threat to validity in almost any situation and, when not well controlled, it carries with it the threats of regression fallacy and potential interactions of selection with other factors (Campbell and Stanley, 1966). As a rule, in community-based campaigns it is not feasible to create many units of analysis and assign them randomly to experimental and control conditions as might be done with, say, sophomores in a psychology class. Even when care is taken to "match" several communities on what seem to be relevant variables (e.g., population, occupational mix, geographical region, media market characteristics) exact equivalence on the criterion of central interest—in this case, knowledge about heart-disease prevention—is unlikely to be achieved.

A primary recommendation, then, would echo the dominant concern other investigators have evinced regarding selection. The lack of initial equivalence of the FCP's education and reference cities created, from the beginning, a threat to validity that cast some doubt on the main research inference and opened up other threats as well.

NOTES

1. The difference betwen the column means in the following two-by-two table is the campaign effect. The difference between the row means is the testing and maturation effect, and the difference between the diagonal means is the sensitization effect:

	No Campaign (Reference)	Campaign (Education)
No Testing or Maturation (Cross-sections)	$(Ij_{ref}\text{-}Ii_{ref})$	$(Ij_{ed}\text{-}Ii_{ed})$
Testing and Maturation (Panel)	$(Cj_{ref}\text{-}Ci_{ref})$	$(Cj_{ed}\text{-}Ci_{ed})$

REFERENCES

Achen, C. (1986). *The statistical analysis of quasi-experiments.* Berkeley: University of California Press.

Alwin, D., & Sullivan, M. (1976). Issues of design and analysis in evaluation research. In I. Bernstein (Ed.), *Validity issues in evaluation research* (pp, 83–106). Beverly Hills, CA: Sage.

Berry, L. (1983). Residential conservation program impacts: Methods of reducing self-selection bias. *Evaluation Review, 7,* 753–775.

Campbell, D. T. (1957). Factors relevant to the validity of experiments in social settings. *Psychological Bulletin, 54,* 297–312.

Campbell, D. T., & Stanley, J. C. (1966). *Experimental and quasi-experimental designs for research.* Chicago: Rand-McNally.

Chaffee, S. H., & McLeod, J. M. (1973). Sensitization in panel design: A coorientational experiment. *Journalism Quarterly, 45,* 661–669.

Cook, T., & Campbell, D. T. (1979) *Quasi-experimentation: Design and analysis issues for field settings.* Chicago: Rand-McNally.

Farquhar, J. W., Fortmann, S. P., Maccoby, N., Haskell, W., Williams, P., Flora, J. A., Taylor, C. B., Brown, B. W., Solomon, D., & Hulley, S. (1985). The Stanford Five City Project: Design and methods. *American Journal of Epidemiology, 122,* 323–334.

Farquhar, J. W., Fortmann, S. P., Flora, J. A., Williams, P. T., Brown, B. W., Rogers, E., & Vranizan, K. (1986). Interim results of the Stanford Five City Project. *CVD Epidemiology Newsletter 39,* 35. (American Heart Association Abstract No. 106.).

Farquhar, J. W., Fortmann, S. P., Flora, J. A., Williams, P. T., Haskell, W., Taylor, C. B., Maccoby, N., & Wood, P. (1988, March). *The Stanford Five City Project: Results after 5 1/3 years of education.* Abstract presented to the 28th Annual Conference on Cardiovascular Disease Epidemiology, Santa Fe, NM.

Heimendinger, J., & Laird, N. (1983). Growth changes: Measuring the effect of an intervention. *Evaluation Review, 7,* 80–95.

Hovland, C. I., Lumsdaine, A. A., & Sheffield, F. D. (1949). *Experiments on mass communication.* Princeton, NJ: Princeton University Press.

Mark, M. (1983). Treatment implementation, statistical power, and internal validity. *Evaluation Review, 7,* 543–549.

Muthen, B., & Joreskog, K. (1983). Selectivity problems in quasi-experimental studies. *Evaluation Review, 7,* 139–174.

Newcomb, T. (1984). Conservation program evaluations: The control of self-selection bias. *Evaluation Review, 8,* 425–440.

Reichardt, C. (1979). The statistical analysis of data from non-equivalent group designs. In T. Cook & D. T. Campbell (Eds.), *Quasi-experimentation: Design and analysis issues for field settings* (pp. 137–205). Palo Alto, CA: Houghton Mifflin.

Roser, C., Chaffee, S., Flora, J., & Farquhar, J. (1988). *Communication for heart disease prevention: The impact on knowledge of a public information campaign.* Paper presented to the International Communication Association convention, New Orleans.

Salmon, C. T., Mrja, E., & Carroll, P. (1983). *Communication in surveys: Examining cognitive effects in survey research.* Paper presented to the Association for Education in Journalism and Mass Communication convention, Corvallis, OR.

Solomon, R. L. (1949). An extension of control group design. *Psychological Bulletin, 46,* 137–150.

Yeaton, W., & Sechrest, L. (1986). Use and misuse of no-difference findings in eliminating threats to validity. *Evaluation Review, 10,* 836–852.

ABOUT THE CONTRIBUTORS

NEIL BRACHT is Professor in the School of Social Work at the University of Minnesota. He is director of community organization for the Minnesota Heart Health Program.

JANE D. BROWN is Professor in the School of Journalism at the University of North Carolina at Chapel Hill. She is editor (with Eli Rubenstein) of *The Media, Social Science and Social Policy for Children,* and is coinvestigator on a five-year public-information campaign and evaluation project sponsored by the National Cancer Institute.

STEVEN H. CHAFFEE is Janet M. Peck Professor of International Communication and Chair of the Department of Communication at Stanford University. He is coauthor (with Michael Petrick) of *Using the Mass Media: Communication Problems in American Society,* editor of *Political Communication: Issues and Strategies for Research,* coeditor (with George Comstock and others) of *Television and Human Behavior* and coeditor (with Charles Berger) of *Handbook of Communication Science.*

PATRICIA G. DEVINE is Assistant Professor in the Department of Psychology at the University of Wisconsin-Madison. Her research interests include stereotypes and prejudice and social cognition.

GEORGE A. DONOHUE is Professor in the Department of Rural Sociology at the University of Minnesota. He is coauthor (with Phillip Tichenor and Clarice Olien) of *Community Conflict and the Press.* His areas of specialization include social theory, socioeconomic development and community organization.

JOHN R. FINNEGAN, Jr. is Assistant Professor in the School of Public Health at the University of Minnesota, specializing in public health and mass communication. He is Associate Director of Education and Director of Mass Media for the Minnesota Heart Health Program.

JUNE FLORA is Assistant Professor in the Department of Communication and the Center for Research in Disease Prevention at Stanford University. She was Education Director of the Stanford Heart Disease Prevention Program and is currently conducting research on prevention and public education campaigns related to cardiovascular diseases and AIDS.

JAMES E. GRUNIG is Professor in the College of Journalism at the University of Maryland. He is coauthor (with Todd Hunt) of *Managing Public Relations* and coeditor (with Larissa Grunig) of *Public Relations Research Annual*. His research specialities include public relations, communication theory, science communication and communication and development.

EDWARD R. HIRT is Assistant Professor in the Department of Psychology at the University of Wisconsin-Madison. His research interests include social cognition and reconstructive processes in memory.

ROBERT HORNIK is Professor in the Annenberg School of Communications at the University of Pennsylvania. He is author of *Development Communication: Information, Agriculture and Nutrition in the Third World*.

GARRETT J. O'KEEFE is Professor in the Department of Agricultural Journalism at the University of Wisconsin-Madison. He is coauthor (with Harold Mendelsohn) of *The People Choose a President: Influences on Voter Decison Making*.

CLARICE N. OLIEN is Associate Professor in the Department of Sociology at the University of Minnesota. She is coauthor (with George Donohue and Phillip Tichenor) of *Community Conflict and the Press*. Her research specialties include community organization, youth development and mass communication.

RICHARD W. POLLAY is Professor of Marketing at the Faculty of Commerce, University of British Columbia, where he also serves as Curator of the History of Advertising Archives. His research is on marketing and advertising's social and cultural impacts. His historical perspective and expertise were recently instrumental in the first cigarette liability suit to be successful against tobacco firms.

LANA F. RAKOW is Assistant Professor in the Department of Communication at the University of Wisconsin-Parkside. She is coeditor (with Cheris Kramarae) of *The Revolution in Words* [forthcoming]. Her interests include feminist communication theory and the application of critical theory to the study of public relations.

CONNIE ROSER is Assistant Professor in the Department of Mass Communication at the University of Denver. She has been a Fellow in the Center for Research in Disease Prevention at Stanford University. Her research interests include information processing and health communication.

CHARLES T. SALMON is Assistant Professor and Head of the Public Relations Sequence in the School of Journalism and Mass Communication at the University of Wisconsin-Madison. His areas of research include issues management, communication and public opinion and evaluation research.

PHILLIP J. TICHENOR is Professor in the School of Journalism and Mass Communication at the University of Minnesota. He is coauthor (with George Donohue and Clarice Olien) of *Community Conflict and the Press*. His research interests include mass communication theory and methodology, mass media and public opinion and science journalism.

K. VISWANATH is a doctoral candidate in the School of Journalism and Mass Communication at the University of Minnesota. He is a research assistant for the Minnesota Heart Health Program and a former community analyst for the Indian National Satellite Project (INSAT).

KIM WALSH CHILDERS is a doctoral student in mass communication research at the University of North Carolina at Chapel

Hill. She has been a graduate fellow at the Bush Institute for Child and Family Policy and was the 1983 recipient of the American Public Health Association's Ray Bruner Fellowship for science and medical writing.

CYNTHIA S. WASZAK is doctoral student in social psychology at the University of North Carolina in Chapel Hill, where she is also a predoctoral trainee at the Carolina Population Center. She worked for six years at Family Health International as a project manager for international family planning studies. She is now Director of Research for the Center for Population Options.